Bloom's Classic Critical Views

EDGAR ALLAN POE

Bloom's Classic Critical Views

Jane Austen

Geoffrey Chaucer

Charles Dickens

Ralph Waldo Emerson

Nathaniel Hawthorne

Herman Melville

Edgar Allan Poe

Walt Whitman

Bloom's Classic Critical Views

EDGAR ALLAN POE

Edited and with an introduction by
Harold Bloom
Sterling Professor of the Humanities
Yale University

BLOOM'S
LITERARY CRITICISM
An imprint of Infobase Publishing

Bloom's Classic Critical Views: Edgar Allan Poe

Copyright © 2008 Infobase Publishing

Introduction © 2008 by Harold Bloom

Bloom's Literary Criticism
An imprint of Infobase Publishing
132 West 31st Street
New York NY 10001

Library of Congress Cataloging-in-Publication Data
Edgar Allan Poe / Harold Bloom.
    p. cm. — (Bloom's classic critical views)
 A selection of important older literary criticism on Edgar Allan Poe
 Includes bibliographical references and index.
 ISBN-13: 978-0-7910-9556-0
 ISBN-10: 0-7910-9556-8
 1. Poe, Edgar Allan, 1809–1849—Criticism and interpretation.
I. Bloom, Harold. II. Title: Bloom's classic critical views : Edgar Allan Poe.
 PS2638.E324 2007
 818'.309—dc22

                                                    2007018428

Series design by Erika K. Arroyo
Cover design by Takeshi Takahashi
Printed in the United States of America
Bang EJB 10 9 8 7 6 5 4 3 2 1

This book is printed on acid-free paper.

Contents

Series Introduction

Bloom's Classic Critical Views is a new series presenting a selection of the most important older literary criticism on the greatest authors commonly read in high school and college classes today. Unlike the Bloom's Modern Critical Views series, which for more than twenty years has provided the best contemporary criticism on great authors, Bloom's Classic Critical Views attempts to present the authors in the context of their time and to provide criticism that has proved over the years to be the most valuable to readers and writers. Selections range from contemporary reviews in popular magazines, which demonstrate how a work was received in its own era, to profound essays by some of the strongest critics in the British and American tradition, including Henry James, G.K. Chesterton, Matthew Arnold, and many more.

Some of the critical essays and extracts presented here have appeared previously in other titles edited by Harold Bloom, such as the New Moulton's Library of Literary Criticism. Other selections appear here for the first time in any book by this publisher. All were selected under Harold Bloom's guidance.

In addition, each volume in this series contains a series of essays by a contemporary expert, who comments on the most important critical selections, putting them in context and suggesting how they might be used by a student writer to influence his or her own writing. This series is intended above all for students, to help them think more deeply and write more powerfully about great writers and their works.

Introduction by Harold Bloom

Together with Walt Whitman, Poe continues to be the most influential of American writers on a worldwide basis, eclipsing even Eliot and Faulkner. For me, this constitutes a considerable irony, since I regard Whitman as the greatest of New World writers and Poe as the worst (among those of repute, obviously). Though I am in the minority of critics on Poe, the plain badness of Poe's various styles, in prose and verse, is merely palpable. Emerson dismissed Poe as "the jingle man," and the Gothic tales were accurately represented (even a touch improved) by the series of horror movies starring Vincent Price.

Poe's verse (I will not call it poetry) is indefensible, though Richard Wilbur, admirable poet, has attempted to argue its case. That Poe is inescapable I concede: he dreamed universal nightmares. I have read his tales in French and German translations, and they are remarkably improved by avoiding his ghastly diction and dubious syntax. Reading his verse in translation is also better than confronting the originals but they remain beyond aesthetic salvation.

The poet-critic John T. Irwin wrote a defense of Poe in a brilliant study, *American Hieroglyphics*, and continued his endeavor with the even more dazzling *The Mystery to a Solution*, which brought together Poe and Jorge Luis Borges as masters of the analytic detective story. For Irwin (himself a considerable poet under the pen-name of "John Bricuth"), what unites Poe and Borges, and many other authors, is an extreme mode of Platonic Idealism, with its valuation of mind (self and soul) over body and the external world. Poe dwells, with the rest of us, in Plato's Cave but wants, more desperately than most do, to find his way out into the disembodied light.

Alas, you can be the most passionate of Platonists and still be incapable of writing yourself out of the proverbial paper bag. Plato, a magnificent stylist, and subtlest of all ironists, does not much resemble his belated disciple, the egregious Poe, whose work shows forth an earnest consciousness ill at ease with irony. Unlike W.B. Yeats, whose supernaturalism always suggests ironic reservations, Poe's phantasmagorias literalize themselves. Even his weirdly systemic cosmology in *Eureka* carries the stigma of barely controlled hysteria.

Poe matters, I suspect, because his prevalent image of the labyrinth has become another Americanization of ancient mythology. As a poet, Poe is an amalgam of English High Romanticism: Coleridge, Byron, Shelley. His tales stem from German Romanticism: Hoffmann, Novalis, Tieck, and others. *Eureka* parodies Emerson's *Nature*, while Poe's now-overpraised criticism travesties Hazlitt, Lamb, and Leigh Hunt. But, as Irwin rightly insists, Poe did invent the analytic detective story, and made of it a Platonic labyrinth. G.K. Chesterton, Borges, and Raymond Chandler all improved upon Poe's new genre, but as their forerunner he deserves John T. Irwin's praise of his inventiveness.

Poe essentially was a religious writer without a religion, unlike Sir Thomas Browne, probably the American Platonist's truest precursor. It is a grim experience reading Poe's *Eureka* side-by-side with Browne's incredibly eloquent baroque reveries, *Urn Burial* and *The Garden of Cyrus*. Thomas De Quincey and Borges can sustain comparison with Browne; Poe sinks without trace. He simply could not write in a Latinate English style. Poe had something to say but little skill in saying it.

◈

BIOGRAPHY

◈

EDGAR ALLAN POE
(1809–1849)

❖

Edgar Allan Poe was born Edgar Poe in Boston on January 19, 1809, the son of traveling actors. Shortly after his birth, his father abandoned the family, and in 1811 his mother died. He was taken into the home of John Allan (from whom Poe derived his middle name), a wealthy merchant living in Richmond, Virginia. In 1815 the Allans took Poe to England, where he attended the Manor House School at Stoke Newington (later the setting of his story "William Wilson"). Poe returned to Richmond with the Allans in 1820. In 1826 he became engaged to Elmira Royster, whose parents broke off the engagement. That fall he entered the University of Virginia. At first he excelled in his studies, but in December 1826 he was taken out of school by John Allan after accumulating considerable gambling debts, which Allan refused to pay. Unable to honor these debts himself, Poe fled to Boston, where he enlisted in the army under the name of Edgar A. Perry.

Poe began his literary career with the anonymous publication of *Tamerlane and Other Poems* (1827) at his own expense. In 1829 he was honorably discharged from the army. Later that year he published a second collection of verse, *Al Aaraaf, Tamerlane, and Minor Poems,* containing revisions of poems from his first collection as well as new material. This volume was well received, leading to a tentative reconciliation with John Allan. In 1830 Poe entered the academy at West Point, but after another falling out with Allan, who withdrew his financial support, Poe deliberately got himself expelled in 1831 through flagrant neglect of his duties. Before leaving, he had managed to gather enough cadet subscriptions to bring out his third collection of verse, *Poems* (1831). In 1833 Poe's final attempt at reconciliation was rejected by the ailing John Allan, who died in 1834 without mentioning Poe in his will.

By the early 1830s, Poe's literary career was progressing. In 1833 he won a prize from the *Baltimore Saturday Visitor* for one of his first short stories, "MS. Found in a Bottle," and in 1835 he was hired as editor of the recently established *Southern Literary Messenger,* which thrived under his direction. In 1836 Poe felt financially

1

secure enough to marry Virginia Clemm, his fourteen-year-old cousin, but later that year he was fired from the *Messenger,* partly because of what appeared to be chronic alcoholism. Poe seems to have suffered from a physical ailment that rendered him so sensitive to alcohol that a single drink could induce a drunken state. Poe was later an editor of *Burton's Gentleman's Magazine* (1839–40), *Graham's Magazine* (1841–42), and the *Broadway Journal* (1845–46). In this capacity he wrote many important reviews—notably of Hawthorne, Dickens, and Macaulay—and occasionally gained notoriety for the severity and acerbity of his judgments. In particular, he wrote a series of polemics against Henry Wadsworth Longfellow, whom he accused of plagiarism.

In addition to his pursuits as an editor and reviewer, Poe continued to write fiction voluminously. His longest tale, *The Narrative of Arthur Gordon Pym* (apparently unfinished), appeared in 1838; *Tales of the Grotesque and Arabesque,* containing "The Fall of the House of Usher" and other important stories, was published in 1840; and *Tales* appeared in 1845. As a fiction writer, Poe wrote not only stories of the macabre and the supernatural ("The Pit and the Pendulum," "The Black Cat," "The Tell-Tale Heart," "Ligeia") but also many humorous or parodic pieces ("King Pest," "Some Words with a Mummy"), prose poems ("Silence—a Fable," "Shadow—a Parable"), and what are generally considered the first true detective stories: "The Murders in the Rue Morgue" (1841), "The Gold-Bug" (1843), and "The Purloined Letter" (1845), among others.

In 1844 Poe moved to New York and in the following year achieved international fame with his poem "The Raven," published in *The Raven and Other Poems* (1845). In 1847 Poe's wife, Virginia, who had been seriously ill since 1842, died, leaving Poe desolate. For the few remaining years of his life, he helped support himself by delivering a series of public lectures, including "The Poetic Principle" (published posthumously in 1850). Among his later publications were the philosophical treatise *Eureka: A Prose Poem* (1848) and the lyric "Annabel Lee" (1849). His *Marginalia* was published serially from 1844 to 1849. After his wife's death, Poe had several romances, including an affair with the Rhode Island poet Sarah Helen Whitman. In 1849 he became engaged for a second time to Elmira Royster (then Mrs. Shelton). Before they could be married, however, Poe died in Baltimore on October 7, 1849, under mysterious circumstances.

Despite the fact that Poe's reputation was initially damaged by his posthumous editor, Rufus Wilmot Griswold, who propagated many longstanding myths about the author's alcoholism and misanthropy, Poe was one of the first American authors to be widely appreciated in Europe. He had a great influence on the development of French Symbolism, with much of his work being translated by Baudelaire and Mallarmé. In England he was greatly admired by such literary figures as Swinburne, Wilde, and Rossetti. By the end of the nineteenth century, Poe was viewed as one of the greatest writers the United States had produced.

◆

PERSONAL

◆

The extracts in this section present various views of Poe. The life of Poe presents almost as much mystery, drama, melancholy, and in some cases fiction as his tales and poems do. Poe's personal image is closely associated with many of the characters and imagery contained in his works: dark, gloomy, half-mad. The portrait of Poe that emerges in the following texts depicts him as an alienated genius, as a suffering artist, and, at other times, as a misanthropic monster. The reality likely lies somewhere in between.

In the first three extracts, readers are offered a glimpse of Poe's image of himself as a young man in his poem "Alone" and then hear of a friend's concern for his well-being and Poe's own worries concerning his professional success in a letter to his beloved wife. The fourth extract is one of the most significant and influential pieces in the history of Poe studies: Rufus Griswold's infamous "Ludwig" obituary, in which Griswold painted the slanderous portrait of Poe that would linger for decades. This obituary was extended into a longer "Memoir of the Author," which became the preface to the collected works of Poe edited by Griswold. He invented slanderous information—Poe's decision to leave the University of Virginia became an "expulsion"—and he emphasized the role of alcohol in the poet's life. He even hinted at criminal behavior that had absolutely no basis in fact. As can be seen in the subsequent texts included in this section, nearly every piece written about Poe in the century following his death either borrows from or attempts to correct the Griswold biography. Even after many other writers tried to defend Poe's reputation from Griswold's libel (see N.P. Willis's entry), the view of Poe as a dissolute misanthrope persists. Modern criticism and biographies have now thoroughly debunked the myth of Poe, but many still see him as a brooding, mentally unbalanced, and suffering artist.

After Griswold's obituary, three other remembrances are included, written by individuals who knew Poe well: a letter from Poe's mother-in-law mourning his death, a piece by N.P. Willis defending Poe's reputation, and an obituary by George Graham, who remembers Poe as a model employee, as well as a misunderstood genius. Even though Poe had died, Thomas Powell included Poe in his *Living Authors of America*, in which he reiterates the opinion put forth by Griswold. Sarah Helen Whitman, to whom Poe was briefly engaged, challenges the false characterization of her former fiancé. The final five entries in the section present passing memories by mere acquaintances, beginning with a humorous note by the journalist Horace Greeley. Maunsell Field remembers a lecture Poe had presented on "The Universe." Algernon Charles Swinburne, a British poet and critic, speaks of Poe's influence on French and English readers, and John Latrobe depicts Poe as an enthusiastic and gentlemanly writer, specifically denying an allegation by Griswold. In the final excerpt, Susan A.T. Weiss remembers the striking physical features of Poe, using phrenology to ascertain his moral character from the shape of his head.

The texts in this section show just how varied the images of Poe, the man as well as the artist, were. Here we see the sensitive artist, the loving husband, the unlucky businessman, the polite gentleman, the raving drunkard, and the literary genius all in one. Which one is the "real" Poe? That is impossible to determine. Rather, we can see how one of the nineteenth century's great artists, in Whitman's apt expression, "contained multitudes."

Edgar Allan Poe "Alone" (1829)

This poem is among Poe's earliest works. Although there is always some danger in confusing a writer's literary output and creations with the biographical details of his own life, this poem invites readers to see Poe thinking back on his own troubled childhood, his orphaned state, and his dreams of making a name for himself. Enunciating a common theme in Romantic literature, the poet here states that he was not like other children: he sees and feels things differently than others do. The middle and end of the poem suggest why this is so: from every aspect of his perception a "demon" stands in the picture. The ability to see the demonic elements of life is indeed a poetic gift. This poem explores the role of a poet in society and gestures to the differences between poetic and realistic perception.

From childhood's hour I have not been
As others were—I have not seen
As others saw—I could not bring
My passions from a common spring—
From the same source I have not taken
My sorrow—I could not awaken
My heart to joy at the same tone—
And all I lov'd—I lov'd alone—
Then—in my childhood—in the dawn
Of a most stormy life—was drawn
From ev'ry depth of good and ill
The mystery which binds me still—
From the torrent, or the fountain—
From the red cliff of the mountain—
From the sun that 'round me roll'd
In its autumn tint of gold—
From the lightning in the sky
As it pass'd me flying by—
From the thunder, and the storm—
And the cloud that took the form
(When the rest of Heaven was blue)
Of a demon in my view—

—Edgar Allan Poe, "Alone," 1829

L.A. WILMER (1843)

Wilmer was a writer and a friend of Poe's. Poe had written a generally favorable review of a work by Wilmer. Here Wilmer alludes to Poe's problems with alcohol, a theme that would characterize the popular view of Poe in the years following his death.

Edgar A. Poe (you know him by character, no doubt, if not personally), has become one of the strangest of our literati. He and I are old friends,—have known each other since boyhood, and it gives me inexpressible pain to notice the vagaries to which he has lately become subject. Poor fellow! he is not a teetotaller by any means, and I fear he is going headlong to destruction, moral, physical and intellectual.

—L.A. Wilmer, Letter to Mr. Tomlin (May 20, 1843),
cited in *Passages from the Correspondence and
Other Papers of Rufus W. Griswold*, ed.
W.M. Griswold, 1898, p. 143

EDGAR ALLAN POE (1846)

Of the many letters Poe wrote to his wife, this is the only one that survives. It conveys the devotion Poe had for her as well as a sense of his professional disappointments. He notes that she is the greatest and only stimulus that keeps him fighting.

My Dear Heart, My dear Virginia! our Mother will explain to you why I stay away from you this night. I trust the interview I am promised, will result in some *substantial good* for me, for your dear sake, and hers—Keep up your heart in all hopefulness, and trust yet a little longer—In my last great disappointment, I should have lost my courage *but for you*—my little darling wife you are my *greatest* and *only* stimulus now, to battle with this uncongenial, unsatisfactory and ungrateful life—I shall be with you tomorrow P.M. and be assured until I see you, I will keep in *loving remembrance* your *last words* and your fervant [*sic*] prayer!

—Edgar Allan Poe, Letter to Virginia Poe
(June 12, 1846)

Rufus Wilmot Griswold (1849)

Rufus Griswold was a "friend" of Poe's, and Poe apparently named Griswold his literary executor—the person in charge of his writings after he died. Poe's decision turned out to be a less than ideal one. As evidenced in this obituary, Griswold wasted no time at all in blackening Poe's name. This text is known as the "Ludwig" article, since it was signed with that name, although it appears that many readers knew Griswold was the author. Beginning with this piece, which was expanded into a full biography and published with the Griswold-edited *Works of Poe* in 1850–56, Griswold painted the libelous portrait of Poe as a disreputable monster who most people would be happy to see dead. Such a view was quickly attacked by others who knew Poe personally, but the image was powerfully drawn and, to a degree, continues to linger in the minds of many modern readers. Students might consult this obituary when contrasting the manufactured or embellished image of Poe with the "real" Poe. Griswold's portrait, though false, is given undue credence by the darkness that infuses much of Poe's work. But does the work necessarily reflect the man? Students writing on Poe could use this excerpt to help discuss the problems with performing biographical readings of the texts.

Edgar Allan Poe is dead. He died in Baltimore the day before yesterday. This announcement will startle many, but few will be grieved by it. The poet was well known personally or by reputation, in all this country; he had readers in England, and in several of the states of Continental Europe; but he had few or no friends; and the regrets for his death will be suggested principally by the consideration that in him literary art lost one of its most brilliant, but erratic stars. . . .

The character of Mr. Poe we cannot attempt to describe in this very hastily written article. We can but allude to some of the more striking phases.

His conversation was at times almost supra-mortal in its eloquence. His voice was modulated with astonishing skill, and his large and variably expressive eyes looked reposed or shot fiery tumult into theirs who listened, while his own face glowed or was changeless in pallor, as his imagination quickened his blood, or drew it back frozen to his heart. His imagery was from the worlds which no mortal can see but with the vision of genius. Suddenly starting from a proposition exactly and sharply defined in terms of utmost simplicity and clearness, he rejected the forms of customary logic, and in a crystalline process of accretion, built up his ocular demonstrations in forms of gloomiest and ghostliest grandeur, or in those of the most airy and delicious beauty, so minutely, and so distinctly, yet so rapidly, that the attention which was yielded to him was chained till it stood among his wonderful creations—till he himself dissolved the spell, and brought his hearers back to common and base existence, by vulgar fancies or by exhibitions of the ignoble passions.

He was at times a dreamer—dwelling in ideal realms—in heaven or hell, peopled with creations and the accidents of his brain. He walked the streets, in madness or melancholy, with lips moving in indistinct curses, or with eyes upturned in passionate prayers, (never for himself, for he felt, or professed to feel, that he was already damned but for their happiness who at that moment were objects of his idolatry); or with his glance introverted to a heart gnawed with anguish, and with a face shrouded in gloom, he would brave the wildest storms; and all night, with drenched garments and arms wildly beating the wind and rain, he would speak as if to spirits that at such times only could be evoked by him from that Aidenn close by whose portals his disturbed soul sought to forget the ills to which his constitution subjected him—close by that Aidenn where were those he loved—the Aidenn which he might never see but in fitful glimpses, as its gates opened to receive the less fiery and more happy natures whose listing to sin did not involve the doom of death. He seemed, except when some fitful pursuit subjected his will and engrossed his faculties, always to bear the memory of some controlling sorrow. The remarkable poem of "The Raven" was probably much more nearly than has been supposed, even by those who were very intimate with him, a reflection and an echo of his own history. He was the bird's

> —unhappy master,
> Whom unmerciful disaster
> Followed fast and followed faster
> Till his song the burden bore—
> Melancholy burden bore
> Of "Nevermore," of "Nevermore."

Every genuine author in a greater or less degree leaves in his works, whatever their design, traces of his personal character; elements of his immortal being, in which the individual survives the person. While we read the pages of the "Fall of the House of Usher," or of "Mesmeric Revelation," we see in the solemn and stately gloom which invests one, and in the subtle metaphysical analysis of both, indications of the idiosyncrasies,—of what was most peculiar—in the author's intellectual nature. But we see here only the better phases of this nature, only the symbols of his juster action, for his harsh experience had deprived him of all faith in man or woman.

He had made up his mind upon the numberless complexities of the social world, and the whole system was with him an imposture. This conviction gave a direction to his shrewd and naturally unamiable character. Still though he regarded society as composed of villains, the sharpness of his intellect was not of that kind which enabled him to cope with villainy, while it continually caused him overshots, to fail of the success of honesty. He was in many respects like Francis Vivian in Bulwer's novel of the *Caxtons*. "Passion, in him, comprehended many of the worst emotions which militate against human happiness. You could not contradict him, but you raised quick choler; you could not speak of wealth, but his cheek paled with gnawing envy. The astonishing natural advantage of this poor boy—his beauty, his readiness, the daring spirit that breathed around him like a fiery atmosphere—had raised his constitutional self-confidence into an arrogance that turned his very claims to admiration into prejudice against him. Irascible, envious—bad enough, but not the worst, for these salient angles were all varnished over with a cold repellant cynicism while his passions vented themselves in sneers. There seemed to him no moral susceptibility; and what was more remarkable in a proud nature, little or nothing of the true point of honor. He had, to a morbid excess, that desire to rise which is vulgarly called ambition, but no wish for the esteem or the love of his species; only the hard wish to succeed—not shine, not serve—succeed, that he might have the right to despise a world which galled his self-conceit."

—Rufus Wilmot Griswold, *New York Tribune*, October 9, 1849

MARIA CLEMM (1849)

Maria Clemm was Poe's beloved aunt as well as his mother-in-law. In this letter, she discusses her arrangement with Griswold to have Poe's works published. With outrage and sadness, she bemoans the slanderous treatment of her late nephew in the press (apparently unaware that Griswold was largely responsible).

———— ———— ————

I am not deceived in you, you *still* wish your poor desolate friend to come to you. I have written to poor Elmira, and have to wait for her answer. They are already making arrangements to publish the works of my *darling lost one*. I have been waited on by several gentlemen, and have finally arranged with Mr. Griswold to arrange and bring them out, and he wishes it done immediately. Mr. Willis is to share with him this labour of love. They say I am to have the *entire* proceeds, so you see, Annie, I will not be entirely destitute. I have had many letters of condolence, and one which has, indeed, comforted me. Neilson Poe, of Baltimore, has written to me, and says he died in the Washington Medical College, not the Hospital, and of congestion of the brain, and not of what the vile, vile papers accuse him. He had many kind friends with him, and was attended to the grave by the literati of Baltimore, and many friends. *Severe excitement* (and no doubt some imprudence) brought this on; he never had one interval of reason. I cannot tell you all now. They now appreciate him and will do justice to his beloved memory. They propose to raise a monument to his memory. Some of the papers, indeed, nearly all, do him justice. I enclose this article from a Baltimore paper. But this, my dear Annie, will not restore him. Never, oh, never, will I see those dear lovely eyes. I feel *so desolate, so wretched, friendless, and alone* . . . I have a beautiful letter from General Morris; he did, indeed, love him. He has many friends, but of what little consequence to him *now*.

—Maria Clemm, Letter to "Annie" [Annie Richmond]
(October 13, 1849), cited in John H. Ingram, *Edgar Allan Poe:
His Life, Letters, and Opinions*, 1880, Vol. 2, pp. 239–40

Nathaniel Parker Willis
"Death of Edgar A. Poe" (1849)

Willis, a poet and writer, defends Poe's reputation against the false image presented in Griswold's obituary. Willis presents Poe as a diligent worker, as well as a perceptive artist and gentleman. He suggests that Poe's irregular behavior may have been the result of his hypersensitivity to alcohol.

Some four or five years since, when editing a daily paper in this city, Mr. Poe was employed by us, for several months, as critic and sub-editor. This was our first personal acquaintance with him. He resided with his wife and mother at Fordham, a few miles out of town, but was at his desk in the office from nine in the morning till the evening paper went to press. With the highest admiration for his genius, and a willingness to let it atone for more than ordinary irregularity, we were led by common report to expect a very capricious attention to his duties, and occasionally a scene of violence and difficulty. Time went on, however, and he was invariably punctual and industrious. With his pale, beautiful, and intellectual face as a reminder of what genius was in him, it was impossible, of course, not to treat him always with deferential courtesy, and to our occasional request that he would not probe too deep in a criticism, or that he would erase a passage colored too highly with his resentments against society and mankind, he readily and courteously assented,—far more yielding than most men, we thought, on points so excusably sensitive. With a prospect of taking the lead in another periodical, he at last voluntarily gave up his employment with us, and through all this considerable period we had seen but one presentment of the man,—a quiet, patient, industrious, and most gentlemanly person, commanding the utmost respect and good feeling by his unvarying deportment and ability.

Residing as he did in the country, we never met Mr. Poe in hours of leisure; but he frequently called on us afterwards at our place of business, and we met him often in the street,—invariably the same sad-mannered, winning, and refined gentleman such as we had always known him. It was by rumor only, up to the day of his death, that we knew of any other development of manner or character. We heard, from one who knew him well (what should be stated in all mention of his lamentable irregularities), that, with a *single glass* of wine, his whole nature was reversed, the demon became uppermost, and, though none of the usual signs of intoxication were visible, his *will* was palpably insane. Possessing his reasoning faculties in excited activity at such times, and seeking his acquaintances with his wonted look and memory, he easily seemed personating only another phase of his natural character, and was accused, accordingly, of insulting arrogance and bad-heartedness. In this reversed character, we repeat, it was never our chance to see him. We know it from hearsay, and we mention it in connection with this sad infirmity of physical constitution, which puts it upon very nearly the ground of a temporary and almost irresponsible insanity.

The arrogance, vanity, and depravity of heart of which Mr. Poe was generally accused seem to us referable altogether to this reversed phase of his character. Under that degree of intoxication which only acted upon him by demonizing his sense of truth and right, he doubtless said and did much that was wholly irreconcilable with his better nature; but when himself, and as we knew him only, his modesty and unaffected humility, as to his own deservings, were a constant charm to his character.

—Nathaniel Parker Willis, "Death of Edgar A. Poe" (1849), cited in *The Complete Works of Edgar Allan Poe*, ed. James A. Harrison, 1902, Vol. 1, pp. 360–62

GEORGE R. GRAHAM
"THE LATE EDGAR ALLAN POE" (1850)

Graham, the editor of *Graham's Magazine*, where Poe worked for two years, extols his employee's intellectual and literary abilities. Graham notes that most of Poe's venom was reserved for those who did not appreciate the value of these realms. As if to counter the Griswold portrait, Graham depicts Poe as a devoted husband and son-in-law, who loves his wife dearly. This version of Poe values money only insofar as it will support his family, and he has little regard for the luxuries of the material world. Like Baudelaire (excerpted later in this volume), Graham sees the later Poe as an outcast, someone justifiably embittered by the vulgarity of capitalist America.

⁓⁓⁓⁓ ⁓⁓⁓⁓ ⁓⁓⁓⁓

Literature with him was religion; and he, its high-priest, with a whip of scorpions scourged the money-changers from the temple. In all else he had the docility and kind-heartedness of a child. No man was more quickly touched by a kindness—none more prompt to atone for an injury. For three or four years I knew him intimately, and for eighteen months saw him almost daily; much of the time writing or conversing at the same desk; knowing all his hopes, his fears, and little annoyances of life, as well as his high-hearted struggle with adverse fate—yet he was always the same polished gentleman— the quiet, unobtrusive, thoughtful scholar—the devoted husband—frugal in his personal expenses—punctual and unwearied in his industry—*and the soul of honor,* in all his transactions. This, of course, was in his better days, and by them *we* judge the man. . . .

I shall never forget how solicitous of the happiness of his wife and mother-in-law he was, whilst one of the editors of *Graham's Magazine*—his whole efforts seemed to be to procure the comfort and welfare of his home. Except for their happiness—and the natural ambition of having a magazine of his own—I never heard him deplore the want of wealth. The truth is, he cared little for money, and knew less of its value, for he seemed to have no personal expenses. What he received from me in regular monthly installments, went directly into the hands of his mother-in-law for family comforts—and *twice* only, I remember his purchasing some rather expensive luxuries for his house, and then he was nervous to the degree of misery until he had, by extra articles, covered what he considered an imprudent indebtedness. His love for his wife was a sort of rapturous worship of the spirit of beauty which he felt was fading before his eyes. I have seen him hovering around her when she was ill, with all the fond fear and tender anxiety of a mother for her first-born—her slightest cough causing in him a shudder, a heart-chill that was visible. I rode out one summer evening with them, and the remembrance of his watchful eyes eagerly bent upon the slightest change of hue in that loved face, haunts me yet as the memory of a sad strain. It was this hourly *anticipation* of her loss, that made him a sad and thoughtful man, and lent a mournful melody to his undying song.

It is true that later in life Poe had much of those morbid feelings which a life of poverty and disappointment is so apt to engender in the heart of man—the sense of having been ill-used, misunderstood, and put aside by men of far less ability, and of none, which preys upon the heart and clouds the brain of many a child of song: A consciousness of the inequalities of life, and of the abundant power of mere wealth allied even to vulgarity, to over-ride all distinctions, and to thrust itself bedaubed with dirt and glittering with tinsel, into the high places of society, and the chief seats of the synagogue; whilst he, a worshiper of the beautiful and true, who listened to the voices of angels, and held delighted companionship with them as the cold throng swept disdainfully by him, and often in danger of being thrust out, houseless, homeless, beggared upon the world, with all his fine feelings strung to a tension of agony when he thought of his beautiful and delicate wife dying hourly before his eyes. What wonder, that he then poured out the vials of a long-treasured bitterness upon the injustice and hollowness of all society around him. . . .

He was a worshiper of INTELLECT—longing to grasp the power of mind that moves the stars—to bathe his soul in the dreams of seraphs. He was himself all ethereal, of a fine essence, that moved in an atmosphere of spirits—of spiritual beauty overflowing and radiant—twin brother with the angels, feeling their flashing wings upon his heart, and almost clasping them in his embrace. Of them, and as an expectant archangel of that high order of intellect, stepping out of himself, as it were, and interpreting the time, he reveled in delicious luxury in a world beyond, with an audacity which we fear in madmen, but in genius worship as the inspiration of heaven.

—George R. Graham, "The Late Edgar Allan Poe"
(letter to N.P. Willis, February 2, 1850),
Graham's Magazine, March 1850, pp. 225–26

THOMAS POWELL "EDGAR ALLAN POE" (1850)

Powell, oddly including a section on the recently deceased Poe in his book on "living" authors of America, takes Griswold's portrait for granted but argues that the truly great are often rather sinful.

We have been told by those who knew Mr. Poe well, that so weakly strung were all his nerves, that the smallest modicum of stimulant had an alarming effect upon him, and produced actions scarcely resolvable by sanity. It may be said that it is not the quantity of stimulant, but the effect produced, which constitutes the drunkard, and that Mr. Poe was as much to blame for the inebriation of a glass as of a bottle; but we would tell these cold-blooded fishes—for they are not men—that it is not given to the common-place men either to feel the raptures of poetical inspiration, or the despondency of prostrated energies. The masses are wisely, as Pope says,

Content to dwell in decencies for ever.

There is a homely verse in an old ballad which was made upon Shakespeare's masterpiece of human philosophy:

Hamlet loved a maid;
Calumny had passed her:
She never had played tricks—
Because nobody had asked her.

This rough and unconditional doggerel gives a graphic insight into the proprieties of the masses: they have neither had the impulse nor the opportunity to be indiscreet. Let our readers clearly understand we are not the apologists of Mr. Poe's errors—as Mark Antony says,

We come to bury Caesar, not to praise him; but, at the same time, we will not allow any undue deference to the opinion of the world.

—Thomas Powell, "Edgar Allan Poe,"
The Living Authors of America, 1850, pp. 123–24

Sarah Helen Whitman (1860)

Sarah Whitman was a close personal friend of Poe's; they were also briefly engaged to be married in 1848. Whitman defends Poe from the harsh treatment he suffered at the hands of many of his critics. Here Poe appears a noble and tormented soul, one whom people should respect and pity, rather than criticize.

The peculiarities of Edgar Poe's organization and temperament doubtless exposed him to peculiar infirmities. We need not discuss them here. They have been already too elaborately and painfully illustrated elsewhere to need further comment. How fearfully he expiated them only those who best knew and loved him can ever know. We are told that ideas of right and wrong are wholly ignored by him—that "no recognitions of conscience or remorse are to be found on his pages." If not *there,* where, then, shall we look for them? In "William Wilson," in "The Man of the Crowd," and in "The Tell-Tale Heart," the retributions of conscience are portrayed with a terrible fidelity. In yet another of his stories, which we will not name, the fearful fatality of crime—the dreadful fascination consequent on the indulgence of a perverse will is portrayed with a relentless and awful reality. May none ever read it who do not need the fearful lesson which it brands on the memory in characters of fire! In the relation of this remarkable story we recognise the power of a genius like that which sustains us in traversing the lowest depths of Dante's *Inferno.* The rapid descent in crime which it delineates, and which becomes at last involuntary, reminds us of the subterranean staircase by which Vathek and Nouronihar reached the Hall of Eblis, where, as they descended, they felt their steps frightfully accelerated till they seemed falling from a precipice.

Poe's private letters to his friends offer abundant evidence that he was not insensible to the keenest pangs of remorse. Again and again did he say to the Demon that tracked his path, "Anathema Maranatha," but again and again did it return to torture and subdue. He saw the handwriting on the wall but had no power to avert the impending doom.

In relation to this, the fatal temptation of his life, he says, in a letter written within a year of his death, "The agonies which I have lately endured have passed my soul through fire. Henceforth I am strong. This those who love me shall know as well as those who have so relentlessly sought to ruin me. I have absolutely *no* pleasure in the stimulants in which I sometimes so madly indulge. It has not been in the pursuit of pleasure that I have perilled life and reputation and reason. It has been in the desperate attempt to escape from torturing memories—memories of wrong and injustice and imputed dishonor—from a sense of insupportable loneliness and a dread of some strange impending doom." We believe these statements to have been sincerely uttered, and we would record here the testimony of a gentleman who, having for years known him intimately and having been near him in his states of utter mental desolation and insanity, assured us that he had never heard from his lips a word that would have disgraced his heart or brought reproach upon his honor.

Could we believe that any plea we may have urged in extenuation of Edgar Poe's infirmities and errors would make the fatal path he trod less abhorrent to others, such would never have been proffered. No human sympathy, no human charity could avert the penalties of the erring life. One clear glance into its mournful corridors—its "halls of tragedy and chambers of retribution," would appal the boldest heart.

Theodore Parker has nobly said that "every man of genius has to hew out for himself, from the hard marbles of life, the white statue of Tranquillity." Those who have best succeeded in this sublime work will best know how to look with pity and reverent awe upon the melancholy torso which alone remains to us of Edgar Poe's misguided efforts to achieve that beautiful and august statue of Peace.

—Sarah Helen Whitman, *Edgar Poe and His Critics,*
1860, pp. 82–85

HORACE GREELEY (1868)

Greeley, the well-known journalist and editor, notes here—with humor, it seems—that the only autograph he had from Poe was that signed on a bad check.

A gushing youth once wrote me to this effect:—

> DEAR SIR: Among your literary treasures, you have doubtless preserved several autographs of our country's late lamented poet, Edgar A. Poe. If so, and you can spare one, please enclose it to me, and receive the thanks of yours truly.

I promptly responded, as follows:—

> DEAR SIR: Among my literary treasures, there happens to be exactly *one* autograph of our country's late lamented poet, Edgar A. Poe. It

is his note of hand for fifty dollars, with my indorsement across the back. It cost me exactly $50.75 (including protest), and you may have it for half that amount. Yours, respectfully.

—Horace Greeley, *Recollections of a Busy Life,*
1868, pp. 196–97

Maunsell B. Field
(1873)

Field, former assistant secretary of the U.S. Treasury under Abraham Lincoln, here recounts a lecture by Poe, recalling Poe's striking physical features and his intellectual bravado, claiming "he solved the whole problem of life."

Edgar A. Poe I remember seeing on a single occasion. He announced a lecture to be delivered at the Society Library building on Broadway, under the title of the "Universe." It was a stormy night, and there were not more than sixty persons present in the lecture-room. I have seen no portrait of Poe that does justice to his pale, delicate, intellectual face and magnificent eyes. His lecture was a rhapsody of the most intense brilliancy. He appeared inspired, and his inspiration affected the scant audience almost painfully. He wore his coat tightly buttoned across his slender chest; his eyes seemed to glow like those of his own raven, and he kept us entranced for two hours and a half. The late Mr. Putnam, the publisher, told me that the next day the wayward, luckless poet presented himself to him with the manuscript of the "Universe." He told Putnam that in it he solved the whole problem of life; that it would immortalize its publisher as well as its author; and, what was of less consequence, that it would bring to him the fortune which he had so long and so vainly been seeking. Mr. Putnam, while an admirer of genius, was also a cool, calculating man of business. As such, he could not see the matter in exactly the same light as the poet did, and the only result of the interview was that he lent Poe a shilling to take him home to Fordham, where he then resided. After poor Poe's death, the late Rufus W. Griswold, not altogether immaculate himself, treated his memory with undue severity.

—Maunsell B. Field, *Memories of Many Men
and Some Women,* 1873, pp. 224–25

ALGERNON CHARLES SWINBURNE (1875)

Swinburne, a well-known English poet and critic, here acknowledges
Poe's greatness and his high reputation in both Great Britain and France.
Swinburne asserts that the esteem afforded Poe will only increase with
the passage of time.

Dear Madam

I have heard with much pleasure of the memorial at length raised to your
illustrious fellow-citizen. The genius of Edgar Poe has won on this side of the
Atlantic such wide and warm recognition that the sympathy which I cannot hope
fitly or fully to express in adequate words is undoubtedly shared at this moment
by hundreds as far as the news may have spread throughout not England only but
France as well; where as I need not remind you the most beautiful and durable
of monuments has been reared to the genius of Poe by the laborious devotion
of a genius equal and akin to his own; and where the admirable translation of
his prose works by a fellow-poet, whom also we have now to lament before his
time, is even now being perfected by a careful and exquisite version of his poems,
with illustrations full of the subtle and tragic force of fancy which impelled
and moulded the original song; a double homage due to the loyal and loving
cooperation of one of the most remarkable younger poets and one of the most
powerful leading painters in France—M. Mallarmé and M. Manet.

It is not for me to offer any tribute here to the fame of your great countryman,
or to dilate with superfluous and intrusive admiration on the special quality of
his strong and delicate genius, so sure of aim and faultless of touch in all the
better and finer part of work he has left us. I would only, in conveying to the
members of the Poe Memorial Committee my sincere acknowledgment of the
honour they have done me in recalling my name on such an occasion, take
leave to express my firm conviction that widely as the fame of Poe has already
spread, and deeply as it is already rooted in Europe, it is even now growing
wider and striking deeper as time advances; the surest presage that time, the
eternal enemy of small and shallow reputations, will prove in this case also the
constant and trusty friend and keeper of a true poet's full-grown fame.

I remain Dear Madam
Yours very truly,
A. C. Swinburne

—Algernon Charles Swinburne, New York
Daily Tribune, November 27, 1875

John H.B. Latrobe
"Reminiscences of Poe" (1877)

Latrobe, one of the judges who awarded Poe the prize for "MS. Found in a Bottle" in 1833, here recalls Poe's gentlemanly traits as well as the excitement and enthusiasm Poe felt for and brought to his own writing. Latrobe also disputes the veracity of Griswold's biography.

The next number of the *Saturday Visitor* contained the "MS. Found in a Bottle," and announced the author. My office, in these days, was in the building still occupied by the Mechanics' Bank, and I was seated at my desk on the Monday following the publication of the tale, when a gentleman entered and introduced himself as the writer, saying that he came to thank me, as one of the committee, for the award in his favor. Of this interview, the only one I ever had with Mr. Poe, my recollection is very distinct indeed, and it requires but a small effort of imagination to place him before me now, as plainly almost as I see any one of my audience. He was, if anything, below the middle size, and yet could not be described as a small man. His figure was remarkably good, and he carried himself erect and well, as one who had been trained to it. He was dressed in black, and his frock-coat was buttoned to the throat, where it met the black stock, then almost universally worn. Not a particle of white was visible. Coat, hat, boots and gloves had very evidently seen their best days, but so far as mending and brushing go, everything had been done, apparently, to make them presentable. On most men his clothes would have looked shabby and seedy, but there was something about this man that prevented one from criticising his garments, and the details I have mentioned were only recalled afterwards. The impression made, however, was that the award in Mr. Poe's favor was not inopportune. *Gentleman* was written all over him. His manner was easy and quiet, and although he came to return thanks for what he regarded as deserving them, there was nothing obsequious in what he said or did. His features I am unable to describe in detail. His forehead was high and remarkable for the great development at the temple. This was the characteristic of his head, which you noticed at once, and which I have never forgotten. The expression of his face was grave, almost sad, except when he was engaged in conversation, when it became animated and changeable. His voice, I remember, was very pleasing in its tone and well modulated, almost rhythmical, and his words were well chosen and unhesitating. Taking a seat, we conversed a while on ordinary topics, and he informed me that Mr. Kennedy, my colleague in the committee, on whom he had already called, had either given, or promised to give him, a letter to the *Southern Literary Messenger*, which he hoped would procure him employment. I asked him whether he was then occupied with any literary labor. He replied that he was engaged on a voyage to the moon, and at once went into a somewhat learned disquisition upon the laws of gravity, the height of the earth's atmosphere and the capacities of balloons, warming in his speech as he proceeded. Presently, speaking in the first person, he began the voyage, after describing the preliminary arrangements, as you will find them set forth in one of his tales, called "The Adventure of One Hans Pfaall," and leaving the earth, and becoming more and more animated, he described his sensation, as he ascended higher and higher, until, at last, he reached the point in space where the moon's attraction overcame that of the earth, when there was a sudden bouleversement of the car and a great confusion among its tenants. By this time the speaker had become so excited, spoke so rapidly, gesticulating much, that when the turn-up-side-down took place, and he clapped his hands and stamped with his foot by way of emphasis, I was carried along with him, and, for aught to the contrary that I now remember, may have fancied myself the companion of his aerial journey. The climax of the tale was the reversal I have mentioned. When he had finished his description he apologised for his excitability, which he laughed at himself. The conversation then turned upon other subjects, and soon afterward he took his leave. I never saw him more. Dr. Griswold's statement "that Mr. Kennedy accompanied him (Poe) to a clothing store and purchased for him a respectable suit, with a change of linen, and sent him to a bath," is a sheer fabrication.

—John H.B. Latrobe, "Reminiscences of Poe,"
Edgar Allan Poe: A Memorial Volume,
ed. Sara Sigourney Rice, 1877, pp. 60–61

Susan A.T. Weiss
"Last Days of Edgar A. Poe" (1878)

Weiss paints a vivid portrait of Poe, describing in detail his striking features, in particular his eyes. Her use of phrenology—now seen as a laughable pseudoscience—confirms a popular view of Poe: that he was supremely intellectual but lacked moral qualities.

I can vividly recall him as he appeared on his visits to us. He always carried a cane, and upon entering the shade of the avenue would remove his hat, throw back his hair, and walk lingeringly, as if enjoying the coolness, carrying his hat in his hand, generally behind him. Sometimes he would pause to examine some rare flower, or to pluck a grape from the laden trellises. He met us always with an expression of pleasure illuminating his countenance and lighting his fine eyes.

Poe's eyes, indeed, were his most striking feature, and it was to these that his face owed its peculiar attraction. I have never seen other eyes at all resembling them. They were large, with long, jet-black lashes,—the iris dark steel-gray, possessing a crystalline clearness and transparency, through which the jet-black pupil was seen to expand and contract with every shade of thought or emotion. I observed that the lids never contracted, as is so usual in most persons, especially when talking; but his gaze was ever full, open, and unshrinking. His usual expression was dreamy and sad. He had a way of sometimes turning a slightly askance look upon some person who was not observing him, and, with a quiet, steady gaze, appear to be mentally taking the caliber of the unsuspecting subject. "What *awful* eyes Mr. Poe has!" said a lady to me. "It makes my blood run cold to see him slowly turn and fix them upon me when I am talking."

Apart from the wonderful beauty of his eyes, I would not have called Poe a very handsome man. He was, in my opinion, rather distinguished-looking than handsome. What he had been when younger I had heard, but at the period of my acquaintance with him he had a pallid and careworn look,—somewhat haggard, indeed,—very apparent except in his moments of animation. He wore a dark mustache, scrupulously kept, but not entirely concealing a slightly contracted expression of the mouth and an occasional twitching of the upper lip, resembling a sneer. This sneer, indeed, was easily excited—a motion of the lip, scarcely perceptible, and yet intensely expressive. There was in it nothing of ill-nature, but much of sarcasm, as when he remarked of a certain pretentious editor, "He can make bold plunges in shallow water;" and again, in reference to an editor presenting a costly book to a lady whose poems he had for years published while yet refusing to pay for them, Poe observed, "He could afford it," with that almost imperceptible curl of the lip, more expressive of contempt than words could have been. The shape of his head struck me, even on first sight, as peculiar. There was a massive projection of the broad brow and temples, with the organ of casualty very conspicuously developed, a marked flatness of the top of the head, and an unusual fullness at the back. I had at this time no knowledge of phrenology; but now, in recalling this peculiar shape, I cannot deny that in Poe what are called the intellectual and animal portions of the head were remarkably developed, while in the moral regions there was as marked a deficiency. Especially there was a slight depression instead of fullness of outline where the organs of veneration and firmness are located by phrenologists. This peculiarity detracted so much from the symmetrical proportions of the head that he sought to remedy the defect by wearing his hair tossed back, thus producing more apparent height of the cranium.

I am convinced that this time of which I speak must have been what Poe himself declared it—one of the brightest, happiest, and most promising of his maturer life. Had he but possessed a will sufficiently strong to preserve him from the temptation which was his greatest bane, how fair and happy might have been his future career!

—Susan A.T. Weiss, "Last Days of Edgar A. Poe,"
Scribner's Monthly, March 1878, pp. 711–12

◆

GENERAL

◆

During his lifetime, Poe was a well-known poet, critic, and fiction writer. His contributions to American literature are almost immeasurable. His verse helped establish American poetry, although writers such as Longfellow were probably more popular and Whitman and Dickinson had probably achieved greater status in the twentieth century. "The Raven," however, remains America's best-known lyric poem. As a critic, Poe did as much to shape the literary sensibilities of his age as anyone in America did. Poe's criticism established a way of viewing and discussing literary art that drew from European Romanticism and prefigured twentieth-century literary theory. But Poe is now best known for his short stories, particularly those that deal with mystery, horror, madness, and suspense. In his own time, he was also known for writing humor and satire. With such stories as "The Murders in the Rue Morgue" and "The Purloined Letter," Poe is considered the founding father of detective fiction.

The extracts in this section collectively present a multifaceted view of Poe the writer. Arranged chronologically, they include reviews by Poe's contemporaries and by later writers that Poe influenced, inspired, or merely puzzled. In general, the critics hold a mixed opinion of the writer; all acknowledge his genius, while many question whether his work contains the essential elements of greatness. Almost all agreed that Poe was able to combine the analytical with the imaginative with skill and flair. But many critics found that Poe's intellectual gifts dwarfed his emotional power; or, to use the popular analogy of the time, he was all head and no heart.

James Russell Lowell opens this section with two pieces: a critical essay praising Poe's genius and a satirical poem poking fun at his overly technical and rational approach to writing. The next three extracts, by

Pendleton Cooke, John Thompson, and James Hannay, respectively, all praise Poe's "genius," especially as it is revealed in his unique combination of rigorous, logical analysis with imaginative or fantastic imagery. The essay by Charles Baudelaire, from which the next entry is taken, is one of the most influential in all of Poe studies. Baudelaire, a major literary figure in his own right, translated much of Poe's work into French, helping to establish Poe's predominant place in late-nineteenth-century French literary culture. Thanks in part to Baudelaire, Poe became one of Europe's most highly regarded American writers. Poe's work significantly influenced the writings of the French *symbolistes* and others. Baudelaire's image of Poe, which presented him as the *poète maudit*—the suffering artist who is unappreciated by the callous, bourgeois society in which he is forced to live—remains most evocative and continues to influence views of Poe today.

George Gilfillan, in his portrait of Poe, identifies a theme that echoes in much of the criticism of Poe's work: Poe's "coldness." Many critics objected to the perceived lack of warmth or human emotion in Poe's writings. Gilfillan says that Poe wrote poetry the way others solve math problems, with cool logic and meticulous intellectual work. This is not a very Romantic image of the poet, of course. Poe's learnedness is also seen as a liability, as when Thomas Chivers accuses him of overusing the "classical" style of poetry. Yet such literary masters as Fyodor Dostoevski and Stéphane Mallarmé admire Poe's style immensely. Dostoevski writes that Poe's realistic approach makes the fantastic elements more material; Mallarmé writes a poem to dedicate Poe's tomb. Richard Henry Horne and Thomas Wentworth Higginson praise Poe's originality, although they both wonder whether Poe's subject matter is always appropriate.

The final entries in this section deal with Poe's work at greater length. Each is penned by a prominent British writer, and each praises Poe, although for differing reasons. Charles Whibley finds that Poe is a truly original writer who employs the same gifts as his fictional detective in unraveling the problems of writing. George Bernard Shaw places Poe alongside Whitman as the greatest writers American democracy had ever produced; he believes that the dehumanizing effects of modern capitalism have proved injurious to Poe, who, despite his own "aloofness" toward the common man, actually represents the best that humankind has to offer. D.H. Lawrence paints a different picture, arguing that Poe is a scientist rather than an artist; Poe's work dissects human emotion and thinking, destroying the object even as it comes to know it. These extracts illuminate the ways in which Poe's work can be so widely admired while also disliked by many. Poe's power is undeniable, but it does not always make for pleasant reading.

James Russell Lowell
"Edgar Allan Poe" (1845)

Lowell was a poet, critic, and scholar who co-edited the first collected works of Poe in 1850. Lowell's *A Fable for Critics* later poked fun at Poe, noting that the poet lacked the proper balance between the heart and the head—a theme common to the Romantic movement. Here, however, Lowell lavishly praises Poe's genius as a critic, poet, and storyteller.

Lowell begins his essay by saying that, "before we can have an American literature, we must have an American criticism." That is, in order to recognize truly great literature, Americans need an appropriate critical apparatus by which to do so. Lowell finds that Poe is among the best critics in America, although he says that Poe is often too harsh ("acid for his inkstand"). Students exploring the interrelations of criticism and literature might turn to Lowell's contentions. Does criticism make literature better? How?

Lowell also discusses Poe's genius. The notion of genius was prominent at the time, and it suggests a certain "natural" or god-given ability. But writing also involved hard work, irrespective of innate ability. Lowell states that talent alone does not approach genius. What, then, is the nature of genius? How does literary genius reveal itself? Is *genius* a useful term for talking about writers?

Like others in this volume, Lowell cites Poe's combination of analytical and imaginative skills. Today it is not uncommon to sharply distinguish between these two intellectual realms. The creative writer or artist is often thought of as having a completely different way of thinking than the scientist, mathematician, or engineer. Yet Poe is praised for combining the two. A student may look at Lowell's piece in exploring Poe's dual use of rationality and creativity.

Another way of discussing this is to revisit the heart-versus-head distinction, alluded to in Lowell's satirical poem. Although many critics praise Poe's gift for bringing together the analytical with the imaginative, Poe is also criticized for being too cold, rational, and intellectual, for lacking real human warmth or feeling. The well-balanced person, presumably, is equal parts heart and head, emotion and reason, passion and intellect. Students might explore these ideas in relation to Poe's tales. Does Poe's style present things in a cool, unemotional way?

In Poe's own literary theory, he asserts that a poem or a tale should have a single effect or a unity of effect. That is, the work should produce the sensation in the reader that the author intended. Lowell points out that Poe's tales do just that, elicit a particular emotion in the reader.

Some have suggested that this is essentially a trick, a technique that may excite or initially shock, but which has no lasting artistic merit. Students examining Poe's effects and approach as a writer may want to look at the way an author in general tries to manipulate the reader's emotions.

———~*//*~— ——~*//*~— ——~*//*~—

Mr. Poe is at once the most discriminating, philosophical, and fearless critic upon imaginative works who has written in America. It may be that we should qualify our remark a little, and say that he *might be,* rather than that he always *is,* for he seems sometimes to mistake his phial of prussic-acid for his inkstand. If we do not always agree with him in his premises, we are, at least, satisfied that his deductions are logical, and that we are reading the thoughts of a man who thinks for himself, and says what he thinks, and knows well what he is talking about. His analytic power would furnish forth bravely some score of ordinary critics. We do not know him personally, but we suspect him for a man who has one or two pet prejudices on which he prides himself. These sometimes allure him out of the strict path of criticism, but, where they do not interfere, we would put almost entire confidence in his judgments. Had Mr. Poe had the control of a magazine of his own, in which to display his critical abilities, he would have been as autocratic, ere this, in America, as Professor Wilson has been in England; and his criticisms, we are sure, would have been far more profound and philosophical than those of the Scotsman. As it is, he has squared out blocks enough to build an enduring pyramid, but has left them lying carelessly and unclaimed in many different quarries.

Remarkable experiences are usually confined to the inner life of imaginative men, but Mr. Poe's biography displays a vicissitude and peculiarity of interest such as is rarely met with. The offspring of a romantic marriage, and left an orphan at an early age, he was adopted by Mr. Allan, a wealthy Virginian, whose barren marriage-bed seemed the warranty of a large estate to the young poet. Having received a classical education in England, he returned home and entered the University of Virginia, where, after an extravagant course, followed by reformation at the last extremity, he was graduated with the highest honors of his class. . . . He now entered the military academy at West Point, from which he obtained a dismissal on hearing of the birth of a son to his adopted father, by a second marriage, an event which cut off his expectations as an heir. The death of Mr. Allan, in whose will his name was not mentioned, soon after relieved him of all doubt in this regard, and he committed himself at once to authorship for a support. Previously to this, however, he had published (in 1827) a small volume of poems, which soon ran through three editions, and excited high expectations of its author's future distinction in the minds of many competent judges. . . .

Mr. Poe's early productions show that he could see through the verse to the spirit beneath, and that he already had a feeling that all the life and grace of the one must depend on and be modulated by the will of the other. We call them the most remarkable boyish poems that we have ever read. We know of none that can compare with them for maturity of purpose, and a nice understanding of the effects of language and metre. Such pieces are only valuable when they display what we can only express by the contradictory phrase of *innate experience.* We copy one of the shorter poems written when the author was only *fourteen!* There is little dimness in the filling up, but the grace and symmetry of the outline are such as few poets ever attain. There is a smack of ambrosia about it.

> To Helen
> Helen, thy beauty is to me
>   Like those Nicean barks of yore,
> That gently, o'er a perfumed sea,
>   The weary, way-worn wanderer bore
>   To his own native shore.
>
> On desperate seas long wont to roam,
>   Thy hyacinth hair, thy classic face,
> Thy Naiad airs have brought me home
>   To the glory that was Greece
>   And the grandeur that was Rome.
>
> Lo! in yon brilliant window-niche
>   How statue-like I see thee stand!
> The agate lamp within thy hand,
>   Ah! Psyche, from the regions which
>   Are Holy Land!

It is the *tendency* of the young poet that impresses us. Here is no "withering scorn," no heart "blighted" ere it has safely got into its teens, none of the drawing-room sansculottism which Byron had brought into vogue. All is limpid and serene, with a pleasant dash of the Greek Helicon in it. The melody of the whole, too, is remarkable. It is not of that kind which can be demonstrated arithmetically upon the tips of the fingers. It is of that finer sort which the inner ear alone can estimate. It seems simple, like a Greek column, because of its perfection. In a poem named "Ligeia," under which title he intended to personify the music of nature, our boy-poet gives us the following exquisite picture:

> Ligeia! Ligeia!
>   My beautiful one,
> Whose harshest idea
>   Will to melody run,
> *Say, is it thy will*
>   On the breezes to toss,
> *Or, capriciously still,*
>   Like the lone albatross,
> *Incumbent on night,*
>   As she on the air,
> *To keep watch with delight*
>   On the harmony there?

John Neal, himself a man of genius, and whose lyre has been too long capriciously silent, appreciated the high merit of these and similar passages, and drew a proud horoscope for their author. The extracts which we shall presently make from Mr. Poe's later poems, fully justify his predictions.

Mr. Poe has that indescribable something which men have agreed to call *genius*. No man could ever tell us precisely what it is, and yet there is none who is not inevitably aware of its presence and its power. Let talent writhe and contort itself as it may, it has no such magnetism. Larger of bone and sinew it may be, but the wings are wanting. Talent sticks fast to earth, and its most perfect works have still one foot of clay. Genius claims kindred with the very workings of Nature herself, so that a sunset shall seem like a quotation from Dante or Milton, and if Shakespeare be read in the very presence of the sea itself, his verses shall but seem nobler for the sublime criticism of ocean. Talent may make friends for itself, but only genius can give to its creations the divine power of winning love and veneration. Enthusiasm cannot cling to what itself is unenthusiastic, nor will he ever have disciples who has not himself impulsive zeal enough to be a disciple. Great wits are allied to madness only inasmuch as they are possessed and carried away by their demon, while talent keeps him as Paracelsus did, securely prisoned in the pommel of its sword. To the eye of genius, the veil of the spiritual world is ever rent asunder, that it may perceive the ministers of good and evil who throng continually around it. No man of mere talent ever flung his inkstand at the devil.

When we say that Mr. Poe has genius, we do not mean to say that he has produced evidence of the highest. But to say that he possesses it at all is to say that he needs only zeal, industry, and a reverence for the trust reposed in him, to achieve the proudest triumphs and the greenest laurels. If we may believe the Longinuses and Aristotles of our newspapers, we have quite too many geniuses of the loftiest order to render a place among them at all desirable, whether for its hardness of attainment or its seclusion. The highest peak of our Parnassus is, according to these gentlemen, by far the most thickly settled portion of the country, a circumstance which must make it an uncomfortable residence for individuals of a poetical temperament, if love of solitude be, as immemorial tradition asserts, a necessary part of their idiosyncrasy. There is scarce a gentleman or lady of respectable moral character to whom these liberal dispensers of the laurel have not given a ticket to that once sacred privacy, where they may elbow Shakespeare and Milton at leisure. A transient visiter, such as a critic must necessarily be, sees these legitimate proprietors in common, parading their sacred enclosure as thick and buzzing as flies, each with "Entered according to act of Congress" labeled securely to his back. Formerly one Phoebus, a foreigner, we believe, had the monopoly of transporting all passengers thither, a service for which he provided no other conveyance than a vicious horse, named Pegasus, who could, of course, carry but one at a time, and even that but seldom, his back being a ticklish seat, and one fall proving generally enough to damp the ardor of the most zealous aspirant. The charges, however, were moderate, as the poet's pocket formerly occupied that position in regard to the rest of his outfit which is now more usually conceded to his head. But we must return from our little historical digression.

Mr. Poe has two of the prime qualities of genius, a faculty of vigorous yet minute analysis, and a wonderful fecundity of imagination. The first of these faculties is as needful to the artist in words, as a knowledge of anatomy is to the artist in colors or in stone. This enables him to conceive truly, to maintain a proper relation of parts, and to draw a correct outline, while the second groups, fills up, and colors. Both of these Mr. Poe has displayed with singular distinctness in his prose works, the last predominating in his earlier tales, and the first in his later ones. In judging of the merit of an author, and assigning him his niche among our household gods, we have a right to regard him from our own point of view, and to measure him by our own standard. But, in estimating his works, we must be governed by his own design, and, placing them by the side of his own ideal, find how much is wanting. We differ with Mr. Poe in his opinions of the objects of art. He esteems that object to be the creation of Beauty, and perhaps it is only in the definition of that word that we disagree with him. But in what we shall say of his writings we shall take his own standard as our guide. The temple of the god of song is equally accessible from every side, and there is room enough in it for all who bring offerings, or seek an oracle.

In his tales, Mr. Poe has chosen to exhibit his power chiefly in that dim region which stretches from the very utmost limits of the probable into the weird confines of superstition and unreality. He combines in a very remarkable manner two faculties which are seldom found united; a power of influencing the mind of the reader by the impalpable shadows of mystery, and a minuteness of detail which does not leave a pin or a button unnoticed. Both are, in truth, the natural results of the predominating quality of his mind, to which we have before alluded, analysis. It is this which distinguishes the artist. His mind at once reaches forward to the effect to be produced. Having resolved to bring about certain emotions in the reader, he makes all subordinate parts tend strictly to the common centre. Even his mystery is mathematical to his own mind. To him x is a known quantity all along. In any picture that he paints, he understands the chemical properties of all his colors. However vague some of his figures may seem, however formless the shadows, to him the outline is as clear and distinct as that of a geometrical diagram. For this reason Mr. Poe has no sympathy with *Mysticism*. The Mystic dwells *in* the mystery, is enveloped with it, it colors all his thoughts; it effects his optic nerve especially, and the commonest things get a rainbow edging from it. Mr. Poe, on the other hand, is a spectator *ab extra*. He analyzes, he dissects, he watches

—with an eye serene,
The very pulse of the machine,

for such it practically is to him, with wheels and cogs and piston-rods all working to produce a certain end. It is this that makes him so good a critic. Nothing baulks him, or throws him off the scent, *except now and then a prejudice*.

This analyzing tendency of his mind balances the poetical, and, by giving him the patience to be minute, enables him to throw a wonderful reality into his most unreal fancies. A monomania he paints with great power. He loves to dissect these cancers of the mind, and to trace all the subtle ramifications of its roots. In raising images of horror, also, he has a strange success; conveying to us sometimes by a dusky hint some terrible *doubt* which is the secret of all horror. He leaves to imagination the task of finishing the picture, a task to which only she is competent.

> For much imaginary work was there;
> Conceit deceitful, so compact, so kind,
> That for Achilles' image stood his spear
> Grasped in an armed hand; himself behind
> Was left unseen, save to the eye of mind.

We have hitherto spoken chiefly of Mr. Poe's *collected* tales, as by them he is more widely known than by those published since in various magazines, and which we hope soon to see collected. In these he has more strikingly displayed his analytic propensity.

Beside the merit of conception, Mr. Poe's writings have also that of form. His style is highly finished, graceful and truly classical. It would be hard to find a living author who had displayed such varied powers. As an example of his style we would refer to one of his tales, "The House of Usher," in the first volume of his *Tales of the Grotesque and Arabesque.* It has a singular charm for us, and we think that no one could read it without being strongly moved by its serene and sombre beauty. Had its author written nothing else it would alone have been enough to stamp him as a man of genius, and the master of a classic style. . . .

Beside his *Tales of the Grotesque and Arabesque,* and some works unacknowledged, Mr. Poe is the author of *Arthur Gordon Pym,* a romance, in two volumes, which has run through many editions in London; of a system of Conchology, of a digest and translation of Lemmonnier's *Natural History,* and has contributed to several reviews in France, in England, and in this country. He edited the *Southern Literary Messenger* during its novitiate, and by his own contributions gained it most of its success and reputation. He was also, for some time, the editor of this magazine, and our readers will bear testimony to his ability in that capacity.

Mr. Poe is still in the prime of life, being about thirty-two years of age, and has probably as yet given but an earnest of his powers. As a critic, he has shown so superior an ability that we cannot but hope that he will collect his essays of this kind and give them a more durable form. They would be a very valuable contribution to our literature, and would fully justify all we have said in his praise. We could refer to many others of his poems than those we have quoted, to prove that he is the possessor of a pure and original vein. His tales and essays have equally shown him a master in prose. It is not for us to assign him his definite rank among contemporary authors, but we may be allowed to say that we know of *none* who has displayed more varied and striking abilities.

—James Russell Lowell, "Edgar Allan Poe,"
Graham's Magazine, February 1845, pp. 49–53

JAMES RUSSELL LOWELL (1848)

There comes Poe, with his raven, like Barnaby Rudge,
Three fifths of him genius and two fifths sheer fudge,
Who talks like a book of iambs and pentameters,
In a way to make people of common sense damn metres,
Who has written some things quite the best of their kind,
But the heart somehow seems all squeezed out by the mind.

—James Russell Lowell, *A Fable for Critics*, 1848

P. PENDLETON COOKE "EDGAR A. POE" (1848)

Cooke, a lawyer and poet who had published work in *Southern Literary Messenger*, included this text as a "postscript" to James Russell Lowell's 1845 essay on Poe. Cooke lavishes praise on Poe, calling "The Raven" a "great triumph of imagination and art." Cooke argues that Poe's tales present the most fantastic ideas but in the guise of utmost truth, so much so that certain foreign journals had published his tales as nonfiction. Cooke asserts that Poe has no equal when it comes to analytical and narrative powers. He contrasts Poe's "truthlike narrative" with Daniel Defoe's *Robinson Crusoe*, the latter being content displaying the familiar "real," whereas Poe drives the reader into the disturbing yet no less "truthful" realms of mystery, monomania, and "convulsions of the soul."

Since the memoir of Mr. Poe, written by James Russell Lowell, appeared, Mr. P. has written some of his best things; amongst them The Raven, and Dreamland—poems—and M. Valdemar's case—a prose narrative.

"The Raven" is a singularly beautiful poem. Many readers who prefer sunshine to the weird lights with which Mr. Poe fills his sky, may be dull to its beauty, but it is none the less a great triumph of imagination and art. Notwithstanding the extended publication of this remarkable poem, I will quote it almost entire—as the last means of justifying the praise I have bestowed upon it.

The opening stanza rapidly and clearly arranges time, place, etc., for the mysteries that follow.

> Once upon a midnight dreary, while I pondered, weak and weary,
> Over many a quaint and curious volume of forgotten lore,
> While I nodded, nearly napping, suddenly there came a tapping
> As of some one gently rapping, rapping at my chamber door,
> ''T is some visiter,' I muttered, tapping at my chamber door—
>   'Only this, and nothing more.'

Observe how artistically the poet has arranged the circumstances of this opening—how congruous all are. This congruity extends to the phraseology; every word is admirably selected and placed with reference to the whole. Even the word "napping" is well chosen, as bestowing a touch of the fantastic, which is subsequently introduced as an important component of the poem. Stanza 2d increases the distinctness and effect of the picture as already presented to us. The "Midnight Dreary" is a midnight "in the bleak December," and the "dying embers" are assuming strange and fantastic shapes upon the student's hearth. We now pass these externals and some words of exquisite melody let us into the secret of the rooted sorrow which has led to the lonely night-watching and fruitless study.

> Vainly I had sought to borrow
> From my books surcease of sorrow—sorrow for the lost Lenore—
> For the rare and radiant maiden, whom *the angels named Lenore,*
>   *Nameless here forever more.*

A death was never more poetically told than in the italicised words:

The "tapping" is renewed—

> And the silken, sad, uncertain, rustling of each purple curtain
> Thrilled me, filled me, with fantastic terrors never felt before,
> So that now, to still the beating of my heart, I stood repeating
> ''T is some visiter entreating entrance at my chamber door,
> Some late visiter entreating entrance at my chamber door,
>   Only this and nothing more.'

After some stanzas, quaint and highly artistical, the raven is found at the window; I quote now continuously to the end. . . .

The rhythm of this poem is exquisite, its phraseology is in the highest degree musical and apt, the tone of the whole is wonderfully sustained and appropriate to the subject, which, full as it is of a wild and tender melancholy, is admirably well chosen. This is my honest judgment; I am fortified in it by high authority. Mr. Willis says:—"It is the most effective single example of fugitive poetry ever published in this country, and unsurpassed in English poetry for subtle, conception, masterly ingenuity of versification, and consistent sustaining of imaginative lift. It is one of those dainties which we *feed on*. It will stick to the memory of every one who reads it."

Miss Barrett says:—"This vivid writing!—this power *which is felt!* 'The Raven' has produced a sensation—a 'fit horror' here in England. Some of my friends are taken by the fear of it, and some by the music. I hear of persons *haunted* by the Nevermore, and one acquaintance of mine, who has the misfortune of possessing a bust of Pallas, never can bear to look at it in the twilight. Our great poet, Mr. Browning, author of Paracelsus, etc., is enthusiastic in his admiration of the rhythm. . . . Then there is a tale of his which I do not find in this volume, but which is going the rounds of the newspapers, about mesmerism, throwing us all into most 'admired disorder,' or dreadful doubts as to whether it can be true, as the children say of ghost stories. The certain thing in the tale in question is the power of the writer, and the faculty he has of making horrible improbabilities seem near and familiar."

The prose narrative, "M. Valdemar's Case"—the story of which Miss Barrett speaks—is the most truth-like representation of the impossible ever written. M. Valdemar is mesmerized *in articulo mortis*. Months pass away, during which he appears to be in mesmeric sleep; the mesmeric influence is withdrawn, and instantly his body becomes putrid and loathsome—*he has been many months dead*. Will the reader believe that men were found to credit this wild story? And yet some very respectable people believed in its truth firmly. The editor of the Baltimore Visiter republished it as a statement of facts, and was at the pains to vouch for Mr. Poe's veracity. If the letter of a Mr. Collier, published just after the original appearance of the story, was not a quiz, he also fell into the same trap. I understand that some foreign mesmeric journals, German and French, reprinted it as being what it purported to be—a true account of mesmeric phenomena. That many others were deceived in like manner by this strange tale, in which, as Miss Barrett says, "the wonder and question are, can it be true?" is very probable.

With Mr. Poe's more recent productions I am not at all acquainted—excepting a review of Miss Barrett's works, and an essay on the philosophy of composition. The first of these contains a great deal of noble writing and excellent criticism; the last is an admirable specimen of analysis. I believe Mr. P. has been for some time ill—has recently sustained a heavy domestic bereavement—and is only now returning to his literary labors. The public will doubtless welcome the return of so favorite an author to pursuits in which heretofore he has done so much and so well.

Unnecessary as the labor may be, I will not conclude this postscript to Mr. Lowell's memoir, without making some remarks upon Mr. Poe's genius and writings generally.

Mr. P.'s most distinguishing power is that which made the extravagant fiction of M. Valdemar's Case sound like truth. He has De Foe's peculiar talent for filling up his pictures with minute life-like touches—for giving an air of remarkable naturalness and truth to whatever he paints. Some of his stories, written many years ago, are wonderful in this fidelity and distinctness of portraiture; "Hans Phaal," "A Descent into the Maelström," and "MS. Found in a Bottle," show it in an eminent degree. In the first of these a journey to the moon is described with the fullness and particularity of an ordinary traveller's journal; entries, astronomical and thermical, and, on reaching the moon, botanical, and zoological, are made with an inimitable matter-of-fact air. In A Descent into the Maelström you are made fairly to feel yourself on the descending round of the vortex, convoying fleets of drift timber, and fragments of wrecks; the terrible whirl makes you giddy as you read. In the "MS. Found in a Bottle" we have a story as wild as the mind of man ever conceived, and yet made to sound like the most matter-of-fact veracious narrative of a seaman.

But in Mr. Poe, the peculiar talent to which we are indebted for Robinson Crusoe, and the memoirs of Captain Monroe, has an addition. Truthlike as nature itself, his strange fiction shows constantly the presence of a singularly adventurous, very wild, and thoroughly poetic imagination. Some sentences from them, which always impressed me deeply, will give full evidence of the success with which this rare imaginative power is made to adorn and ennoble his truthlike pictures. Take this passage from Ligeia, a wonderful story, written to show the triumph of the human will even over *death*. Ligeia, in whom the struggle between the will to live, and the power of death, has seemed to terminate in the defeat of the passionate will, is consigned to the tomb. Her husband married a second wife, "the fair-haired and blue-eyed Lady Rowena." By the sick bed of this second wife, who is dying from some mysterious cause, he sits.

[quotes from "The Fall of the House of Usher"]

These quoted passages—the "white and ghastly spectrum of the teeth" in "Berenice"—the visible vulture eye, and audible heart-beat in the "Tell-tale Heart"—the resemblance in "Morella" of the living child to the dead mother, becoming gradually fearful, until the haunting eyes gleam out a terrible *identity*, and prove as in Ligeia the final conquest of the will over death—these and a thousand such clinging ideas, which Mr. P.'s writings abound in, prove indisputably that the fires of a great poet are seething under those analytic and narrative powers *in which no living writer equals him*.

This added gift of a daring and wild imagination is the source of much of the difference between our author and De Foe. De Foe loves and deals always with the homely. Mr. Poe is nervously afraid of the homely—has a creed that Beauty is the goddess of the Poet:—not Beauty with swelling bust, and lascivious carriage, exciting passions of the blood, but Beauty sublimated and cherished by the soul—the beauty of the Uranian, not Dionean Venus. De Foe gives us in the cheerful and delightful story of his colonist of the desert isles, (which has as sure a locality in a million minds as any genuine island has upon the maps,) a clear, plain, true-sounding narrative of matters that might occur any day. His love for the real makes him do so. The "real" of such a picture has not strangeness enough in its proportions for Mr. Poe's imagination; and, with the same talent for truthlike narrative, to what different results of creation does not this imagination, scornful of the soberly real, lead him! Led by it he loves to adventure into what in one of his poems he calls—

a wild weird clime
Out of space, out of time;—

deals in mysteries of "life in death," dissects monomanias, exhibits convulsions of soul—in a word, wholly leaves beneath and behind him the wide and happy realm of the common cheerful life of man.

That he would be a greater favorite with the majority of readers if he brought his singular capacity for vivid and truth-like narrative to bear on subjects nearer ordinary life, and of a more cheerful and happy character, does not, I think, admit of a doubt. But whether with the few he is not all the more appreciable from the difficult nature of the fields which he has principally chosen, is questionable. For what he has done, many of the best minds of America, England and France, have awarded him praise; labors of a tamer nature might not have won it from such sources. For my individual part, having the seventy or more tales, analytic, mystic, grotesque, arabesque, always wonderful, often great, which his industry and fertility have already given us, I would like to read one cheerful book made by his *invention*, with little or no aid from its twin brother imagination—a book in his admirable style of full, minute, never tedious narrative—a book full of homely doings, of successful toils, of ingenious shifts and contrivances, of ruddy firesides—a book healthy and happy throughout, and with no poetry in it at all anywhere, except a good old English "poetic justice" in the end. Such a book, such as Mr. Poe could make it, would be a book for the million, and if it did nothing to exalt him with the few, would yet certainly *endear* him to them.

Mr. Lowell has gone deeply and discriminatingly into Mr. Poe's merits as a poet. Any elaborate remarks of mine on the same subject, would be out of place here. I will not, however, lose this opportunity of expressing an admiration which I have long entertained of the singular mastery of certain externals of his art which he everywhere exhibits in his verse. His rhythm, and his vocabulary, or phraseology, are perhaps perfect. The reader has perceived the beauty of the rhythm in The Raven. Some other verses from poems to which Mr. Lowell has referred, are quite as remarkable for this beauty. Read these verses from Lenore:—

. . . And take these, in the most graceful of all measures—they are from "To One in Paradise."

> And all my days are trances
>   And all my nightly dreams
> Are where thy dark eye glances,
>   And where thy footstep gleams—
> In what ethereal dances,
>   By what eternal streams.

Along with wonderful beauty of rhythm, these verses show the exquisite taste in phraseology, the nice sense of melody and aptness in words, of which I spoke. We have direct evidence of this nice sense of verbal melody in some quotations which are introduced into the dramatic fragment "Politian."

[. . .]

I must conclude these insufficient remarks upon a writer worthy of high and honorable place amongst the leading creative minds of the age.

As regards the Wiley & Putnam publication of Mr. Poe's tales—a volume by which his rare literary claims have been most recently presented to the public—I think the book in some respects does him injustice. It contains twelve tales out of more than seventy; and it is made up almost wholly of what may be called his analytic tales. This is not *representing* the author's mind in its various phases. A reader gathering his knowledge of Mr. Poe from this Wiley & Putnam issue would perceive nothing of the diversity and variety for which his writings are in fact remarkable. Only the publication of all his stories, at one issue, in one book, would show this diversity and variety in their full force; but much more might have been done to represent his mind by a judicious and not wholly one-toned selection.

—P. Pendleton Cooke, "Edgar A. Poe,"
Southern Literary Messenger, January 1848

John R. Thompson
"The Late Edgar A. Poe" (1849)

Thompson was the editor of the *Southern Literary Messenger*, a magazine that Poe had previously edited and in which he had published many works. In this obituary, Thompson praises Poe's originality, unconventionality, and overall genius. He marvels at how artfully Poe could combine both wildly imaginative and patiently analytical thinking.

Unquestionably he was a man of great genius. Among the *litterateurs* of his day he stands out distinctively as an original writer and thinker. In nothing did he conform to established custom. Conventionality he contemned. Thus his writings admit of no classification. And yet in his most eccentric vagaries he was always correct. The fastidious reader may look in vain, even among his earlier poems—where "wild words wander here and there"—for an offence against rhetorical propriety. He did not easily pardon solecisms in others; he committed none himself. It is remarkable too that a mind so prone to unrestrained imaginings should be capable of analytic investigation or studious research. Yet few excelled Mr. Poe in power of analysis or patient application. Such are the contradictions of the human intellect. He was an impersonated antithesis.

—John R. Thompson, "The Late Edgar A. Poe,"
Southern Literary Messenger, November 1849, p. 694

James Hannay "The Life and Genius of Edgar Allan Poe" (1852)

Hannay acknowledges Poe's combination of analytical and imaginative powers, but asserts that all fine intellects exhibit this combination. Students interested in the distinction, whether valid or not, between artistic or poetic sensibilities and practical, calculating, or mathematical gifts might cite Hannay's article.

―――――――――――

It has been remarked of him that he united singularly the qualities of the Poet with the faculties of the Analyst. He wrote charming little ballads, and was a curious disentangler of evidence—criminal evidence, for instance—and fond of problems and cipher. The union is indubitable; but I scarcely think it should have been so much dwelt upon. Every man of fine intellect of the highest class includes a capacity more or less for all branches of inquiry. Carlyle was distinguished in arithmetic long before he became the Teacher which we hail him as, now. On the other hand, inventors in the regions of mechanics partake of something poetic in their inspiration. Brindley was as eccentric as Goldsmith. Watt would muse over a tea-kettle as Rousseau did over *la pervenche,* or over the lake into which he dropped sentimental tears. One very curious theory was hit upon by a solid critic a little while ago to explain Poe's two-handedness. He knew that Poe wrote fine poetry—he knew Poe made subtle calculations; and what was his inference? *Credite posteri!* He insisted that the calculating faculty was *the* fact, and that the poetry was calculation! I scarcely ever remember a more curious instance of the "cart being put before the horse"—by the ass! Nothing can be more clear, to be sure, than that Poe employed a great deal of ingenuity and calculation in the finishing of his Tales and polishing of his poems. But all this leaves the poetic inspiration pure at the bottom as the essential fact. Otherwise, if we are to make the calculating the predominant faculty, we may look out for a volume of Sonnets by Cocker! Poe has admitted us, in one of his essays, to the *genesis* of "The Raven," and has even told us which stanza he wrote first, and on what mechanical principles he managed the arrangement of the story. But surely all this presupposes the pure creative genius necessary to the conception?

Keeping the distinction in view, we shall easily see that all his Tales—analytic and other—resolve themselves into poems, instead of the poems resolving themselves into machinery. The "Gold Bug," for example, makes a most ingenious use of a cipher, but the cipher is only *materiel*. Without creative genius mere cipher is an affair for the Foreign Office—which still remains a very inferior place to Parnassus. The same remark applies to his other poetical exercises—for such they are—in Mesmerism, Physics, Circumstantial Evidence, &c. Far from being a narrow student of the details of these, he always has clearly an eye in using them to the poetic goal or result

—James Hannay, "The Life and Genius of Edgar Allan Poe,"
The Poetical Works of Edgar Allan Poe, 1852, pp. xxv–xxvi

CHARLES BAUDELAIRE "EDGAR ALLAN POE: HIS LIFE AND WORKS" (1852)

A great poet in his own right, Baudelaire (author of *Les fleurs du mal* or *Flowers of Evil*) translated much of Poe's work and is largely responsible for Poe's popularity in France. In this essay, Baudelaire emphasizes the "unlucky" life of the poetic genius. For Baudelaire, Poe is indisputably America's greatest writer, but, ironically, America is poorly suited for such an artist. Baudelaire complains that, in the United States, Poe's genius was wasted, since Americans value only the "making-money author" (a phrase Baudelaire derisively states in English, as if the French language itself should not be tainted with it). According to Baudelaire, Poe suffered in this crass, materialistic, and commercial society, but he was also able to create the finest literature of his age. Thus, Poe's life and work are set at odds; he is unappreciated and unlucky in life, but his works represent the higher realm of Art.

Baudelaire's portrait of Poe presents the famous image of the *poète maudit* (literally, "accursed poet"), the outcast who is spurned by society for revealing the truth, especially about society's spiritual emptiness. For Baudelaire, this image is particularly apt in a society that revels in its own commercial and democratic ideals and in which the artist will remain an outsider or outcast. Students exploring the role of the artist in society might look at Baudelaire's view that the artist should stand above the common man. A sociological study of Poe could also use Baudelaire's essay to examine how social classes relate to literary works. Many of Poe's characters are frequently outsiders who do not seem to "fit" within their society. A student using a psychoanalytic approach to Poe could cite Baudelaire's exploration of the mind of Poe, whether seen through the madness of his characters or through the traumas of his personal life.

In addition to the sociological and psychological elements, Baudelaire emphasizes the originality and simplicity of Poe's style. Poe uses the first-person pronoun "with cynical monotony." His stories almost all employ a straightforward narration by the main character. Students might refer to this aspect of Baudelaire's criticism when comparing different kinds of narrative techniques. Poe's technique seems to lend his utterly fantastic works greater credibility: the unbelievable tale is presented in a detached, almost scientific fashion. This can be seen in the detective stories (such as "The Murders in the Rue Morgue") and science fiction ("The Mesmeric Revelation"). Students could contrast this style with other writers, such as Irving or Hawthorne, who often employ third-person narration in their tales.

Baudelaire's essay represents an important event in comparative literature: a major French *litterateur* writing about a major American one. Students interested in a comparative study might look at the influence of Poe's ideas, poems, or short stories on European literature, including Baudelaire's own *Les fleurs du mal*. Poe was himself so influenced by certain European writers that he defended the originality of his own stories, declaring that "terror is not of Germany, it is of the soul." Students writing about transatlantic influences can use Baudelaire's essay as a starting point. Is Poe better suited to a European audience, as Baudelaire suggests? What is particularly American or un-American about Poe? Baudelaire's reading might offer material for students who want to examine Poe in relation to world literature.

I

Some destinies are fatal. In the literature of every country there are men who bear the word *unlucky* written with mysterious letters in the sinuous folds of their foreheads. Some time ago a wretch with the strange tattoo *no luck* on his forehead was led before the court. He carried the label of his life with him everywhere, as a book bears its title, and the questioning proved that his existence conformed to his advertisement. In literary history there are similar fates. One might say that the blind Angel of Expiation, seizing certain men, whips them with all his might for the edification of the others. Yet if we study their lives attentively we find they have talent, virtue and grace. Society pronounces a special anathema and condemns them for the very vices of character that its persecution has given them. What did Hoffman fail to do to disarm destiny? What did Balzac fail to do to exorcize fortune? Hoffmann was obliged to destroy himself at the very moment, so long desired, when he began to be safe from necessity, when bookstores fought over his tales, when at last he possessed his beloved library. Balzac had three dreams: a well-organized, complete edition of his works; the settling of his debts; and a marriage long savored in the depths of his heart. Thanks to an amount of labor which stuns the most ambitious and painstaking imagination the edition was made, the debts were paid and the marriage accomplished. Balzac was happy, no doubt. But malevolent destiny, having permitted him to put one foot on the promised land, wrenched it away at once. Balzac experienced a horribly agony worthy of his strength.

Is there a Providence preparing men for misfortune from the cradle? These men whose somber and desolate talent awes us have been cast *with premeditation* into a hostile milieu. A tender and delicate spirit, a Vauvenargues, slowly unfolds its frail leaves in the gross atmosphere of a garrison. A mind that loves the open air and adores free nature struggles for a long time behind the stifling wall of a seminary. This ironic and ultragrotesque comic talent, whose laugh sometimes resembles a gasp or a sob, has been imprisoned in vast offices with green boxes and men with gold spectacles. Are there then some souls dedicated to the altar, *sanctified,* so to speak, who must march to their death and glory through perpetual self-immolation? Will the nightmare of *Tenebrae* always envelop these chosen spirits? They defend themselves in vain, they take all precautions, they perfect prudence. Let us block all the exits, close the door with a double lock, stop up the chinks in the windows. Oh! we forgot the keyhole; the Devil has already entered.

Leur chien même les mord et leur donne la rage.
Un ami jurera qu'ils ont trahi le roi.

Alfred de Vigny has written a book demonstrating that the poet's place is in neither a republic, nor an absolute monarchy, nor a constitutional monarchy; and no one has answered him.

The life of Edgar Poe is a wretched tragedy, and the horror of its ending is increased by its triviality. The various documents that I have just read have persuaded me that the United States was a vast cage for Poe, a great accounting establishment. All his life he made grim efforts to escape the influence of that antipathetic atmosphere. One of his biographers says that if Poe had wanted to regularize his genius and apply his creative faculties in a way more appropriate to the American soil he could have been an author with money, *a making-money author.* He said that after all, the times were not so hard for a talented man; he always found enough to live on, provided that he behaved with order and economy and used material wealth with moderation. Elsewhere, a critic shamelessly declares that however fine the genius of Poe might be, it would have been better to have merely had talent because talent is more easily turned to cash than genius is. A note written by one of his friends states that Poe was difficult to employ on a magazine, and he had to be paid less than the others because he wrote in a style too far above the ordinary. All of that reminds me of the odious paternal proverb, *"Make money, my son, honestly, if you can,* BUT MAKE MONEY." *What a smell of department stores,* as J. de Maistre said concerning Locke.

If you talk to an American and speak to him of Poe, he will admit Poe's genius, willingly even; perhaps he will be proud, but he will end by saying, in his superior tone, "But I am a practical man." Then, with a sardonic air, he will speak to you of the great minds that cannot retain anything; he will speak to you of Poe's loose life—his alcoholic breath, which would have caught fire by a candle's flame, his nomadic habits. He will tell you that he was an erratic creature, a planet out of orbit, that he roved from New York to Philadelphia, from Boston to Baltimore, from Baltimore to Richmond. And if, your heart already moved by these signs of a calamitous existence, you remind him that Democracy certainly has its defects—in spite of its benevolent mask of liberty, it does not always permit, perhaps, the growth of individuality; it is often very difficult to think and write in a country where there are twenty or thirty million sovereigns; moreover, *you have heard it said* that there was a tyranny much more cruel and inexorable than that of a monarchy, in the United States (that of opinion)—then you will see his eyes open wide and cast off sparks. The froth of wounded patriotism mounts to his lips, and America, by his mouth, will heap insults on metaphysics and on Europe, its old mother. America is a practical creature, vain about its industrial power and a little jealous of the old continent. It does not have time to have compassion for a poet who could be maddened by pain and isolation. It is so proud of its young immensity, so naively trusting in the omnipotence of industry, so convinced that it will finally devour the Devil, that it has a certain pity for all these incoherent dreams. Onward it says; onward and ignore the dead. It would gladly walk over solitary, free spirits and trample them as lightheartedly as the immense railways overrun the leveled forests and the monster ships overrun the debris of a ship burned the previous evening. It is in a hurry to arrive. Time and money are everything.

Some time before Balzac descended into the final abyss while uttering the noble plaints of a hero who still has great things to do, Edgar Poe, who is similar to him in many ways, was stricken by a frightful death. France lost one of her greatest geniuses and America lost a novelist, critic and philosopher scarcely made for her. Many people here are ignorant of the death of Edgar Poe; many others believe that he was a rich young gentleman, writing little, producing his strange and terrible creations in the most agreeable leisure, and knowing literary life only through rare and striking successes. The reality was quite the opposite. . . .

Poe's death caused real emotion in America. Authentic testimony of pain rose from various parts of the Union. Sometimes death causes many things to be forgiven. We are happy to mention a letter from Longfellow, which does him all the more honor because Poe had treated him badly: "What a melancholy end, that of Mr. Poe, a man so richly endowed with genius! I have never known him personally, but I have always had great esteem for his power as a prose writer and as a poet. His prose is remarkably vigorous and direct, yet copious, and his verse breathes a special melodious charm, an atmosphere of true poetry, which is all-pervasive. The harshness of his criticism I have never attributed to anything but the irritability of an overly sensitive nature, exasperated by all manifestations of falseness."

The prolix author of *Evangeline* is amusing when he talks of *copiousness*. Does he take Edgar Poe for a mirror?

II

Comparing the character of a great man with his works is a very great and rewarding pleasure. A very legitimate curiosity has always been stimulated by biographies, by notes on manners and habits and by the physical appearance of artists and writers. People seek Erasmus' acuity of style and precision of idea in the cut of his profile; we examine the heads of Diderot and Mercier, where a little swagger mingles with goodfellowship, to find the warmth and show of their work. Voltaire's battle face reveals his stubborn irony, and his horizon-searching eye reveals his power of command or of prophecy. The solid countenance of Joseph de Maistre is that of the eagle and the bull at the same time. And who has not cudgeled his brains to decipher the *Human Comedy* by means of the powerful and complex forehead and face of Balzac?

Edgar Poe was a little below average in stature, but his body was solidly built; his feet and hands were small. Before his health was undermined, he was capable of marvelous feats of strength. I believe that it has often been noticed that Nature makes life very hard for those of whom she expects great things. Although they appear frail sometimes, they are built like athletes, and are as good for pleasure as for suffering. Balzac corrected the proofs for his books while attending the rehearsals of the *Resources de Quinola* and directing and playing all the roles himself; he dined with the actors, and when everyone was exhausted and had retired to sleep, he returned to work with ease. Everyone knows that he committed great excesses of insomnia and sobriety. Edgar Poe, in his youth, distinguished himself in all exercises of skill and strength and—as is revealed in his work—calculations and problems. One day he made a bet that he could leave one of the Richmond docks, swim upstream seven miles in the James River, and return on foot the same day; and he did it. It was a boiling summer day, and he did not carry it off badly. Expression of face, gestures, gait posture of head—everything singled him out, in his good days, as a man of great distinction. He was *marked* by Nature as one of those who, in a social circle, at a cafe, or in the street, *compel* the eye of the observer and engross him. If ever the word *strange* (which has been much abused in modern descriptions) has been aptly applied to anything, it is certainly to Poe's type of beauty. His features were not large, but quite regular. His complexion was a light brunette, his expression sad, distraught, and, although neither angry nor insolent, somehow displeasing. His singularly fine eyes seemed at first glance to be dark grey, but on closer examination they appeared frosted with a light indefinable violet. His forehead was superb. It did not have the ridiculous proportions invented by bad artists when, in order to flatter a genius, they transform him into a hydrocephalic, but an overflowing inner force seemed to push forward the organs of reflection and construction. The parts to which phrenologists attribute the sense of the picturesque were not absent, however; they merely seemed disturbed, jostled by the haughty and usurping tyranny of comparison, construction and causation. The sense of ideality and absolute beauty, the esthetic sense par excellence, also reigned in this forehead with calm pride. In spite of all these qualities, the head did not present an agreeable and harmonious impression. Seen full-face, it was striking and commanded attention by the domineering and inquisitorial effect of the forehead, but the profile revealed certain lacks; there was an immense mass of brain in front and back, and a moderate amount in the middle. In short, there was enormous animal and intellectual power, but weakness in the area of veneration and the affections. The despairing echoes of melancholy running through the works of Poe have a penetrating tone, it is true, but one must also admit that it is a very solitary melancholy, uncongenial to the ordinary man. I cannot help laughing when I think of some lines that a writer highly esteemed in the United States wrote about Poe some time after his death. I quote from memory, but I will answer for the meaning. "I have just reread the works of the regrettable Poe. What an admirable poet! What an amazing storyteller! What a prodigious and superhuman mind! He was really the original mind of our country. Well, I would give all of his seventy mystic, analytic and grotesque tales, so brilliant and full of ideas, for the good little hearthside book, the family book, that he could have written with the marvelously pure style that gives him such superiority over us. How much greater Mr. Poe would be!" To ask a family book of Edgar Poe! It is true, then, that human folly is the same in all climates, and the critic always wants to tie gross vegetables to ornamental shrubs.

Poe had black hair, shot through with some white threads, and a bristling moustache which he neglected to trim and to comb properly. He dressed with good taste but was a little negligent, like a gentleman who has many other things to do. His manners were excellent, very polished and self-assured, but his conversation deserves special comment. The first time that I questioned an American about it, he answered me, laughing, "Oh! oh! His conversation was not at all coherent!" After some explanation, I understood that Mr. Poe took great leaps in the world of ideas, like a mathematician who demonstrates for very intelligent students, and that he often carried on monologs. In fact, it was an essentially meaty conversation. He was not a *fine talker.* Moreover, he had a horror of conventionality, in speaking as in writing, but his vast knowledge, acquaintance with several languages, profound studies and ideas gathered in several countries made his conversation an excellent instruction. In short, he was the proper man for people who measure friendship according to the spiritual profit that they can make. Yet it seems that Poe was very indiscriminate in his choice of listeners. He scarcely troubled to discover whether his hearers were capable of understanding his tenuous abstractions or admiring the glorious conceptions which constantly flashed through the somber sky of his mind. He sat in a tavern beside a sordid ruffian and gravely expounded the great lines of his terrible book *Eureka* with a relentless coolness, as though he were dictating to a secretary or disputing with Kepler, Bacon or Swedenborg. That is a special trait of his. No man has ever freed himself more completely from the rules of society, or troubled himself less about passersby; that is why, on certain days, he was received in low class cafes but was refused entrance to the places where *respectable people* drink. No society has ever forgiven such things, still less an English or American society. Besides, Poe already had to be forgiven his genius. In the *Messenger* he had ferociously pursued mediocrity; his criticism had been hard and disciplinary, like that of a superior, solitary man who is interested only in ideas. A moment of disgust for all things human had arrived, when only metaphysics mattered to him. Dazzling his young, unformed country with his intelligence and shocking men who thought themselves his equals with his manners, Poe inevitably became one of the most unfortunate of writers. Hostility came in crowds; solitude surrounded him. In Paris or Germany he would have found friends to give him understanding and solace. In America he had to fight for his bread. In this way his intoxication and perpetual moving are explained. He traveled through life as though it were a Sahara, and he changed abodes like an Arab.

But there are other reasons—his deep domestic sorrows, for example. We have seen his precocious youth suddenly cast into the asperity of life. Poe was almost always alone; in addition, the terrible battle in his mind and the harshness of his work must have made him seek the delight of oblivion in wine and liquor. What fatigues others gave him solace. Finally, Poe escaped literary animosity, the vertigo of the infinite, domestic sorrows and the outrages of misery in the darkness of intoxication, like the darkness of the tomb. He did not drink like a glutton but like a barbarian. The alcohol had scarcely touched his lips before he rooted himself at the counter and drank glass after glass until his good Angel was drowned and his faculties were annihilated. It is a miraculous fact, verified by all who knew him, that neither the purity and perfection of his style, nor the precision of his thought, nor his eagerness for work and difficult study was disturbed by his terrible habit. The composition of most of the good pieces preceded or followed one of his attacks. After the appearance of *Eureka,* he gave himself over furiously to drink. The very morning when the *Whig Review* published "The Raven" and the name of Poe was on every tongue, with everyone discussing his poem, he crossed Broadway in New York, stumbling and staggering against the buildings.

Literary intoxication is one of the most common and lamentable phenomena of modern life, but perhaps there are many extenuating circumstances. In the time of Saint-Amant, Chapelle and Colletet, literature was also intoxicated, but joyfully, in the company of nobles who were highly literate and who had no fear of the cabaret. Even certain ladies would not have blushed to have a taste for wine, as is proved by the adventure of one whose servant found her with Chapelle, both of them weeping hot tears after supper because of the death of poor Pindar, dead through the fault of ignorant doctors. In the eighteenth century the tradition continues, a little impaired. The school of Retif drinks, but it is already a school of pariahs, a subterranean world. Mercier, very old, is found in Cor-Honore Street. Napoleon has conquered the eighteenth century; Mercier is a little drunk, and he says that *he* no *longer lives except by curiosity.* Today, literary drunkenness has assumed a somber and sinister character. Now there is no particularly literate class that does itself the honor of associating with men of letters. Their absorbing work and aversion for schools hinders their uniting. As for women, their formless education and political and literary incompetence keep many authors from seeing anything in them but household utensils or objects of lust. Once dinner is digested and the animal satisfied, the poet enters the vast solitude of his thought; sometimes he is exhausted by his craft. What then? His mind grows accustomed to the idea of its invincible strength, and he can no longer resist the hope of finding again in drink the serene or terrible visions which are already his old friends. The same transformation of customs that makes the literate world a class apart is also undoubtedly responsible for the immense consumption of tobacco in the new literature.

III

I shall try to give an idea of the general character of the works of Edgar Poe. Giving an analysis of each work would be impossible without writing a book, for this singular man, in spite of his disordered and diabolic life, produced a great deal.

When he was appointed editor of the *Southern Literary Messenger,* it was stipulated that he receive 2500 francs a year. In exchange for this paltry salary, he was responsible for reading and selecting pieces for each month's issue and composing the part called *editorial*—that is to say, he evaluated all the works that appeared and weighed all of the literary events. In addition, he very often contributed a novella or a bit of poetry. He plied this trade for nearly two years. Thanks to his active direction and the originality of his criticism, the *Literary Messenger* soon attracted all eyes. Before me I have the issues of those two years. The editorial part is considerable, and the articles are very long. In the same issue, we often find reviews of a novel, a book of poetry, a medical book and a book on physics or history. All the reviews are written with the greatest care and indicate a knowledge of various literatures and a scientific aptitude reminiscent of French writers of the eighteenth century. Apparently Poe had put his time to good use during his previous misfortunes, and had turned over many ideas. He wrote a remarkable quantity of critical reviews of the principal English and American authors, and often of French memoirs. The source of an idea, its origin and end, the school to which it belonged, the salutary or noxious method of the author—all of these were neatly, clearly and rapidly explained. Although Poe attracted much attention, he also made many enemies. Profoundly absorbed in his opinions, he waged tireless war on false reasoning, stupid pastiches, solecisms, barbarisms and all the literary crimes daily committed in books and newspapers. Yet he could not be reproached, for he preached by example. His style is pure; it is adequate to his ideas and renders their precise impression. Poe is always correct. It is very remarkable that a man of such roving and ambitious imagination should at the same time be so fond of rules and so capable of careful analysis and patient research. He could be called an antithesis made flesh. But his fame as a critic damaged his literary future a great deal. Many wanted to be avenged, and every possible reproach was cast in his face as the number of his works increased. Everyone knows the long, banal litany: immorality, lack of tenderness, absence of conclusions, extravagance, useless literature. French criticism has never forgiven Balzac for *Le grand homme de province a Paris*.

In poetry, Edgar Poe is a solitary spirit. Almost alone on the other side of the ocean he represents the Romantic movement. Properly speaking, he is the first American to make his style a tool. His profound and plaintive poetry is nevertheless finely wrought, pure, correct and brilliant as a crystal jewel. In spite of the amazing qualities which have made soft, tender spirits adore them, Alfred de Musset and Alphonse de Lamartine would obviously not have been his friends if he had lived here. They do not have enough will and self-mastery. Although Edgar Poe loved complicated rhythms, he shaped them in a profound harmony no matter how complicated they were. One of his short poems, "The Bells," is a veritable literary curiosity, but it is totally untranslatable. "The Raven" had a huge success. In the judgment of Longfellow and Emerson, it is a marvel. The content is slight; it is a pure work of art. . . . The tone is grave and almost supernatural, like insomniac thoughts; the lines fall one by one, like monotonous tears. In "Dreamland," he tried to portray the series of dreams and fantastic images besieging the soul when the body's eye is closed. Other poems, such as "Ulalume" and "Annabel Lee" enjoy equal fame. But the poetic stock of Edgar Poe is slight. His condensed and finely-worked poetry undoubtedly cost much effort, and he was often in need of money in order to surrender himself to that delightful and fruitless pain.

As a novelist and storyteller, Edgar Poe is unique in his field, just as Maturin, Balzac and Hoffmann were in theirs. The various pieces scattered throughout the magazines have been gathered into two sheaves, *Tales of the Grotesque and Arabesque* and *Edgar A. Poe's Tales* in the edition of Wiley and Putnam. There are approximately 72 pieces. Some are purely grotesque, some are preoccupied with magnetism, some are wild clownings, some are unleashed aspirations towards the infinite. The tiny volume of tales has had great success in Paris as well as in America because it contains stories that are highly dramatic, but dramatic in a special way.

I should like to characterize Poe's work very briefly and exactly, for it is a totally new creation. The qualities that essentially define it and distinguish it from others are (if I may be pardoned these strange words) *conjecturisme* and *probabilisme*. My assertions can be verified by examining some of his subjects.

"The Gold Bug": an analysis of a succession of methods for deciphering a cryptogram which will help to disclose hidden treasure. I cannot help thinking regretfully that the unfortunate E. Poe must have dreamed more than once of means of discovering treasure. The explanation of this method, which becomes the odd literary specialty of certain police secretaries, is eminently logical and lucid. The description of the treasure is fine; what a good sense of warmth and dazzlement one has! For the treasure is found. *It was not a dream* as usually happens in novels—the author awakening us brutally after having aroused our spirits by whetting our hopes. This time it is a *real* treasure and the decipherer has truly won it. Here is the exact sum: in money, $450,000 (not an ounce of silver, but all gold and very ancient, enormous, weighty pieces with unreadable inscriptions), 110 diamonds, 18 rubies, 310 emeralds, 21 sapphires, one opal, 200 rings and massive earrings, some 30 chains, 83 crucifixes, 5 censors, an enormous punchbowl of gold with vine leaves and bacchantes, 2 sword-handles and 197 watches adorned with precious stones. The content of the coffer is first valued at a million and a half dollars, but the sale of the jewels brings the total above that. The description of this treasure makes one dizzy with largesse and ambitions of benevolence. The coffer hidden by the pirate Kidd contained enough, certainly, to ease many unknown desperations.

"The Maelstrom": Would it not be possible to descend into an abyss whose bottom has never been sounded, in studying the laws of gravity in a new way?

"The Murders in the Rue Morgue" could instruct prosecuting attorneys. A murder has been committed. How? By whom? This affair contains some inexplicable and contradictory facts, and the police have given up. A young man who is gathering evidence for the love of the art presents himself.

Through extreme concentration of thought and successive analysis of all the phenomena of understanding, he happens upon the law of the generation of ideas. Between one word and the next, between two ideas which are apparently unrelated, he can establish a complete intermediary series before the dazzled eyes of the police, and fill in the lacuna of unexpressed and almost unconscious ideas. He has closely studied all the possibilities and all the probable associations. He has ascended from induction to induction until he succeeds in showing decisively that an ape has committed the crime.

"The Mesmeric Revelation": The author's point of departure has evidently been this question: With the help of the unknown power called magnetic fluid, could we discover the law that rules the ultimate worlds? The beginning is full of dignity and solemnity. The physician has put his patient to sleep simply to ease him. "What do you think about your illness?—I will die.—Will that cause you sorrow?—No." The patient complains that he is badly questioned. "Direct me, says the doctor.—Begin at the beginning.—What is the beginning?—(*Very low*) It is GOD.—Is God a spirit?—No.—Is he matter, then?—No." A vast theory of matter follows, of gradations of matter and the hierarchy of beings. I published this story in an issue of *Liberte de Penser* in 1848.

Elsewhere there is an account of a spirit that had lived on an extinguished planet. This was the point of departure: Can one, by means of induction and analysis, determine what physical and moral phenomena would occur among the inhabitants of a world approached by a murderous comet?

At other times we find the purely fantastic modeled on nature, without explanation, in the manner of Hoffman: "The Man of the Crowd" plunges endlessly into the heart of the crowd; he swims with delight in the human sea. When the shadowy twilight full of tremulous lights descends, he flies from the silenced districts and ardently seeks the places where human matter swarms busily. As the circle of light and life shrinks, he seeks the center uneasily. Like men in a flood, he clings desperately to the last culminating points of public movement. And that is all we know. Is he a criminal who has a horror of solitude? Is he an imbecile who cannot endure himself? . . .

Poe usually suppresses the minor details or gives them a minimal value. Because of this harsh severity, the generating idea is more evident and the subject stands out vividly against the bare background. His method of narration is simple. He overuses the first person pronoun with cynical monotony. One might say that he is so sure of being interesting that he does not bother to vary his technique. His tales are nearly always the account or manuscript of the main character. As for his ardent exploration of the horrible, I have noticed it in various men, and it is often the result of a great unoccupied vital energy, of an obstinate chastity sometimes, and also of a profound sensibility which has been thwarted. The supernatural pleasure that a man can experience in seeing his own blood run—the brusque, useless movements, the cries almost involuntarily piercing the air—is a similar phenomenon. Pain is a release from pain, and action is a relaxation from repose.

Another peculiar trait of his work is that it is completely anti-feminine. Let me explain. Women write and write in a swift overflow; their hearts prattle by the ream. Generally, they know neither art, nor measure, nor logic. Their style trains and coils like their garments. In spite of her superiority, the very great and justly famous George Sand has not entirely escaped this law of temperament; she throws her masterpieces into the mail as though they were letters. It is said that she writes her books on letter paper.

In Poe's books the style is condensed, tightly linked. The ill will or laziness of the reader cannot slip through the mesh of this logically woven net. All ideas, like obedient arrows, fly to the same target.

I have followed a long trail of tales without finding one love story. This man is so intoxicating that I did not think about it until the end. Without claiming to extol the ascetic system of an ambitious mind absolutely, I think that such an austere literature would be a useful weapon against the invading fatuity of women, who are more and more stimulated by the disgusting idolatry of men. And I am very lenient toward Voltaire, who thought it well in the preface to his womanless tragedy, *La Mort de César*, to emphasize his glorious tour de force by feigning excuses for his impertinence.

In Edgar Poe there are no enervating whines, but always a tireless ardor for the ideal. Like Balzac, who died perhaps saddened because he was not a pure scholar, Poe is enchanted by science. He wrote a *Manual for the Conchologist*, which I have forgotten to mention. Like conquerors and philosophers, he has a compelling aspiration toward unity and he assimilates morality into physical things. It could be said that he attempts to apply the procedures of philosophy to literature, and the methods of algebra to philosophy. In the constant ascent toward the infinite, one loses his breath. In this literature the air is rarefied as in a laboratory. We endlessly contemplate the glorification of will applied to induction and analysis. Poe seems to intend to wrench language from the prophets and to monopolize rational explanation. Thus, the landscapes which sometimes serve as background for his feverish fictions are pale as ghosts. Poe scarcely shared the passions of other men; he sketched trees and clouds that seem to be the dream of clouds and trees, or strange characters shaken by a supernatural, galvanic shiver.

Once, however, he set himself to write a purely human book. *The Narrative of Arthur Gordon Pym*, which has had no great success, is a story of sailors who, after severe damage to the ship, have been becalmed in the South Seas. The author's genius delights in these terrible scenes and in the amazing sketches of tribes and islands which are not indicated on the maps. The style of this book is extremely simple and detailed. . . .

Although *Eureka* was undoubtedly the long-cherished dream of Edgar Poe, I cannot write a precise account of it here, for it is a book that requires a special article. Whoever has read the "Mesmeric Revelation" knows the metaphysical tendencies of the author. *Eureka* attempts to develop the process and show the law by which the universe assumed its present visible form and organization. It shows that the same law which began creation will act to destroy the world and absorb it. One readily comprehends why I do not care to engage lightly in discussion of such an ambitious attempt. I would be afraid of erring and slandering an author for whom I have the deepest respect. Edgar Poe has already been accused of pantheism, and although I may be forced to agree that appearances lead to such a conclusion, I can assert that, like many other great men bewitched by logic, he sometimes contradicts himself. It is to his credit. Thus his pantheism is counteracted by his ideas on the hierarchy of beings and by many passages that obviously affirm the permanence of personality.

Edgar Poe was very proud of this book, which naturally did not have the same success as his tales. One must read it cautiously and verify his strange ideas by checking them against similar and opposite systems.

IV

I had a friend who was also a metaphysician in his fashion, obsessed and absolute, with the air of a Saint Just. He often said to me, taking an example from the world and looking at me from the corner of his eye, "Every mystic has a hidden vice." And I continued his thought: Then he must be destroyed. But I laughed, because I did not understand. One day, as I was chatting with a well-known, busy bookseller whose specialty is to cater to the enthusiasms of all the mystical band and the obscure courtesans of occult sciences, I asked for information on his clientele. He said to me, "Remember that every mystic has a hidden vice, often a very material one—drunkenness, gormandizing, lewdness. One will be avaricious, the other cruel, etc. . . ."

Good Lord! I said to myself. Then what is the fatal law that binds us, dominates us, and avenges the violation of its insufferable despotism by degrading and sapping our moral being? The visionaries have been the greatest of men. Why must they be punished for their greatness? Hasn't their ambition been the most noble? Will man eternally be so limited that one of his faculties cannot expand except at the expense of the others? If wanting to know the truth at all costs is a great crime, or if it can lead to great error, if stupidity and indifference are virtues and guarantees of balance, I think we should be very forbearing towards these illustrious criminals, for we children of the eighteenth and nineteenth centuries can all be accused of the same vice.

I say this shamelessly, because I feel it comes from a profound feeling of pity and tenderness: Edgar Poe—drunkard, pauper, oppressed, pariah— pleases me more than do the calm and virtuous Goethe and W. Scott. I would readily say of him and of a particular class of men what the catechism says of our Lord: "He has suffered much for us."

We could write on his tomb, "All you who have passionately sought to discover the laws of your being, who have aspired to infinity, you whose rebuffed feelings have had to seek a frightful relief in the wine of debauchery, pray for him. His corporeal being, now purified, floats among the beings whose existence he glimpsed. Pray for him who sees and knows: he will intercede for you."

—Charles Baudelaire, "Edgar Allan Poe:
His Life and Works," tr. Jean Alexander
Revue de Paris, March–April 1852, pp. 90–110

George Gilfillan "Edgar Poe" (1854)

Gilfillan was a Scottish poet and critic. His "galleries" of *Literary Portraits* included many of the most important writers of the Victorian era.

He begins with a play on words, comparing and contrasting the notions of genius and geniality. If genius is understood by its connection to imagination, fancy, and originality, then Poe is a genius. But if geniality is also required, then Poe lacks genius. Gilfillan says that without geniality, genius is cold, forbidding, and can cause resentment. Gilfillan suggests that only the intrepid few will attempt to know the genius who is not genial. Essayists might compare this idea with similar sentiments expressed by other critics, particularly Cooke (in this volume), who praises Poe but wishes he had written more "homely" or comfortable pieces, to be enjoyed by the millions.

The discussion of geniality raises an issue that always hounded Poe and continues to resound in Poe studies today: his coldness. In his own time, Poe was viewed (unfavorably) as a lawyer-like writer, meaning one who analyzed without feeling. His coolly calculating reason seemed to snuff out any heat from passion, and passion was generally thought of as the primary material of poetry. Probably drawing from Poe's own analysis of "The Raven" in "The Philosophy of Composition," Gilfillan says that Poe constructed his poem as if solving a math problem. Students might want to look at Gilfillan's essay for insight into the relation between cool reason and heated passion in literary production.

Poe's apparent coldness is sometimes cited as a flaw, sometimes as a strength. To be sure, the *realism* (a term not yet coined in Poe's era) of the tales is enhanced by the quasi-scientific method and narration. Many critics cite the vividness of Poe's details. But the supposed lack of "heart" makes Poe seem like an architect of sensations only, someone who titillates or horrifies briefly but who does not leave a lasting impression. Students may want to examine the ways that rational and emotional ideas are presented in stories or poems. Gilfillan suggests that the two may be at odds.

Poe's choice of subject matter, particularly in his well-known tales, might relate to his analytical sensibilities as well as to his own fears. Mysteries, natural disasters, madness, and above all death, these test the limits and ultimately defeat the cool, calculating reason that tries to comprehend them. In the "puzzle" stories, we see that riddle being solved, but in most of Poe's stories, the inexplicable is presented without being solved. As Gilfillan notes, Poe either gives a realistic portrait of unreal things or he casts familiar things in an unfamiliar light. This effect is somewhat like the "estrangement" that Russian formalist literary theorists discuss. The literary aspect of Poe is connected to the way he blurs the boundaries between fact and fiction, real and unreal. Gilfillan, citing Dante but quoting Milton, provides an apt metaphor for Poe's style: the "cold performs the effect of fire."

A case so strange as Poe's compels us into new and more searching forms of critical, as well as of moral analysis. Genius has very generally been ascribed to him; but some will resist and deny the ascription—proceeding partly upon peculiar notions of what genius is, and partly from a very natural reluctance to concede to a wretch so vile a gift so noble, and in a degree, too, so unusually large. Genius has often been defined as something inseparably connected with the *genial* nature. If this definition be correct, Poe was not a genius any more than Swift, for geniality neither he nor his writings possessed. But if genius means a compound of imagination and inventiveness, original thought heated by passion, and accompanied by power of fancy, Poe was a man of great genius. In wanting geniality, however, he wanted all that makes genius lovely and beloved, at once beautiful and dear. A man of genius, without geniality, is a mountain clad in snow, companioned by tempests, and visited only by hardy explorers who love sublime nakedness, and to snatch a fearful joy from gazing down black precipices; a man whose genius is steeped in the genial nature, is an autumn landscape, suggesting not only images of beauty, and giving thrills

of delight, but yielding peaceful and plenteous fruits, and in which the heart
finds a rest and a home. From the one the timid, the weak, and the gentle
retire in a terror which overpowers their admiration; but in the other the
lowest and feeblest find shelter and repose. Even Dante and Milton, owing
to the excess of their intellectual and imaginative powers over their genial
feelings, are less loved than admired; while the vast supremacy of Shakspere is
due, not merely to his universal genius, but to the predominance of geniality
and heart in all his writings. Many envy and even hate Dante and Milton; and
had Shakspere only written his loftier tragedies, many might have hated and
envied him too; but who can entertain any such feelings for the author of
the *Comedy of Errors* and *Twelfth Night,* the creator of Falstaff, Dogberry, and
Verres? If genius be the sun, geniality is the atmosphere through which alone
his beams can penetrate with power, or be seen with pleasure.

Poe is distinguished by many styles and many manners. He is the author
of fictions as matter-of-fact in their construction and language as the stories
of Defoe, and of tales as wierd and wonderful as those of Hoffman; of amatory
strains trembling, if not with heart, with passion, and suffused with the purple
glow of love, and of poems, dirges either in form or in spirit, into which the
genius of desolation has shed its dreariest essence; of verses, gay with apparent,
but shallow joy, and of others dark with a misery which reminds us of the
helpless, hopeless, infinite misery, which sometimes visits the soul in dreams.
But, amid all this diversity of tone and of subject, the leading qualities of his
mind are obvious. These consist of strong imagination—an imagination,
however, more fertile in incidents, forms, and characters, than in images; keen
power of analysis, rather than synthetic genius; immense inventiveness; hot
passions, cooled down by the presence of art, till they resemble sculptured
flame, or "lightning in the hand of a painted Jupiter;" knowledge rather
recherche and varied, than strict, accurate, or profound; and an unlimited
command of words, phrases, musical combinations of sound, and all the
other materials of an intellectual workman. The direction of these powers
was controlled principally by his habits and circumstances. These made him
morbid; and his writings have all a certain morbidity about them. You say at
once, cool and clear as most of them are, these are not the productions of a
healthy or happy man. But surely never was there such a calm despair—such
a fiery torment so cased in ice! When you compare the writings with the
known facts of the author's history, they appear to be so like, and so unlike,
his character. You seem looking at an inverted image. You have the features, but
they are discovered at an unexpected angle. You see traces of the misery of a
confirmed debauchee, but none of his disconnected ravings, or of the partial

imbecility which often falls upon his powers. There is a strict, almost logical, method in his wildest productions. He tells us himself that he wrote "The Raven" as coolly as if he had been working out a mathematical problem. His frenzy, if that name must be given to the strange fire which was in him, is a conscious one; he feels his own pulse when it is at the wildest, and looks at his foaming lips in the looking-glass.

Poe was led by a singular attraction to all dark, dreadful, and disgusting objects and thoughts: maelstroms, mysteries, murders, mummies, premature burials, excursions to the moon, solitary mansions surrounded by mist and weighed down by mysterious dooms, lonely tarns, trembling to the winds of autumn, and begirt by the shivering ghosts of woods—these are the materials which his wild imagination loves to work with, and out of them to weave the most fantastic and dismal of worlds. Yet there's "magic in the web." You often revolt at his subjects; but no sooner does he enter on them, than your attention is riveted, you lend him your ears—nay, that is a feeble word, you surrender your whole being to him for a season, although it be as you succumb, body and soul, to the dominion of a nightmare. What greatly increases the effect, as in *Gulliver's Travels,* is the circumstantiality with which he recounts the most amazing and incredible things. His tales, too, are generally cast into the autobiographical form, which adds much to their living vraisemblance and vivid power. It is Coleridge's "Old Mariner" over again. Strange, wild, terrible, is the tale he has to tell; haggard, wo-begone, unearthly, is the appearance of the narrator. Every one at first, like the wedding guest, is disposed to shrink and beat his breast; but he holds you with his glittering eye, he forces you to follow him into his own enchanted region, and once there, you forget everything, your home, your friends, your creed, your very personal identity, and become swallowed up like a straw in the maelstrom of his story, and forget to breathe till it is ended, and the mysterious tale-teller is gone. And during all the wild and whirling narrative, the same chilly glitter has continued to shine in his eye, his blood has never warmed, and he has never exalted his voice, above a thrilling whisper.

Poe's power may perhaps be said to be divisible into two parts: first, that of adding an air of circumstantial verity to incredibilities; and, secondly, that of throwing a weird lustre upon commonplace events. He tells fiction so minutely, and with such apparent simplicity and sincerity, that you almost believe it true; and he so combines and so recounts such incidents as you meet with every day in the newspapers, that you feel truth to be stranger far than fiction. Look, as a specimen of the first, to his "Descent into the Maelstrom," and to his "Hans Pfaal's Journey to the Moon." Both are impossible; the former as much so as the latter; but he tells them with such Dante-like directness, and such Defoe-like minuteness, holding his watch, and marking, as it were, every second in the progress of each stupendous lie, that you rub your eyes at the close, and ask the question, Might not all this actually have occurred? And then turn to the "Murders in the Rue St Morgue," or to the "Mystery of Marie Roget," and see how, by the disposition of the drapery he throws over little or ordinary incidents, connected, indeed, with an extraordinary catastrophe, he lends

The light which never was on sea or shore

to streets of revelry and vulgar sin, and to streams whose sluggish waters are never disturbed save by the plash of murdered victims, or by the plunge of suicides desperately hurling their bodies to the fishes, and their souls to the flames.

In one point, Poe bears a striking resemblance to his own illustrious countryman, Brockden Brown—neither resort to agency absolutely supernatural, in order to produce their terrific effects. They despise to start a ghost from the grave—they look upon this as a cheap and *fade* expedient— they appeal to the "mightier might" of the human passions, or to those strange unsolved phenomena in the human mind, which the terms mesmerism and somnambulism serve rather to disguise than to discover, and sweat out from their native soil superstitions far more powerful than those of the past. Once only does Poe approach the brink of the purely preternatural—it is in that dreary tale, the "Fall of the House of Usher;" and yet, nothing so discovers the mastery of the writer, as the manner in which he avoids, while nearing, the gulf. There is really nothing, after all, in the strange incidents of that story, but what natural principles can explain. But Poe so arranges and adjusts the singular circumstances to each other, and weaves around them such an artful mist, that they produce a most unearthly effect. Perhaps some may think that he has fairly crossed the line in that dialogue between Charmian and Iras, describing the conflagration of the world. But, even there, how admirably does he produce a certain feeling of probability, by the management of the natural causes which he brings in to produce the catastrophe. He burns his old witch-mother, the earth, scientifically! We must add that the above is the only respect in which Poe resembles Brown. Brown was a virtuous and amiable man, and his works, although darkened by unsettled religious views, breathe a fine spirit of humanity. Poe wonders at, and hates man; Brown wonders at, but at the same time pities, loves, and hopes in him. Brown mingled among men like a bewildered angel; Poe like a prying fiend.

We have already alluded to the singular power of analysis possessed by this strange being. This is chiefly conspicuous in those tales of his which turn upon circumstantial evidence. No lawyer or judge has ever equalled Poe in the power he manifests of sifting evidence—of balancing probabilities—of finding the *multum* of a large legal case in the *parvum* of some minute and well-nigh invisible point—and in constructing the real story out of a hundred dubious and conflicting incidents. What scales he carries with him! how fine and tremulous with essential justice! And with what a microscopic eye he watches every footprint! Letters thrown loose on the mantelpiece, bell-ropes, branches of trees, handkerchiefs, &c., become to him instinct with meaning, and point with silent finger to crime and to punishment. And to think of this subtle algebraic power, combined with such a strong ideality, and with such an utterly corrupted moral nature! Surely none of the hybrids which geology has dug out of the graves of chaos, and exhibited to our shuddering view, is half so strange a compound as was Edgar Poe. We have hitherto scarcely glanced at his poetry. It, although lying in a very short compass, is of various merit: it is an abridgment of the man in his strength and weakness. Its chief distinction, as a whole, from his prose, is its peculiar music. *That,* like all his powers, is fitful, changeful, varying; but not more so than to show the ever-varying moods of his mind, acting on a peculiar and indefinite theory of sound. The alpha and omega of that theory may be condensed in the word "reiteration." He knows the effect which can be produced by ringing changes on particular words. The strength of all his strains consequently lies in their chorus, or "oure turn," as we call it in Scotland. We do not think that he could have succeeded in sustaining the harmonies or keeping up the interest of a large poem. But his short flights are exceedingly beautiful, and some of his poems are miracles of melody. All our readers are familiar with "The Raven." It is a dark world in itself; it rises in your sky suddenly as the cloud like a man's hand rose in the heaven of Palestine, and covers all the horizon with the blackness of darkness. As usual in his writings, it is but a common event idealised; there is nothing supernatural or even extraordinary in the incident recounted; but the reiteration of the one dreary word "nevermore;" the effect produced by seating the solemn bird of yore upon the bust of Pallas; the manner in which the fowl with its fiery eyes becomes the evil conscience or memory of the lonely widower; and the management of the time, the season, and the circumstances—all unite in making the Raven in its flesh and blood a far more terrific apparition than ever from the shades made night hideous, while "revisiting the glimpses of the moon." The poem belongs to a singular class of poetic uniques, each of which is itself enough to make a reputation, such as Coleridge's *Rime of the Anciente Marinere,* or *Christabel,* and Aird's "Devil's Dream upon Mount Acksbeck"—poems in which some one new and generally dark idea is wrought out into a whole so strikingly complete and self-contained as to resemble creation, and in which thought, imagery, language, and music combine to produce a similar effect, and are made to chime together like bells. What entireness of effect, for instance, is produced in the "Devil's Dream," by the unearthly theme, the strange title, the austere and terrible figures, the singular verse, and the knotty and contorted language; and in the *Rime of the Anciente Marinere,* by the ghastly form of the narrator—the wild rhythm, the new mythology, and the exotic diction of the tale he tells! So Poe's "Raven" has the unity of a tree blasted, trunk, and twigs, and root, by a flash of lightning. Never did melancholy more thoroughly "mark for its own" any poem than this. All is in intense keeping. Short as the poem is, it has a beginning, middle, and end. Its commencement how abrupt and striking—the time a December midnight—the poet a solitary man, sitting, "weak and weary," poring in helpless fixity, but with no profit or pleasure, over a black-letter volume; the fire half expired, and the dying embers haunted by their own ghosts, and shivering above the hearth! The middle is attained, when the raven mounts the bust of Pallas, and is fascinating the solitary wretch by his black, glittering plumage, and his measured, melancholy croak. And the end closes as with the wings of night over the sorrow of the unfortunate, and these dark words conclude the tale:—

> And my soul from out that shadow that lies floating
> > on the floor,
> Shall be lifted Nevermore.

You feel as if the poem might have been penned by the finger of one of the damned.

The same shadow of unutterable wo rests upon several of his smaller poems, and the effect is greatly enhanced by their gay and song-like rhythm. That madness or misery which sings out its terror or grief, is always the most desperate. It is like a burden of hell set to an air of heaven. "Ulalume" might have been written by Coleridge during the sad middle portion of his life. There is a sense of dreariness and desolation as of the last of earth's autumns, which we find nowhere else in such perfection. What a picture these words convey to the imagination:—

> The skies they were ashen and sober;
> The leaves they were crisped and sere—

The leaves they were withering and sere,
It was night in the lonesome October
Of my most immemorial year.
It was hard by the dim lake of Auber,
In the misty mid-region of Weir—
It was down by the dark tarn of Auber,
In the ghoul-haunted woodland of Weir.

These to many will appear only words; but what wondrous words. What a spell they wield! Like a wasted haggard face, they have no bloom or beauty; but what a tale they tell! Weir—Auber—where are they? They exist not, except in the writer's imagination, and in yours, for the instant they are uttered, a misty picture, with a tarn, dark as a murderer's eye, below, and the last thin, yellow leaves of October fluttering above—exponents both of a misery which scorns the name of sorrow, and knows neither limit nor termination—is hung up in the chamber of your soul for ever. What power, too, there is in the "Haunted Palace," particularly in the last words, "They laugh, but smile no more!" Dante has nothing superior in all those chilly yet fervent words of his, where "the ground burns frore, and cold performs the effect of fire."

We must now close our sketch of Poe; and we do so with feelings of wonder, pity, and awful sorrow, tempted to look up to heaven, and to cry, "Lord, why didst thou make this man in vain?" Yet perhaps there was even in him some latent spark of goodness, which may even now be developing itself under a kindlier sky. He has gone far away from the misty mid-region of Weir; his dreams of cosmogonies have been tested by the searching light of Eternity's truth; his errors have received the reward that was meet; and we cannot but say, ere we close, Peace even to the well-nigh putrid dust of Edgar Poe.

—George Gilfillan, "Edgar Poe,"
A Third Gallery of Portraits, 1854, pp. 380–88

THOMAS HOLLEY CHIVERS (1856)

Chivers, a friend and fellow poet, unleashes here a somewhat harsh critique of Poe's poetry. Chivers points out that Poe's work was derivative, especially of classical works, and that Poe lacked the "boldness" or "manliness" to make his otherwise ingenious ideas into great literary works.

Poe's Art consisted mostly in classical imitation. Not that he exactly aped the finished refinement of Greek Art, but that, possessing the highest poetic sense—a sense made affluent by the most polished education—he essayed not exactly to create a New Epoch, but to teach a servile race of mannerists how to avoid that everlasting platitude which is the besetting sin of the Age. I do not mean, by this, that he did not possess the genius for high things; but that he chose rather to make use of already existing materials than to suffer the intellectual travail necessary to create new. I allude now more especially to the "Raven." When I say this I mean to be understood that America never produced a man—nor indeed, any other Country—who possessed a higher *sense* of the Poetic Art than he did—not that grotesqueness of abandon, any more than the bizarrerie of fantasqueness, constitutes the *true* Poetic Art. Had he lived, he would have redeemed the platitude of the Age not only from its wantonness of affection, but also from its insipid sentimentality. One of his greatest faults was, his want of profound meditation—or, what Balzac beautifully calls—*La patience Angelique du genie.*

He had the genius to conceive, but not the boldness to execute. His ideal was great, but he had not the audacity to realize it in any creation passionately tangible to the soul. It was the statue of Pygmalion without the immortal soul to animate it. He could conceive of the grandeur, invention and grace which characterized the immortal works of the Carracci family; but he wanted the passion of Claude to suffuse them with that roseate glow of vitality necessary to true Beauty. But what distinguished him above every one of his contemporaries, was, his ability to see the imperfections in which they reveled. But one of his unaccountable deficiencies was, his utter inability to see that any work, to be perfect—or even to *approach* perfection,—must be the result of an equal blending of Art and Passion—that is, the highest Passion united with the most exalted Art—the passion moulding the Art.

His Ideal of Art was Raffaelesque, as his forms were Michaelangelesque; but he wanted the Venetian vitality to give living warmth to his Picture. Like Lodovico Carracci, he possessed the power to mingle in one form all the forms of all the other Artists that had preceeded him but, being destitute of that very quality which gave him the power to create a New School—namely, Nature,—his work will not remain a Model for all.

His Art was nothing but Art, without a particle of Nature to enliven it— was wanting in the very essentials of true genius—that which makes all Art glorious—the true Shekinah of Inspiration, namely—*fortuitousness.* He was deficient in that very power which Bellari says was the peculiar characteristic of Domenichino, *delinea gli animi, colorisce la vita*—for he neither drew the soul, nor coloured the life. He possessed the grace of Albano, and the delicacy of Guido, without possessing those other vivifying qualities which made their faces look like people from Paradise.

He was rather an Ambrosial Eclecticist than the *Fons ingeniorum,* the En-Ador, or Fons Pythonis of his Age—for he lacked the *Festina lente* necessary to the *crystalline revelation of the Divine Idea*—that is, the utterable sigh of an unutterable love breathed from the depths of our souls—which is the revelation of true Poesy.

Perhaps I can better describe the nature of his mind by saying that it was *feminine* and lacked *manliness.* Nor do I mean by this that the female mind is not perfectly adapted for Poetic contemplation; but, that, where man's mind partakes of this nature, it argues an inability to achieve great things. This was not only the case with Poe, but he was the most *boyish* man that I ever met. When I say this, I do not mean that a certain kind *of naivete* is not necessary to Poetical composition, but that Poe did not possess it. But, what I mean by his femininness is, that he was wanting in *manly decision.* Nothing would have pleased him better than being considered the Hero of Dante's *Inferno* for he was always, in imagination, at least, making toilsome Pilgrimages through the dim Regions of Pluto.

—Thomas Holley Chivers,
New Life of Edgar Allan Poe, c. 1856

FYODOR M. DOSTOEVSKI
"THREE TALES OF EDGAR POE" (1861)

Dostoevski, one of the greatest writers of the nineteenth century, is best known for such novels as *Crime and Punishment* and *The Brothers Karamazov.* Here he introduces three stories by Poe, newly translated into Russian. Dostoevski praises Poe's use of what we would now call "science" fiction. He notes that Poe does not so much produce fantasy, as he shows how something unnatural could be logically possible. Dostoevski contrasts Poe with the German writer E.T.A. Hoffmann, to whom Poe was often compared. Dostoevski disputes their similarity, though, saying that Poe's work is quite realistic, whereas Hoffmann's remains fantastic. Dostoevski notes that Poe is so realistic that certain tales (he cites "The Balloon Hoax") were taken to be true. Dostoevski states that, in Poe, the fantastic is "material." Essayists examining issues of realism or the interrelation of fact and fiction would be well served to consult this brief essay.

Two or three stories by Edgar Poe have already been translated and published in Russian magazines. Here we present to our readers three more. What a strange, though enormously talented writer, that Edgar Poe! His work can hardly be labeled as purely fantastic, and in so far as it falls into this category, its fantasticalness is a merely external one, if one may say so. He admits, for instance, that an Egyptian mummy that had lain five thousand years in a pyramid, was recalled into life with the help of galvanism. Or he presumes that a dead man, again by means of galvanism, tells the state of his mind, and so on, and so on. Yet such an assumption alone does not make a story really fantastic. Poe merely supposes the outward possibility of an unnatural event, though he always demonstrates logically that possibility and does it sometimes even with astounding skill; and this premise once granted, he in all the rest proceeds quite realistically. In this he differs essentially from the fantastic as used for example by Hoffmann. The latter personifies the forces of Nature in images, introduces in his tales sorceresses and specters, and seeks his ideals in a far-off utterly unearthly world, and not only assumes this mysterious magical world as superior but seems to believe in its real existence. . . . Not so Edgar Poe. Not fantastic should he be called but capricious. And how odd are the vagaries of his fancy and at the same time how audacious! He chooses as a rule the most extravagant reality, places his hero in a most extraordinary outward or psychological situation, and, then, describes the inner state of that person with marvellous acumen and amazing realism. Moreover, there exists one characteristic that is singularly peculiar to Poe and which distinguishes him from every other writer, and that is the vigor of his imagination. Not that his fancy exceeds that of all other poets, but his imagination is endowed with a quality which in such magnitude we have not met anywhere else, namely the power of details. Try, for instance, yourselves to realize in your mind anything that is very unusual or has never before occurred, and is only conceived as possible, and you will experience how vague and shadowy an image will appear before your inner eye. You will either grasp more or less general traits of the inward image or you will concentrate upon the one or the other particular, fragmentary feature. Yet Edgar Poe presents the whole fancied picture or events in all its details with such stupendous plasticity that you cannot but believe in the reality or possibility of a fact which actually never has occurred and even never could happen. Thus he describes in one of his stories a voyage to the moon, and his narrative is so full and particular, hour by hour following the imagined travel, that you involuntarily succumb to the illusion of its reality. In the same way he once told in an American newspaper the story of a balloon that crossed the ocean from Europe to the

New World, and his tale was so circumstantial, so accurate, so filled with unexpected, accidental happenings, in short was so realistic and truthful that at least for a couple of hours everybody was convinced of the reported fact and only later investigation proved it to be entirely invented. The same power of imagination, or rather combining power, characterizes his stories of the Purloined Letter, of the murder committed by an orangutan, of the discovered treasure, and so on.

Poe has often been compared with Hoffmann. As we have said before, we believe such a comparison to be false. Hoffmann is a much greater poet. For he possesses an ideal, however wrong sometimes, yet an ideal full of purity and of inherent human beauty. You find this ideal embodied even oftener in Hoffmann's non-fantastic creations, such as "Meister Martin" or the charming and delightful "Salvator Rosa," to say nothing of his masterpiece, "Kater Murr." In Hoffmann, true and ripe humor, powerful realism as well as malice, are welded with a strong craving for beauty and with the shining light of the ideal. Poe's fantasticalness, as compared with that, seems strangely "material," if such expression may be allowed. Even his most unbounded imagination betrays the true American. To acquaint our readers with this capricious talent we present meanwhile three of his tales.

—Fyodor M. Dostoevski, "Three Tales of Edgar Poe,"
Wremia, 1861

Stéphane Mallarmé
"Le Tombeau d'Edgar Poe" (1876)

Mallarmé, an influential French poet and leading figure in the Symbolist poetry movement, also translated much of Poe's work. This sonnet was written for the dedication of Poe's tomb in Baltimore.

Such as into Himself at last eternity changes
him, the Poet stirs with a naked sword
his century dismayed to have ignored
that death still triumphed in this voice so strange!
With a hydra-spasm, once hearing the angel endow
with a sense more pure the words of the tribe,
they loudly proclaimed the sortilege imbibed
from the dishonorable flood of some black brew.

Alas, from the warring heaven and earth, if
our concept cannot carve a bas-relief
with which to adorn Poe's dazzling sepulcher,
calm block fallen down here from some dark
disaster, let this granite forever mark
bounds to dark flights of Blasphemy scarce in the future.

—Stéphane Mallarmé, "Le Tombeau d'Edgar Poe," 1876

RICHARD HENRY HORNE (1876)

Horne, an English poet and critic, praises Poe's originality as well as the
patient, careful approach he took to storytelling. Horne remembers Poe's
story "The Spectacles," in which a vain young man, refusing to wear his
glasses, winds up marrying his own great-great-grandmother; he then
vows to behave less rashly in the future, and to always wear them. It
is somewhat understandable that cautious publishers might shy away
from such a tale.

No cunning barrister preparing an important brief; no great actor studying
a new part; no machinist brooding over the invention of an engine, or a
change subversive of the old machinery; no analytic chemist seeking to
establish the fact of a murder by the discovery and proof of blood or poison in
some unexpected substance; no Dutch painter working for months on the
minute finish of all sorts of details in the background as well as foreground
of his picture,—ever took more pains than did Edgar Allan Poe in the
production of most of his principal works. The more impossible his story, the
more perseveringly, learnedly, patiently, and plausibly he laboured to prove
the facts as he saw them. And, unless you throw the book down, he always
succeeds. If you read on steadily, you must go with him. You must believe
in his mesmerism, his mummy, and his more than "detective" acumen in
tracing a horrible murder to the "escaped convict" of a menagerie; you are
with him in the unswamped, frantic little boat, whirling round the interior of
the maelstrom; and you most certainly make a voyage with Hans Pfaall to the
moon, admiring all his scientific previsions and manoeuvres, and delighted
with all the somewhat alarming wonders through which he navigates you.
Since the voyage of Mr. Lemuel Gulliver to the island of Laputa, there has
been nothing of this class comparable to the reasoned-out story, or lunatic
"log"—for it is both—of Hans Pfaall.

Not that the story is any imitation, or bears anything beyond an aerial resemblance to the wonderful narrative of Dean Swift. Among all literary men, Poe stands very much alone, and should be judged by his own standard. It will be well if we tried to do this in all cases of original genius. If it be true that we judge of all things by comparison, still there is, no doubt, a stupid and slavish degree to which this is often carried. In the power of describing imaginary, and even miraculous scenes, actions and events, Poe possesses a kind of similarity to Swift, and also to some of the writers in the *Arabian Nights,* and among the Hebrews, ancient Persians, and other Oriental fabulists; but while Poe's narratives excite an equally rivetting interest and apprehension, they are not, for the most part, beautiful or poetical though we must admit several marked exceptions of somewhat depressing loveliness and melancholy fascination. We have heard people say that they wished they had never read some of the stories, so painfully penetrating had been the influence. Let no one endeavour to imitate Edgar Allan Poe. Without his genius and acquirements, such subjects would be intolerable, and the copyist would be discovered and denounced in an instant. The great majority of the fashionable novels of the day are no better than doll-houses by the side of his brain-haunted structures.

During a certain period of Poe's troubled circumstances, he wrote to me, I being then in London, and inclosed a manuscript, saying that he had singled me out, though personally a stranger, to ask the friendly service of handing a certain story to the editor of one of the magazines, with a view, of course, to some remittance. Without waiting to read the story, I replied at once that I considered his application to me a great compliment, and that I would certainly do the best I could in the business. But when I read the story, my heart of hope sank within me: it was "The Spectacles." I tried several magazines. Not an editor would touch it. In vain I represented the remarkable tact with which the old lady, under the very trying task she had set herself, did, nevertheless, maintain her female delicacy and dignity. I met with nothing beyond a deaf ear, an uplifted eyebrow, or the ejaculations of a gentleman pretending to feel quite shocked. It may be that false modesty, and social, as well as religious, hypocrisy, are the concomitant and counterpart of our present equivocal state of civilisation; but if I were not an Englishman, it is more than probable I should say that those qualities were more glaringly conspicuous in England than in any other country.

With regard to the poems of Edgar Allan Poe, they have been in certain instances mistaken by admirers in many parts of the world,—not for any rare qualities they really possess, but for something they have not. General readers of poetry, especially youthful readers, have been led away—we will not call it "led astray"—by his weird music. Also by the studied artifice of his selection, or coinage, of liquid and sonorous sounds and words, such as (to spell them phonetically) *ullaleume—annabellee—ells* (in the "Bells") *ore*, in "The Raven," which abounds in that long-drawn tone. It is too obviously artificial, and seems to supersede inspiration. The poet himself appears to have taken a strange pleasure in describing the almost mechanical plan and execution of the poem for which he is most celebrated. A critic has suggested that this statement was probably an afterthought. Possibly it was one of Poe's analytic freaks; and yet, when we see clearly the forethought he must have devoted to the working-out of his stories, I regret to say that I more than half believe his statement about the very unpoetical hatching of his Raven. "Heresy and schism!" As for the charming melody, liquid flow, and luring pathos of some of his lyrics, there can be no question of the success of the versification, by whatever means produced. Now and then the poems look deep, but that is often owing to their pellucid clearness, and there is not very much at the bottom. It is in the unique invention, and mastery of execution in his prose tales, that the genius of Poe most potently displays itself. There is nothing like them in the English, or any other language.

—Richard Henry Horne (April 8, 1876),
Edgar Allan Poe: A Memorial Volume,
ed. Sara Sigourney Rice, 1877, pp. 81–84

THOMAS WENTWORTH HIGGINSON "POE" (1879)

Higginson was a Unitarian minister and writer who is perhaps best known for discovering and posthumously publishing Emily Dickinson's poetry. Here he remembers seeing Poe give a reading when Higginson was still in college. He also praises Poe's poetry and ranks Poe alongside Nathaniel Hawthorne as the greatest writers of imaginative prose. He suggests that Hawthorne is superior, since he provides a solid foundation to go with the lofty ideas, but nevertheless praises Poe. Students might compare Poe and Hawthorne, using Higginson's comments to see how the writers differ. Higginson notes that Poe has become well respected in France, one of the first American writers to achieve popularity there. Alternately, students might compare Higginson's comments with Baudelaire's, looking at the difference between an American and European point of view. Higginson disagrees with Poe's criticism, especially of Hawthorne, and suggests that Poe led a sad, miserable life. He ends by remembering Poe's fiancée, Sarah

Helen Whitman, whose own memories of Poe are included in this volume. Students interested in biographical criticism might examine Higginson's "memoir" in relation to Griswold's or Whitman's.

It happens to us but few times in our lives to come consciously into the presence of that extraordinary miracle we call genius. Among the many literary persons whom I have happened to meet, at home or abroad, there are not half a dozen who have left an irresistible sense of this rare quality; and, among these few, Poe stands next to Hawthorne in the vividness of personal impression he produced. I saw him but once, and it was on that celebrated occasion, in 1845, when he startled Boston by substituting his boyish production, "Al Aaraaf," for the more serious poem which he was to have delivered before the Lyceum. There was much curiosity to see him, for his prose-writings had been eagerly read, at least among college students, and his poems were just beginning to excite still greater attention. After a rather solid and very partisan address by Caleb Cushing, then just returned from his Chinese embassy, the poet was introduced. I distinctly recall his face, with its ample forehead, brilliant eyes, and narrowness of nose and chin; an essentially ideal face, not noble, yet anything but coarse; with the look of over-sensitiveness which when uncontrolled may prove more debasing than coarseness. It was a face to rivet one's attention in any crowd; yet a face that no one would feel safe in loving. It is not perhaps strange that I find or fancy in the portrait of Charles Baudelaire, Poe's French admirer and translator, something of the traits that are indelibly associated with that one glimpse of Poe.

I remember that when introduced he stood with a sort of shrinking before the audience and then began in a thin, tremulous, hardly musical voice, an apology for his poem, and a deprecation of the expected criticism of a Boston audience; reiterating this in a sort of persistent, querulous way, which did not seem like satire, but impressed me at the time as nauseous flattery. It was not then known, nor was it established for long after—even when he had himself asserted it—that the poet was himself born in Boston; and no one can ever tell, perhaps, what was the real feeling behind the apparently sycophantic attitude. When, at the end, he abruptly began the recitation of his rather perplexing poem, the audience looked thoroughly mystified. The verses had long since been printed in his youthful volume, and had re-appeared within a few days, if I mistake not, in Wiley & Putnam's edition of his poems; and they produced no very distinct impression on the audience until Poe began to read the maiden's song in the second part. Already his tones had been softening to a finer melody than at first, and when he came to the verse:

> Ligeia! Ligeia,
>   My beautiful one!
> Whose harshest idea
>   Will to melody run,
> O! is it thy will
>   On the breezes to toss?
> Or capriciously still
>   Like the lone albatross
> Incumbent on night
>   (As she on the air)
> To keep watch with delight
>   On the harmony there?

his voice seemed attenuated to the finest golden thread; the audience became hushed, and, as it were, breathless; there seemed no life in the hall but his; and every syllable was accentuated with such delicacy, and sustained with such sweetness as I never heard equaled by other lips. When the lyric ended, it was like the ceasing of the gipsy's chant in Browning's "Flight of the Duchess"; and I remember nothing more, except that in walking back to Cambridge my comrades and I felt that we had been under the spell of some wizard. Indeed, I feel much the same in the retrospect to this day.

The melody did not belong, in this case, to the poet's voice alone; it was already in the words. His verse, when he was willing to give it natural utterance, was like that of Coleridge in rich sweetness, and like that was often impaired by theories of structure and systematic experiments in meter. Never in American literature, I think, was such a fountain of melody flung into the air as when "Lenore" first appeared in the *Pioneer*; and never did fountain so drop downward as when Poe rearranged it in its present form. The irregular measure had a beauty as original as that of "Christabel," and the lines had an ever-varying, ever-lyrical cadence of their own until their author himself took them and cramped them into couplets. What a change from

> *Peccavimus!*
>   But rave not thus!
>   And let the solemn song
> Go up to God so mournfully that *she* may feel no wrong!

to the amended version, portioned off in regular lengths, thus:

Peccavimus! but rave not thus! and let a Sabbath song
Go up to God so solemnly, the dead may feel no wrong.

Or worse yet, when he introduced that tedious jingle of slightly varied
repetition which reached its climax in lines like these:

Till the fair and gentle Eulalie became my blushing bride.
Till the yellow-haired young Eulalie became my
    smiling bride.

This trick, caught from Poe, still survives in our literature; made more
permanent, perhaps, by the success of his "Raven." This poem, which made
him popular, seems to me far inferior to some of his earlier and slighter
effusions; as those exquisite verses "To Helen" which are among our
American classics, and have made

The glory that was Greece
And the grandeur that was Rome,

a permanent phrase in our language.

Poe's place in purely imaginative prose-writing is as unquestionable as
Hawthorne's. He even succeeded, which Hawthorne did not, in penetrating
the artistic indifference of the French mind; and it was a substantial triumph,
when we consider that Baudelaire put himself or his friends to the trouble
of translating even the prolonged platitudes of "Eureka," and the wearisome
narrative of "Arthur Gordon Pym." Neither Poe nor Hawthorne has ever
been fully recognized in England; and yet no Englishman of our time, except
possibly De Quincey, has done any prose imaginative work to be named
with theirs. But in comparing Poe with Hawthorne, we see that the genius of
the latter has hands and feet as well as wings, so that all his work is solid as
masonry, while Poe's is broken and disfigured by all sorts of inequalities and
imitation and stucco; he not disdaining, for want of true integrity, to disguise
and falsify, to claim knowledge that he did not possess, to invent quotations
and references, and even, as Griswold showed, to manipulate and exaggerate
puffs of himself. I remember the chagrin with which I looked through Tieck,
in my student-days, to find the "Journey into the Blue Distance" to which Poe
refers in the "House of Usher"; and how one of the poet's intimates laughed
me to scorn for being deceived by any of Poe's citations; saving that he hardly
knew a word of German.

But making all possible deductions, how wonderful remains the power
of Poe's imaginative tales, and how immense is the ingenuity of his puzzles

and disentanglements. The conundrums of Wilkie Collins never renew their interest after the answer is known; but Poe's can be read again and again. It is where spiritual depths are to be touched that he shows his weakness; where he attempts it, as in "William Wilson," it seems exceptional; where there is the greatest display of philosophic form he is often most trivial, whereas Hawthorne is often profoundest when he has disarmed you by his simplicity. The truth is that Poe lavished on things comparatively superficial those great intellectual resources which Hawthorne reverently husbanded and used. That there is something behind even genius to make or mar it, this is the lesson of the two lives.

Poe makes one of his heroes define another as "that *monstrum horrendum*, an unprincipled man of genius." It is in the malice and fury of his own critical work that his low moral tone most betrays itself. No atmosphere can be more belittling than that of his "New York Literati"; it is a mass of vehement dogmatism and petty personalities; opinions warped by private feeling, and varying from page to page. He seemed to have absolutely no standard of critical judgment, though it is true that there was very little anywhere in America, during those acrimonious days, when the most honorable head might be covered with insult or neglect, while any young poetess who smiled sweetly on Poe or Griswold or Willis might find herself placed among the muses. Poe complimented and rather patronized Hawthorne; but found him only "peculiar and not original"; saying of him, "He has not half the material for the exclusiveness of literature that he has for its universality," whatever that may mean; and finally he tried to make it appear that Hawthorne had plagiarized from himself. He returned again and again to the attack on Longfellow as a willful plagiarist, denouncing the trivial resemblance between his "Midnight Mass for the Dying Year" and Tennyson's "Death of the Old Year," as "belonging to the most barbarous class of literary piracy (Works, ed. 1853, III, 325). To make this attack was "to throttle the guilty" (III, 300); and while dealing thus ferociously with Longfellow, thus condescendingly with Hawthorne, he was claiming a foremost rank among American authors for obscurities now forgotten, such as Mrs. Amelia B. Welby and Estelle Anne Lewis. No one ever did more than Poe to lower the tone of literary criticism in this country; and the greater his talent, the greater the mischief. As a poet he held for a time the place earlier occupied by Byron, and later by Swinburne, as the patron saint of all willful boys suspected of genius, and convicted at least of its infirmities. He belonged to the melancholy class of wasted men, like the German Hoffmann, whom perhaps of all men of genius he most resembled. No doubt, if we are to apply any standard of moral weight or sanity to literary men—a proposal which Poe would doubtless have ridiculed—it can only be in a very large and generous way. If a career has only a manly ring to it we can forgive many errors—as in reading, for instance, the autobiography of Benvenuto Cellini, carrying always his life in his hand amid a brilliant and reckless society. But the existence of a poor Bohemian, besotted when he has money, angry and vindictive when the money is spent, this is a dismal tragedy, for which genius only makes the footlights burn with more luster. There is a passage in Keats's letters, written from the haunts of Burns, in which he expresses himself as filled with pity for the poet's life; "he drank with blackguards, he was miserable; we can see horribly clear in the works of such a man his life, as if we were God's spies." Yet Burns's sins and miseries left his heart unspoiled, and this cannot be said of Poe. After all, the austere virtues—the virtues of Emerson, Hawthorne, Whittier—are the best soil for genius.

I like best to think of Poe as associated with his gifted betrothed, Sarah Helen Whitman, whom I saw sometimes in her later years. She had outlived her early friends and loves and hopes, and perhaps her literary fame, such as it was; she had certainly outlived her recognized ties with Poe, and all but his memory. There she dwelt in her little suite of rooms, bearing youth still in her heart and in her voice, and on her hair also, and in her dress. Her dimly-lighted parlor was always decked, here and there, with scarlet; and she sat, robed in white, her back always to the light, with a discreetly-tinted shadow over her still thoughtful and noble face. She seemed a person embalmed while still alive; it was as if she might dwell forever there, prolonging into an indefinite future the tradition of a poet's love; and when we remembered that she had been Poe's betrothed, that his kisses had touched her lips, that she still believed in him and was his defender, all criticism might well, for her sake, be disarmed, and her saintly life atone for his stormy and sad career.

—Thomas Wentworth Higginson, "Poe,"
Literary World, March 15, 1879

JORIS-KARL HUYSMANS (1884)

Huysmans was a French Symbolist novelist. He is best known for *À Rebours* (usually translated as *Against Nature* or *Against the Grain*), from which this passage is taken. The novel deals with a single character, Des Esseintes, who is deeply affected by the writings of Poe, among others.

Better perhaps than anyone else, Poe possessed those intimate affinities that could satisfy the requirements of Des Esseintes' mind.

If Baudelaire had made out among the hieroglyphics of the soul the critical age of thought and feeling, it was Poe who, in the sphere of morbid psychology, had carried out the closest scrutiny of the will.

In literature he had been the first, under the emblematic title "The Imp of the Perverse," to study those irresistible impulses which the will submits to without fully understanding them, and which cerebral pathology can now explain with a fair degree of certainty; he had been the first again, if not to point out, at least to make known the depressing influence fear has on the will, which it affects in the same way as anaesthetics which paralyse the senses and curare which cripples the motory nerves. It was on this last subject, this lethargy of the will, that he had concentrated his studies, analysing the effects of this moral poison and indicating the symptoms of its progress—mental disturbances beginning with anxiety, developing into anguish, and finally culminating in a terror that stupefies the faculties of volition, yet without the intellect, however badly shaken it may be, giving way.

As for death, which the dramatists had so grossly abused, he had in a way given it a sharper edge, a new look, by introducing into it an algebraic and superhuman element; though to tell the truth, it was not so much the physical agony of the dying he described as the moral agony of the survivor, haunted beside the death-bed by the monstrous hallucinations engendered by grief and fatigue. With awful fascination he dwelt on the effects of terror, on the failures of will-power, and discussed them with clinical objectivity, making the reader's flesh creep, his throat contract, his mouth go dry at the recital of these mechanically devised nightmares of a fevered brain.

Convulsed by hereditary neuroses, maddened by moral choreas, his characters lived on their nerves; his women, his Morellas and Ligeias, possessed vast learning steeped in the mists of German philosophy and in the cabbalistic mysteries of the ancient East, and all of them had the inert, boyish breasts of angels, all were, so to speak, unsexed.

—Joris-Karl Huysmans, *À Rebours,*
tr. Robert Baldick, 1884, Ch. 14

HALLAM TENNYSON (1897)

O American poets (Tennyson said): "I know several striking poems by American poets, but I think that Edgar Poe is (taking his poetry and prose together) the most original American genius." When asked to write an epitaph of one line for Poe's monument in Westminster Churchyard, Baltimore, he answered: "How can so strange and so fine a genius, and so sad a life, be exprest and comprest in one line."

—Hallam Tennyson, *Alfred Lord Tennyson: A Memoir*,
1897, Vol. 2, pp. 292–93

CHARLES WHIBLEY "EDGAR ALLAN POE" (1896)

Whibley, an influential British literary critic, praises Poe's talents as a writer of tales, criticism, and poetry. Whibley notes that, although Poe drew from known sources of inspiration, he is an original. Poe's tales seem to lie outside any particular place, time period, or national tradition. Indeed, with Poe's international fame, he seems to belong to no one location in particular, but rather to a "fairy-land" of his own making.

Whibley notes that Poe's tales seem to combine the horrific with the comical, mixing terror and laughter, suggesting a sinister "theory of the ludicrous." Students could refer to this essay when comparing Poe's tales of terror to his humorous writings and how these areas overlap and inform each other in Poe's work. Whibley examines the character of C. Auguste Dupin, Poe's amateur detective who solves mysteries in "The Murders in the Rue Morgue," "The Mystery of Marie Claire," and "The Purloined Letter." Through these tales, Poe is credited with inventing the detective story, and Whibley marvels at how original Dupin is. By 1896 such a figure had many imitators. Students examining Poe's detective stories might use Whibley's analysis of Dupin's techniques.

Whibley examines Poe's style as well. Whibley says that Poe is a great maker of stories, but not a great writer. He complains about Poe's awkward sentences and bombastic phrasing. Whibley also states that Poe should have known better, especially since he was familiar with great writers such as Coleridge. A student writing about Poe's style could examine Whibley's criticism. Is Whibley right in suggesting that Poe's prose is excessive? How does the style of storytelling affect the story? How does Poe's writing differ from other esteemed writers such as Coleridge or Flaubert?

Whibley commends Poe's work as a critic. In addition to being a writer of fiction and poetry, Poe was one of the most influential literary critics in the United States in his day. Whibley notes that Poe's trademark critical severity was always "in defence of literature" and thus justified. He compares Poe the critic to Dupin the detective: each uses insight and reason to pierce through the veils obscuring "true" literature. Calling Poe a prophet, Whibley marvels at how Poe anticipates the critiques of realism and naturalism to come in the late nineteenth century. A student looking at Poe's theory of literature, especially his theory of poetry or of "art for art's sake," might cite Whibley's comments on Poe. Finally, Whibley examines Poe's poetry, remarking that he was able to see "with his ear." That is, the poetry is musical, designed to be heard rather than to be interpreted. Students might want to examine the way that "sound" and "sense" interact in Poe's poetry.

―――――   ―――――   ―――――

His first success was achieved (in 1833) with "The MS. Found in a Bottle," which won a prize offered by *The Saturday Visitor*. Henceforth, with varying fortune, he earned his living by his pen. He wrote stories, satires, poems; his criticism became the terror of the incompetent; and though his Southern descent, his genius, his reasonable contempt, rendered him unpopular in the North, he was, many years before his death, the best hated and most highly respected of his class. The one constant ambition of his life—to start a magazine of his own—was disappointed; but alone of his contemporaries he captured a reputation in Europe, and neither ill-health nor misfortune shook for an instant his legitimate confidence in himself, his determination to set in their place the pigmies who surrounded him. Meanwhile, his strange marriage with Virginia Clemm, who, at the ceremony, was not yet fourteen, with his unfailing devotion to his fragile wife and her mother, disproved the boorish cruelty wherewith he was so complacently charged. On the other hand, the affection, required yet unsuccessful, which he cherished at the end for Mrs. Whitman, for "Annie," and for Mrs. Shelton, does not suggest the humour of one who had a strong, rational hold upon existence. But he lived his own life, as he died his own death, and it is for the Griswolds to hold their peace in the presence of genius.

At least his works remain to confute the blasphemer, and it is certain that no writer ever bequeathed so many examples to posterity. Although he went not beyond the tradition of his time, although he owed something to Maturin and Mrs. Radclyffe, something also, in decoration and decay, to the *romantiques* of 1830, he was essentially an inventor. He touched no kind of story without making it a type for all time. Even *The Narrative of Arthur Gordon Pym*, which you confess to be tiresome and elaborate, has been a stimulus to a whole generation of romance-mongers; and you feel, despite its faults, that it displays a greater verisimilitude, if not a greater knowledge, than the best of its successors. Before all things, Poe had the faculty of detaching himself from the present and of imagining unseen continents. With seamanship, science, erudition, mysticism, with all the branches of human knowledge he feigned an acquaintance. He tells you with pride that "The MS. Found in a Bottle" was written many years before he had seen the maps of Mercator; and you find yourself eagerly forgiving the amiable pedantry. But it is in *The Tales of the Grotesque and Arabesque* that Poe first revealed his personal imagination—an imagination rather of tone than of incident. "The House of Usher," "Ligeia," and the rest surpass all other stories in economy of method and suggestion. Death, catalepsy, and the supernatural are the material of them all. They know neither time nor place; they are enwrapped in an atmosphere only substantial enough to enclose phantoms; spectral castles frown upon sombre tarns, destined to engulph them; clouds, fantastically outlined, chase one another across an imagined sky; ancient families totter to their doom, overwhelmed in misery and disease; ruined halls are resplendent with red lanterns and perfumed with swinging censers; the heroine's hand is cold as marble, marble-cold also is her forehead, but she is learned in all the sciences, and the castle library contains the works of Caslius Secundus Curio and Tertullian. Everywhere there is a sombre splendour, a forbidding magnificence. No wonder that the dweller in an English abbey shudders at "the Bedlam patterns of the carpets of tufted gold." Naught save the names, which are of no country and of no age, heightens the colour of the monotone romance. Madeleine, Berenice, Ligeia, Morella, Eleonora—do they not sing in your ear, and by their beauty make more horrible the cold tragedy of their deaths? To analyse these fantasies closely is impossible; you must leave them to the low, dim-tinted atmosphere wherein Poe has enveloped them. They are vague, fleeting, mystical—a sensation of tapestry, wherein spectral figures wander hand in hand. Silence and horror are their cult, and there is not one of the ladies whose ever-approaching death would not be hastened by a breath of reality. Ligeia dwells in "a dim and decaying city by the Rhine," but who would seek to discover her habitation? It were as infamous as to discover beneath a tropical sun, "the Valley of the Many-coloured Grass," where pined the hapless Eleonora. The best of the fancies are rather poetry than prose, and already Poe had perfected his artifice of the refrain. The finest passage in "Eleonora" is repeated with the stateliest effect, and the horror of "Silence" is increased tenfold by the oft-recurring phrase: "And the man trembled in the solitude, but the night waned, and he sat upon the rock." In these grotesque imaginings even laughter becomes a terror. At Sparta, says the monster of "The Assignation," "the altar of Laughter survived all the others," and he chuckles at the very point of death. When, in "The Cask of Amontillado," the last stone is fitted to Fortunato's living tomb, "there came from out the niche a low laugh," which might well have sent Montresor's hair on end. Not even did Morella's lover meet his doom with tears. "I laughed with a long and bitter laugh," he says, "as I found no trace of the first in the charnel where I laid the second—Morella." But, worst of all, the demon laughs when the whole world is cursed to silence: wherefrom you may deduce as sinister a theory of the ludicrous as you please.

And then he turned to another kind, and created at a breath M. Dupin, that master of insight, who proved that the complex was seldom profound, and who discovered by the natural transition from a colliding fruiterer, through street stones, stereotomy, Epicurus, Dr. Nicholls and Orion, that Chantilly was a very little fellow, and would do better for the Theatre des Varietes. Now, Monsieur Charles A. Dupin was of good family—so much you are ready to believe; he was also young—a statement you decline to accept on the word of a creator, unless, indeed, he be the Wandering Jew. But whatever his age and breeding, he is a master of analysis, and plays at ratiocination as a boy plays with a peg-top. He knows by long experience that in pitting your intelligence against another's you are sure to win if you identify yourself with your adversary. And when once this principle is understood, it is as easy as a game of marbles, and more profitable. M. Dupin loves darkness better than light, not because his deeds are evil, but because, being a poet and a mathematician, he works better by lamplight. Hence it was his practice to live through the day by the glimmer of two flickering candles, and to walk abroad at night under the spell of the gas-lamps. When serious work was toward, or he was forced to interview the doltish Prefect of Police, then he sat in the dark, and silently puffed his meerschaum. The smallest indication was sufficient for him, and while the police fumbled over the murders in the Rue Morgue, arresting a harmless bank-clerk, he not only discovered the true culprit, but was convinced that the culprit's master was a sailor, belonging to a Maltese vessel. "How was it possible?" asked his incredulous accomplice, "that you should know the man to be a sailor, and belonging to a Maltese vessel?" "I do not *know* it," said Dupin. "I am not *sure* of it! Here, however, is a small piece of ribbon, which from its form, and from its greasy appearance, has evidently been used in tying the hair in one of those long *queues* of which sailors are so fond. Moreover, this knot is one which few besides sailors can tie, and is peculiar to the Maltese." Imagine the joy of happening upon this masterpiece of combined observation and analysis, in the days before the trick had not been vulgarised beyond recognition! And yet, despite this flash of genius, M. Dupin affected to despise ingenuity, which he regarded as the cheapest of human qualities; and he would persuade you that all his finest effects were produced by pure reason! His most daring deed was done in the Rue Morgue: the instant discovery of the inhuman murderer was adroitness itself; and the advertisement of the recovered Ourang-Outang was even more brilliant. Unhappily there is a touch of melodrama in the locked door, the pistol upon the table, and the extorted confession. But M. Dupin is seldom guilty of such an indiscretion, and you readily forgive him. A more subtle achievement was the recovery of the purloined letter, for in this exploit he opposed the great Minister D, and proved the superior at all points. In brief, his shining qualities are as stars in the night, nor have they been dimmed by the unnumbered imitators, who to-day are mimicking the tone and the manner of the inimitable Dupin.

Though "The Gold Bug" is a masterpiece of another kind, it is nearly related to "The Purloined Letter." It displays the perfect logic, the complete lucidity, the mastery of analysis, which make M. Dupin immortal. No step in the adventure but is foreseen and inevitable. Never before nor since has use so admirable been made of ciphers and buried treasure. The material, maybe, was not new, but the treatment, as of a glorified problem in mathematics, was Poe's own invention. In his hands the slightest incident ceased to be curious, and became (so to say) a link in the chain of fate. Not only was he unrivalled in the art of construction, but he touched the simplest theme with a clairvoyant intelligence, which seemed at the same moment to combine and analyse the materials of his story. Thus, also, the best of his scientific parables convince the imagination, even if they leave the reason refractory. But the purpose of these is too obvious, their central truths too heavily weighted with pretended documents for immortality. It is upon the grotesque, the horrible, and the ingenious that Poe has established his reputation. And surely the author of "Ligeia," of "Silence," of "William Wilson," of the Dupin Cycle, of "The Gold Bug," and of "The Mask of the Red Death" need not defend his title to undying fame.

Though Poe was a maker of great stories, he was not a great writer. That he might have been is possible, for none ever showed in fragments a finer sense of words; that he was not is certain. Mr. Stedman attempts to excuse him upon the ground that he lived before Pater, Flaubert, and Arnold. Never was a more preposterous theory formulated. As though the art of prose were newly invented! The English tongue, accurate, noble, coloured, is centuries older than Pater; and even in Poe's own time there were models worth the following. He knew Coleridge from end to end, and did not profit by his example. So conscious is he of style in others, that he condemns the Latinity of Lamb, but he rarely knits his own sentences to perfection.

The best he wraps round with coils of useless string, and he is not incapable of striking false notes upon the Early-Victorian drum. He shocks you, for instance, by telling you that William Wilson at Oxford "vied in profuse-ness of expenditure with the haughtiest heirs of the wealthiest earldoms in Great Britain"—a sentence equally infamous whether it appeal to the ear or to the brain. Egeaus, again, the ghoulish lover of Berenice, boasts with a pride which Mrs. Radclyffe might envy that "there are no towers in land more time-honoured than my gloomy, gray, hereditary halls." This is fustian, and you regret it the more because in construction, in idea, Poe was seldom at fault. The opening of his stories is commonly perfect. How could you better the first page of "The House of Usher," whose weird effect is attained throughout by the simplest means? Another writer would take five pages to explain what Poe has touched off in the first five lines of "The Oval Portrait"; and to how many writers has this rejection of all save the essential been a noble example? But Poe, writing on the impulse of a whim, let the style which he knew elude his grasp, and if his carelessness cast a shadow upon his true masterpieces, it reduces the several volumes of properly forgotten fantasies to the lower level of journalism.

The criticism of Poe inaugurated a new era, a new cult of taste and beauty. Whether in theory or in practice he was ahead not only of his time, but of all time. That same keen intelligence which created M. Dupin, tore to pieces the prevailing superstitions and disclosed in a few pages the true qualities of literature. Beauty is his cult; poetry for him is "the rhythmical creation of beauty." He is neither preacher nor historian. Being an artist, he esteems facts as lightly as morals. Art, he says, has "no concern whatever either with Duty or with Truth." A poem is written solely for the poem's sake. "Perseverance," again, "is one thing, genius quite another," and the public has as little to do with the industry as with the inspiration of the artist. To us who have lived through the dark age of naturalism his passage upon Truth rings like a prophecy: "The demands of Truth," he writes in "The Poetic Principle," "the demands of Truth are severe; she has no sympathy with the myrtles. All *that* which is so indispensable in Song, is precisely all *that* with which *she* has nothing whatever to do. It is but making her a flaunting paradox to wreath her in gems and flowers." Even more precise and bitter is his epigrammatic indictment of Realism. "The defenders of this pitiable stuff"—you will find the lines in *Marginalia*—"uphold it on the ground of its truthfulness. Taking the thesis into question, the truthfulness is the one overwhelming defect. An original idea that—to laud the accuracy with which the stone is hurled that knocks us in the head. A little less accuracy might have left us more brains. And here are critics absolutely commending the truthfulness with which only the disagreeable is conveyed! In my view, if an artist must paint decayed cheeses, his merit will lie in their looking as little like decayed cheeses as possible." And that was written twenty years before the advent of Zola!

In "The Philosophy of Composition," moreover, he explains, what should never have needed explanation, that a work of art is the result not of accident but of a reasoned artifice; and he illustrates his thesis by a whimsical, far-fetched analysis of his own "Raven." He treats the poem with the same impartial intelligence which M. Dupin would have brought to the detection of a murderer or the discovery of a missing trinket. In truth, Poe might be called the Dupin of Criticism. For he looked, with his keen eye and rapid brain, through the innumerable follies wherewith literature was obscured, and he rejected the false hypotheses as scornfully as M. Dupin set aside the Prefect's imbecilities. As a practical critic Poe was a fighter. His sense of honour knew neither civility nor favouritism. He alone among critics has come forth with a chivalrous defence of his craft, in which he took a fierce pride. He was no adulator ready-made to serve some Society of Authors: he was a judge, condemning the guilty with an honourable severity. "When we attend less to authority," he wrote, "and more to principles, when we look *less* at merit and *more* at demerit, we shall be better critics than we are." Is that not enough to make the Popular Novelist turn green with fury, especially since it is the deliberate utterance of a man, whose example has furnished forth a whole library of popular novels? Twice he quotes the parable of the critic who "presented to Apollo a severe censure upon an excellent poem. The god asked him for the beauties of the work. He replied that he only troubled himself about the errors. Apollo presented him with a sack of unwinnowed wheat, and bade him pick out the chaff for his pains." Now, this is the critic's severest condemnation, and yet Poe is honest enough to declare that he is not sure that the god was in the right.

Being a severe judge, he was generously misunderstood. Longfellow was magnanimous enough to attribute "the harshness of his criticism to the irritation of a sensitive nature, chafed by some indefinite sense of wrong." Thus the Illiterate Novelist is wont to ascribe the lightest censure to a critic's envy. And they do not see, neither Longfellow nor the Illiterate Novelist, that they are bringing superfluous charges of bad faith. Is it possible that Longfellow could not imagine the necessity of censure? Is it possible that he, like the bleating lambs of fiction, believed that criticism was written, not for its own sake, but for the voidance of gall? If such were his creed, if he, being a critic, would never have written a line, unblotted by hatred or irritation, it is fortunate that he never lapsed from his devotion to poetry. But Poe was not always harsh, and when he used the scourge, he used it in defence of literature. It was his misfortune to review his contemporaries; and they, though they resented his censure, have already justified his severity by crawling, one and all, into oblivion. A bolder editor, indeed, would have suppressed the two volumes of books reviewed—articles which served their turn at the moment, which are ill-written, and which dimly reflect the brilliant insight of *Marginalia*. But when Poe encountered a master, he was eager in appreciation. His praise of Alfred Tennyson was as generous as it was wise. "In perfect sincerity," he wrote, "I regard him as the noblest poet that ever lived." And, again, remembering that this was written in 1843, you recognise in Poe the gift of prophecy.

But to complete the cycle of his accomplishments he was also a poet, and it is as a poet that he wears the greener bays. Here his practice coincided accurately with his theory. He believed that a long poem was a contradiction in terms, and he only erred once against the light, when he called *Eureka,* a tedious treatise upon all things and nothing, "a prose poem." In his eyes the sole aim of poetry was beauty, and such beauty as should touch the ear rather than the brain. His musical art eludes analysis, and he esteemed it great in proportion as it receded from the hard shapes and harder truths of life. Of him it might be said truly that "he seemed to see with his ear." You do not question "Annabel Lee" and "Ulalume." You do not attempt to drag a common meaning from their gossamer loveliness. You listen to their refrains and repeated cadences; you delight in their rippling sound and subtle variations; and you are content to find yourself in the presence of an art, which, like music, does not represent, but merely presents, an emotion. And because Poe acknowledged the artifice of his poetry, some have denied him imagination. As though imagination did not most clearly manifest herself in artistic expression!

It is not surprising that Poe's multiform genius should have proved a dominant influence upon European literature. Not only was he a sombre light to the decadence, not only was he a guiding flame in the pathway of the mystics; but also he revived the novel of adventure and lost treasure, of the South Seas and of Captain Kidd. The atrocities which have been committed in the name of his Dupin are like the sands for number, and the detective of fact, as of romance, has attempted to model himself upon this miracle of intelligence. Thus he has been an example to both houses—to Huysmans, who has emulated his erudition, and to Gaboriau, who has cheapened his mystery. It is his unique distinction to have anticipated even the trivialities of life. His title, "The Man That Was Used Up," has let in upon us the legion of imbeciles who did or didn't, who would or wouldn't. And stranger still, he it was that imagined the philosopher, who, in the vanity of his heart, should spell his god with a little g! His influence came not from America but from France. No sooner was "The Murders in the Rue Morgue" published in America, than it appeared as a *feuilleton* in *Le Commerce,* and in 1846 was printed a volume of *Contes,* translated by Isabelle Meunier. Ten years later Baudelaire began the brilliant series of translations, which added the glory of Poe to French literature. That Poe gained in the transference there is no doubt: the looseness of his style—his most grievous fault—was tightened in the distinguished prose of Baudelaire; and henceforth Poe was free to shape the literary future of France. It was his example that moulded the *conte* to its ultimate completion. His talents of compression and facile exposition, his gift of building up a situation in a hundred words, were imitated by the army of writers, who first perfected the short story, and then sent it across the Channel. Nor is Baudelaire the only poet who has done Poe into French. M. Stephane Mallarme, also, has proved his sympathy with the author of "The Raven" in a set of matchless translations. He has turned the verse of Poe into a rhythmical prose, and withal he has kept so close to the original, that the prose echoes not only the phrase but the cadence of the verse. And from France Poe penetrated every country in Europe. He is known and read in those remote corners which he described, yet never saw. He is as familiar in Spain as in Scandinavia, and but a year ago "The Raven" was translated "direct from English" in far-off Valparaiso.

And here is the final contrast of his life. The prophet of silence and seclusion is blown to the four winds of heaven. But he has conquered glory without stooping one inch from his proper attitude of aristocracy. He is still as exclusive and morose as his stories. Between him and his fantasies there is no discord. You imagine him always stern-faced and habited in black, with Virginia Clemm at his side, Virginia shadowy as Ligeia, amiable as the mild Eleonora in the Valley of the Many-coloured Grass. He dwelt in mid America, and he was yet in fairy-land. Though the squalor of penury and the magazines gave him neither "ancestral hall" nor "moss-grown abbey," he lived and died enclosed within the impregnable castle of his mind.

—Charles Whibley, "Edgar Allan Poe," *New Review,*
January 1896, pp. 617–25

WILLIAM BUTLER YEATS (1899)

In this excerpt, Yeats, one of Ireland's greatest poets, criticizes Poe's poetry and fiction, claiming that Poe's work seems artificial and insincere. In particular, Yeats finds Poe's "appeal to the nerves" to be a trick, unworthy of great literature.

—————

My dear Horton, I have been a long time without writing to thank you for your Poe. I like the Raven on the head of Pallas about best. I like next the drawing on page 18—a really admirable grotesque. I do not know why you or indeed anybody should want to illustrate Poe however. His fame always puzzles me. I have to acknowledge that even after one allows for the difficulties of a critic who speaks a foreign language, a writer who has had so much influence on Baudelaire and Villiers de L'Isle Adam has some great merit. I admire a few lyrics of his extremely and a few pages of his prose, chiefly in his critical essays, which are sometimes profound. The rest of him seems to me vulgar and commonplace and the Pit and the Pendulum and the Raven do not seem to me to have permanent literary value of any kind. Analyse the Raven and you find that its subject is a commonplace and its execution a rhythmical trick. Its rhythm never lives for a moment, never once moves with an emotional life. The whole thing seems to me insincere and vulgar. Analyse the Pit and the Pendulum and you find an appeal to the nerves by tawdry physical affrightments, at least so it seems to me who am yet puzzled at the fame of such things. No, your book is the *Pilgrim's Progress*. You could do that in a fine ancient spirit, full of a sincere naivety.

—William Butler Yeats, Letter to W.T. Horton,
September 3, 1899

GEORGE BERNARD SHAW
"EDGAR ALLAN POE" (1909)

Shaw was one of the greatest playwrights of his age. He was also an ardent socialist, which explains the political critique attached to his appreciation of Poe. Like Baudelaire, Shaw notes that Poe does not seem to belong to the United States. Unlike Baudelaire, however, Shaw does not think that Poe's aristocratic bearing places him above the democratic rabble; he thinks that Poe represents the "Land of the Free" that America's capitalist powers had forgotten it once was. Shaw ultimately places Poe alongside Whitman as the great poets of American democracy. Students examining the interrelations of art and politics might look to Shaw's essay. Essayists could compare Poe's and Whitman's approaches to art as well as to democracy.

Shaw alludes to Poe's curious status in American literature, specifically referring to Poe's omission from the "Pantheon" of American writers. Ironically, Shaw suggests that Poe's literary supremacy is a reason, since Poe is so much more accomplished than others that he is not even mentioned in their company. Shaw claims that Poe's imagination is so powerful that readers often stand in awe of his works, rather than actively engaging them. Essayists writing about the reception of Poe or the development of an American literary canon might examine Shaw's comments closely. Is it possible to be *too good* to be admired?

Shaw acknowledges that Poe was aloof when it came to the common individual (unlike Whitman). Shaw believes that Poe's distance from reality has something to do with it, since the common individual was less of a concern to the unrealistic worlds where all houses are haunted and all forests are enchanted. Shaw notes, somewhat prudishly, that Poe does not deal in the vulgarities of life, but focuses on the ideas. This is another, more positive way of saying that Poe was more concerned with the head than the heart, the mind rather than the body. Critics (such as Lowell) have counted that asceticism against Poe, but Shaw suggests that this characteristic elevates Poe above his fellow American writers. Shaw also argues that this is why Poe is underappreciated in the United States and England. Anticipating the critique of consumerist society perhaps, Shaw states that readers in wealthy nations are wallowing in sensuality. He suggests that, when the world's wealth is more evenly distributed and values are accordingly adjusted, writers such as Poe will receive their proper due.

—⦅∿∿⦆— —⦅∿∿⦆— —⦅∿∿⦆—

There was a time when America, the Land of the Free, and the birthplace of Washington, seemed a natural fatherland for Edgar Allan Poe. Nowadays the thing has become inconceivable: no young man can read Poe's works without asking incredulously what the devil he is doing in that galley. America has been found out; and Poe has not; that is the situation. How did he live there, this finest of fine artists, this born aristocrat of letters? Alas! he did not live there: he died there, and was duly explained away as a drunkard and a failure, though it remains an open question whether he really drank as much in his whole lifetime as a modern successful American drinks, without comment, in six months.

If the Judgment Day were fixed for the centenary of Poe's birth, there are among the dead only two men born since the Declaration of Independence whose plea for mercy could avert a prompt sentence of damnation on the entire nation; and it is extremely doubtful whether those two could be persuaded to pervert eternal justice by uttering it. The two are, of course, Poe and Whitman; and there is between them the remarkable difference that Whitman is still credibly an American, whereas even the Americans themselves, though rather short of men of genius, omit Poe's name from their Pantheon, either from a sense that it is hopeless for them to claim so foreign a figure, or from simple Monroeism. One asks, has the America of Poe's day passed away, or did it ever exist?

Probably it never existed. It was an illusion, like the respectable Whig Victorian England of Macaulay. Karl Marx stripped the whitewash from that sepulchre; and we have ever since been struggling with a conviction of social sin which makes every country in which industrial capitalism is rampant a hell to us. For let no American fear that America, on that hypothetic Judgment Day, would perish alone. America would be damned in very good European company, and would feel proud and happy, and contemptuous of the saved. She would not even plead the influence of the mother from whom she has inherited all her worst vices. If the American stands today in scandalous preeminence as an anarchist and a ruffian, a liar and a braggart, an idolater and a sensualist, that is only because he has thrown off the disguises of Catholicism and feudalism which still give Europe an air of decency, and sins openly, impudently, and consciously, instead of furtively, hypocritically, and muddle-headedly, as we do. Not until he acquires European manners does the American anarchist become the gentleman who assures you that people cannot be made moral by Act of Parliament (the truth being that it is only by Acts of Parliament that men in large communities can be made moral, even when they want to), or the American ruffian hand over his revolver and bowie knife to be used for him by a policeman or soldier; or the American liar and braggart adopt the tone of the newspaper, the pulpit, and the platform; or the American idolater write authorized biographies of millionaires; or the American sensualist secure the patronage of all the Muses for his pornography.

Howbeit, Poe remains homeless. There is nothing at all like him in America; nothing, at all events, visible across the Atlantic. At that distance we can see Whistler plainly enough, and Mark Twain. But Whistler was very American in some ways: so American that nobody but another American could possibly have written his adventures and gloried in them without reserve. Mark Twain, resembling Dickens in his combination of public spirit and irresistible literary power with a congenital incapacity for lying and bragging, and a congenital hatred of waste and cruelty, remains American by the local color of his stories. There is a further difference. Both Mark Twain and Whistler are as Philistine as Dickens and Thackeray. The appalling thing about Dickens, the greatest of the Victorians, is that in his novels there is nothing personal to live for except eating, drinking, and pretending to be happily married. For him the great synthetic ideals do not exist, any more than the great preludes and toccatas of Bach, the symphonies of Beethoven, the paintings of Giotto and Mantegna, Velasquez and Rembrandt. Instead of being heir to all the ages, he came into a comparatively small and smutty literary property bequeathed by Smollett and Fielding. His criticism of Fechter's Hamlet, and his use of a speech of Macbeth's to illustrate the character of Mrs. Macstinger, shew how little Shakespear meant to him. Thackeray is even worse: the notions of painting he picked up at Heatherley's school were further from the mark than Dickens' ignorance; he is equally in the dark as to music; and though he did not, when he wished to be enormously pleasant and jolly, begin, like Dickens, to describe the gorgings and guzzlings which make Christmas our annual national disgrace, that is rather because he never does want to be enormously pleasant and jolly than because he has any higher notions of personal enjoyment. The truth is that neither Dickens nor Thackeray would be tolerable were it not that life is an end in itself and a means to nothing but its own perfection; consequently any man who describes life vividly will entertain us, however uncultivated the life he describes may be. Mark Twain has lived long enough to become a much better philosopher than either Dickens or Thackeray; for instance, when he immortalized General Funston by scalping him, he did it scientifically, knowing exactly what he meant right down to the foundation in the natural history of human character. Also, he got from the Mississippi something that Dickens could not get from Chatham and Pentonville. But he wrote A Yankee at the Court of King Arthur just as Dickens wrote A Child's History of England. For the ideal of Catholic chivalry he had nothing but derision; and he exhibited it, not in conflict with reality, as Cervantes did, but in conflict with the prejudices of a Philistine compared to whom Sancho Panza is an Admirable Crichton, an Abelard, even a Plato. Also, he described Lohengrin as "a shivaree," though he liked the wedding chorus; and this shews that Mark, like Dickens, was not properly educated; for Wagner would have been just the man for him if he had been trained to understand and use music as Mr. Rockefeller was trained to understand and use money. America did not teach him the language of the great ideals, just as England did not teach it to Dickens and Thackeray. Consequently, though nobody can suspect Dickens or Mark Twain of lacking the qualities and impulses that are the soul of such grotesque makeshift bodies as Church and State, Chivalry, Classicism, Art, Gentility, and the Holy Roman Empire; and nobody blames them for seeing that these bodies were mostly so decomposed as to have become intolerable nuisances, you have only to compare them with Carlyle and Ruskin, or with Euripides and Aristophanes, to see how, for want of a language of art and a body of philosophy, they were so much more interested in the fun and pathos of personal adventure than in the comedy and tragedy of human destiny.

Whistler was a Philistine, too. Outside the corner of art in which he was a virtuoso and a propagandist, he was a Man of Derision. Important as his propaganda was, and admired as his work was, no society could assimilate him. He could not even induce a British jury to award him substantial damages against a rich critic who had "done him out of his job"; and this is certainly the climax of social failure in England.

Edgar Allan Poe was not in the least a Philistine. He wrote always as if his native Boston was Athens, his Charlottesville University Plato's Academy, and his cottage the crown of the heights of Fiesole. He was the greatest journalistic critic of his time, placing good European work at sight when the European critics were waiting for somebody to tell them what to say. His poetry is so exquisitely refined that posterity will refuse to believe that it belongs to the same civilization as the glory of Mrs. Julia Ward Howe's lilies or the honest doggerel of Whittier. Tennyson, who was nothing if not a virtuoso, never produced a success that will bear reading after Poe's failures. Poe constantly and inevitably produced magic where his greatest contemporaries produced only beauty. Tennyson's popular pieces, The May Queen and The Charge of the Six Hundred, cannot stand hackneying: they become positively nauseous after a time. The Raven, The Bells, and Annabel Lee are as fascinating at the thousandth repetition as at the first.

Poe's supremacy in this respect has cost him his reputation. This is a phenomenon which occurs when an artist achieves such perfection as to place himself *hors concours*. The greatest painter England ever produced is Hogarth, a miraculous draughtsman and an exquisite and poetic colorist. But he is never mentioned by critics. They talk copiously about Romney, the Gibson of his day; freely about Reynolds; nervously about the great Gainsborough; and not at all about Rowlandson and Hogarth, missing the inextinguishable grace of Rowlandson because they assume that all caricatures of this period are ugly, and avoiding Hogarth instinctively as critically unmanageable. In the same way, we have given up mentioning Poe: that is why the Americans forgot him when they posted up the names of their great in their Pantheon. Yet his is the first—almost the only name that the real connoisseur looks for.

But Poe, for all his virtuosity, is always a poet, and never a mere virtuoso. Poe put forward his Eureka, the formulation of his philosophy, as the most important thing he had done. His poems always have the universe as their background. So have the figures in his stories. Even in his tales of humor, which we shake our heads at as mistakes, they have this elemental quality. Toby Dammit himself, though his very name turns up the nose of the cultured critic, is more impressive and his end more tragic than the serious inventions of most story-tellers. The short-sighted gentleman who married his grandmother is no common butt of a common purveyor of the facetious: the grandmother has the elegance and free mind of Ninon de l'Enclos, the grandson the *tenue* of a marquis. This story was sent by Poe to Horne, whose Orion he had reviewed as poetry ought to be reviewed, with a request that it might be sold to an English magazine. The English magazine regretted that the deplorable immorality of the story made it for ever impossible in England!

In his stories of mystery and imagination Poe created a world-record for the English language: perhaps for all the languages. The story of the Lady Ligeia is not merely one of the wonders of literature: it is unparalleled and unapproached. There is really nothing to be said about it: we others simply take off our hats and let Mr. Poe go first. It is interesting to compare Poe's stories with William Morris. Both are not merely stories: they are complete works of art, like prayer carpets; and they are, in Poe's phrase, stories of imagination. They are masterpieces of style; what people call Macaulay's style is by comparison a mere method But they are more different than it seems possible for two art works in the same kind to be. Morris will have nothing to do with mystery. "Ghost stories," he used to say, "have all the same explanation: the people are telling lies." His Sigurd has the beauty of mystery as it has every other sort of beauty, being, as it is, incomparably the greatest English epic; but his stories are in the open from end to end, whilst in Poe's stories the sun never shines.

Poe's limitation was his aloofness from the common people. Grotesques, negroes, madmen with delirium tremens, even gorillas, take the place of ordinary peasants and courtiers, citizens and soldiers, in his theatre. His houses are haunted houses, his woods enchanted woods; and he makes them so real that reality itself cannot sustain the comparison. His kingdom is not of this world.

Above all, Poe is great because he is independent of cheap attractions, independent of sex, of patriotism, of fighting, of sentimentality, snobbery, gluttony, and all the rest of the vulgar stock-in-trade of his profession. This is what gives him his superb distinction. One vulgarized thing, the pathos of dying children, he touched in Annabel Lee, and devulgarized it at once. He could not even amuse himself with detective stories without purifying the atmosphere of them until they became more edifying than most of Hymns, Ancient and Modern. His verse sometimes alarms and puzzles the reader by fainting with its own beauty; but the beauty is never the beauty of the flesh. You never say to him as you have to say uneasily to so many modern artists: "Yes, my friend, but these are things that men and women should live and not write about. Literature is not a keyhole for people with starved affections to peep through at the banquets of the body." It never became one in Poe's hands. Life cannot give you what he gives you except through fine art; and it was his instinctive observance of this distinction, and the fact that it did not beggar him, as it would beggar most writers, that makes him the most legitimate, the most classical, of modern writers.

It also explains why America does not care much for him, and why he has hardly been mentioned in England these many years. America and England are wallowing in the sensuality which their immense increase of riches has placed within their reach. I do not blame them: sensuality is a very necessary, and healthy and educative element in life. Unfortunately, it is ill distributed; and our reading masses are looking on at it and thinking about it and longing for it, and having precarious little holiday treats of it, instead of sharing it temperately and continuously, and ceasing to be preoccupied with it. When the distribution is better adjusted and the preoccupation ceases, there will be a noble reaction in favor of the great writers like Poe, who begin just where the world, the flesh, and the devil leave off.

—George Bernard Shaw, "Edgar Allan Poe," *Nation*,
[London], January 16, 1909

D.H. LAWRENCE "EDGAR ALLAN POE" (1923)

D.H. Lawrence, the British novelist best known for *Lady Chatterley's Lover* and *Sons and Lovers*, made a major contribution to literary criticism with his book *Studies in Classic American Literature*, from which this excerpt is taken. Lawrence's style is a bit impressionistic, with broad themes interwoven through terse, clipped sentences or even sentence fragments. Note that his criticism of Poe's overly wrought sentences marks a sharp contrast to his own style.

While Baudelaire had said that Poe never wrote a love story, Lawrence asserts that Poe wrote about "love" constantly, in all of his tales. Lawrence focuses on "Ligeia" and "The Fall of the House of Usher," two "love stories" that involve premature death and ghastly resurrection. Poe had said that the death of a beautiful woman was "the most poetical topic in the world," and he often employed this device in his tales and poems. For Lawrence, this love was also its own undoing, since, at the extreme, the lover would destroy the object of his devotion. Thus, love inevitably leads to death and destruction, as evidenced in Poe's tales. One topic readers might want to examine is Lawrence's argument in connection with a psychological approach to Poe's stories. Lawrence suggests that love is itself a longing for oneness, for unity. How do Poe's stories strive for such unity? Lawrence uses psychoanalytical terms to describe the effects of Poe's tales. Students learning about Freudian interpretation could look to Lawrence's essay for some interesting suggestions. How does Poe's work fit within a psychoanalytical framework?

Lawrence says that Poe is more of a scientist than an artist, by which he seems to be suggesting that Poe is more interested in analyzing or breaking down a given sensation or emotion; an artist, by contrast, would create impressions, not just boil down their essences. Students examining Poe's analytical and aesthetic modes might examine Lawrence's distinctions between science and art. Lawrence says that an artist must both create and destroy, whereas Poe is only interested in the destructive, or disintegrative, half of this process. Does Poe really lack the creative side of art? Science, of course, deals with knowing (the word comes from the Latin *scio*, meaning "to know"); Lawrence implies that the desire to know is a vampire-like impulse. The knower feeds off the thing it tries to know. In this way, it also kills the known thing. Students might explore this notion of science, particularly as it applies to art. Does knowing necessarily lead to destruction? Is consciousness itself a destructive force?

———   ———   ———

Poe has no truck with Indians or Nature. He makes no bones about Red Brothers and Wigwams.

He is absolutely concerned with the disintegration-processes of his own psyche. As we have said, the rhythm of American art-activity is dual.

1. A disintegrating and sloughing of the old consciousness.
2. The forming of a new consciousness underneath.

Fenimore Cooper has the two vibrations going on together. Poe has only one, only the disintegrative vibration. This makes him almost more a scientist than an artist.

Moralists have always wondered helplessly why Poe's "morbid" tales need have been written. They need to be written because old things need to die and disintegrate, because the old white psyche has to be gradually broken down before anything else can come to pass.

Man must be stripped even of himself. And it is a painful, sometimes a ghastly, process.

Poe had a pretty bitter doom. Doomed to seethe down his soul in a great continuous convulsion of disintegration, and doomed to register the process. And then doomed to be abused for it, when he had performed some of the bitterest tasks of human experience, that can be asked of a man. Necessary tasks, too. For the human soul must suffer its own disintegration, *consciously*, if ever it is to survive.

But Poe is rather a scientist than an artist. He is reducing his own self as a scientist reduces a salt in a crucible. It is an almost chemical analysis of the soul and consciousness. Whereas in true art there is always the double rhythm of creating and destroying.

This is why Poe calls his things "tales." They are a concatenation of cause and effect.

His best pieces, however, are not tales. They are more. They are ghastly stories of the human soul in its disruptive throes. Moreover, they are "love" stories.

Ligeia and *The Fall of the House of Usher* are really love stories.

Love is the mysterious vital attraction which draws things together, closer, closer together. For this reason sex is the actual crisis of love. For in sex the two blood-systems, in the male and female, concentrate and come into contact, the merest film intervening. Yet if the intervening film breaks down, it is death.

So there you are. There is a limit to everything. There is a limit to love.

The central law of all organic life is that each organism is intrinsically isolate and single in itself.

The moment its isolation breaks down, and there comes an actual mixing and confusion, death sets in.

This is true of every individual organism, from man to amoeba.

But the secondary law of all organic life is that each organism only lives through contact with other matter, assimilation, and contact with other life, which means assimilation of new vibrations, nonmaterial. Each individual organism is vivified by intimate contact with fellow organisms: up to a certain point. So man. He breathes the air into him, he swallows food and water. But more than this. He takes into him the life of his fellow men, with whom he comes into contact, and he gives back life to them. This contact draws nearer and nearer, as the intimacy increases. When it is a whole contact, we call it love. Men live by food, but die if they eat too much. Men live by love, but die, or cause death, if they love too much.

There are two loves: sacred and profane, spiritual and sensual.

In sensual love, it is the two blood-systems, the man's and the woman's, which sweep up into pure contact, and *almost* fuse. Almost mingle. Never quite. There is always the finest imaginable wall between the two blood-waves, through which pass unknown vibrations, forces, but through which the blood itself must never break, or it means bleeding.

In spiritual love, the contact is purely nervous. The nerves in the lovers are set vibrating in unison like two instruments. The pitch can rise higher and higher. But carry this too far, and the nerves begin to break, to bleed, as it were, and a form of death sets in.

The trouble about man is that he insists on being master of his own fate, and he insists on *oneness*. For instance, having discovered the ecstasy of spiritual love, he insists that he shall have this all the time, and nothing but this, for this is life. It is what he calls "heightening" life. He wants his nerves to be set vibrating in the intense and exhilarating unison with the nerves of another being, and by this means he acquires an ecstasy of vision, he finds himself in glowing unison with all the universe.

But as a matter of fact this glowing unison is only a temporary thing, because the first law of life is that each organism is isolate in itself, it must return to its own isolation.

Yet man has tried the glow of unison, called love, and he *likes* it. It gives him his highest gratification. He wants it. He wants it all the time. He wants it and he will have it. He doesn't want to return to his own isolation. Or if he must, it is only as a prowling beast returns to its lair to rest and set out again.

This brings us to Edgar Allan Poe. The clue to him lies in the motto he chose for *Ligeia*, a quotation from the mystic Joseph Glanvill: "And the will therein lieth, which dieth not. Who knoweth the mysteries of the will, with its vigour? For God is but a great will pervading all things by nature of its intentness. Man doth not yield himself to the angels, nor unto death utterly, save only through the weakness of his feeble will."

It is a profound saying: and a deadly one.

Because if God is a great will, then the universe is but an instrument.

I don't know what God is. But He is not simply a will. That is too simple. Too anthropomorphic. Because a man wants his own will, and nothing but his will, he needn't say that God is the same will, magnified *ad infinitum*.

For me, there may be one God, but He is nameless and unknowable.

For me, there are also many gods, that come into me and leave me again. And they have very various wills, I must say. But the point is Poe.

Poe had experienced the ecstasies of extreme spiritual love. And he wanted those ecstasies and nothing but those ecstasies. He wanted that great gratification, the sense of flowing, the sense of unison, the sense of heightening of life. He had experienced this gratification. He was told on every hand that this ecstasy of spiritual, nervous love was the greatest thing in life, was life itself. And he had tried it for himself, he knew that for him it was life itself. So he wanted it. And he *would have it*. He set up his will against the whole of the limitations of nature.

This is a brave man, acting on his own belief, and his own experience. But it is also an arrogant man, and a fool.

Poe was going to get the ecstasy and the heightening, cost what it might. He went on in a frenzy, as characteristic American women nowadays go on in a frenzy, after the very same thing: the heightening, the flow, the ecstasy. Poe tried alcohol, and any drug he could lay his hands on. He also tried any human being he could lay his hands on.

His grand attempt and achievement was with his wife; his cousin, a girl with a singing voice. With her he went in for the intensest flow, the heightening, the prismatic shades of ecstasy. It was the intensest nervous vibration of unison, pressed higher and higher in pitch, till the blood-vessels of the girl broke, and the blood began to flow out loose. It was love. If you call it love. Love can be terribly obscene.

It is love that causes the neuroticism of the day. It is love that is the prime cause of tuberculosis.

The nerves that vibrate most intensely in spiritual unisons are the sympathetic ganglia of the breast, of the throat, and the hind brain. Drive this vibration over-intensely, and you weaken the sympathetic tissues of the chest—the lungs—or of the throat, or of the lower brain, and the tubercles are given a ripe field. But Poe drove the vibrations beyond any human pitch of endurance.

Being his cousin, she was more easily keyed to him.

Ligeia is the chief story. Ligeia! A mental-derived name. To him the woman, his wife, was not Lucy. She was Ligeia. No doubt she even preferred it thus.

Ligeia is Poe's love-story, and its very fantasy makes it more truly his own story.

It is a tale of love pushed over a verge. And love pushed to extremes is a battle of wills between the lovers.

Love is become a battle of wills.

Which shall first destroy the other, of the lovers? Which can hold out longest, against the other?

Ligeia is still the old-fashioned woman. Her will is still to submit. She wills to submit to the vampire of her husband's consciousness. Even death.

"In stature she was tall, somewhat slender, and, in her latter days, even emaciated. I would in vain attempt to portray the majesty, the quiet ease, of her demeanour, or the incomprehensible lightness and elasticity of her footfall. . . . I was never made aware of her entrance into my closed study, save by the dear music of her low sweet voice, as she placed her marble hand upon my shoulder."

Poe has been so praised for his style. But it seems to me a meretricious affair. "Her marble hand" and "the elasticity of her footfall" seem more like chair-springs and mantelpieces than a human creature. She never was quite a human creature to him. She was an instrument from which he got his extremes of sensation. His *machine à plaisir*, as somebody says.

All Poe's style, moreover, has this mechanical quality, as his poetry has a mechanical rhythm. He never sees anything in terms of life, almost always in terms of matter, jewels, marble, etc.,—or in terms of force, scientific. And his cadences are all managed mechanically. This is what is called "having a style."

What he wants to do with Ligeia is to analyse her, till he knows all her component parts, till he has got her all in his consciousness. She is some strange chemical salt which he must analyse out in the test-tubes of his brain, and then—when he's finished the analysis—*E finita la commedia*!

But she won't be quite analysed out. There is something, something he can't get. Writing of her eyes, he says: "They were, I must believe, far larger than the ordinary eyes of our own race"—as if anybody would want eyes "far larger" than other folks'. "They were even fuller than the fullest of the gazelle eyes of the tribe of the valley of Nourjahad"—which is blarney. "The hue of the orbs was the most brilliant of black and, far over them, hung jetty lashes of great length"—suggests a whiplash. "The brows, slightly irregular in outline, had the same tint. The 'strangeness,' however, which I found in the eyes, was of a nature distinct from the formation, or the colour, or the brilliancy of the features, and must, after all, be referred to the *expression*."—Sounds like an anatomist anatomizing a cat—"Ah, word of no meaning! behind whose vast latitude of mere sound we entrench our ignorance of so much of the spiritual. The expression of the eyes of Ligeia! How for long hours have I pondered upon it! How have I, through the whole of a midsummer night, struggled to fathom it! What was it—that something more profound than the well of Democritus—which lay far within the pupils of my beloved! What was it? I was possessed with a passion to discover. . . ."

It is easy to see why each man kills the thing he loves. To *know* a living thing is to kill it. You have to kill a thing to know it satisfactorily. For this reason, the desirous consciousness, the SPIRIT, is a vampire.

One should be sufficiently intelligent and interested to know a good deal *about* any person one comes into close contact with. *About* her. Or *about* him.

But to try to know any living being is to try to suck the life out of that being.

Above all things, with the woman one loves. Every sacred instinct teaches one that one must leave her unknown. You know your woman darkly, in the blood. To try to know her mentally is to try to kill her. Beware, oh woman, of the man who wants to *find out what you are*. And, oh men, beware a thousand times more of the woman who wants to *know* you, or *get* you, what you are.

It is the temptation of a vampire fiend, is this knowledge.

Man does so horribly want to master the secret of life and of individuality *with his mind*. It is like the analysis of protoplasm. You can only analyse *dead* protoplasm, and know its constituents. It is a death-process.

Keep KNOWLEDGE for the world of matter, force, and function. It has got nothing to do with being.

But Poe wanted to know—wanted to know what was the strangeness in the eyes of Ligeia. She might have told him it was horror at his probing, horror at being vamped by his consciousness.

But she wanted to be vamped. She wanted to be probed by his consciousness, to be KNOWN. She paid for wanting it, too. Nowadays it is usually the man who wants to be vamped, to be KNOWN.

Edgar Allan probed and probed. So often he seemed on the verge. But she went over the verge of death before he came over the verge of knowledge. And it is always so.

He decided, therefore, that the clue to the strangeness lay in the mystery of will. "And the will therein lieth, which dieth not. . ."

Ligeia had a "gigantic volition." . . . "An intensity in thought, action, or speech was possibly, in her, a result, or at least an index" (he really meant indication) "of that gigantic volition which, during our long intercourse, failed to give other and more immediate evidence of its existence."

I should have thought her long submission to him was chief and ample "other evidence."

"Of all the women whom I have ever known, she, the outwardly calm, the ever-placid Ligeia, was the most violently a prey to the tumultuous vultures of stern passion. And of such passion I could form no estimate, save by the miraculous expansion of those eyes which at once so delighted and appalled me—by the almost magical melody, modulation, distinctness, and placidity of her very low voice—and by the fierce energy (rendered doubly effective by contrast with her manner of utterance) of the wild words which she habitually uttered."

Poor Poe, he had caught a bird of the same feather as himself. One of those terrible cravers, who crave the further sensation. Crave to madness or death. "Vultures of stern passion" indeed! Condors.

But having recognized that the clue was in her gigantic volition, he should have realized that the process of this loving, this craving, this knowing, was a struggle of wills. But Ligeia, true to the great tradition and mode of womanly love, by her will kept herself submissive, recipient. She is the passive body who is explored and analysed into death. And yet, at times, her great female will must have revolted. "Vultures of stern passion!" With a convulsion of desire she desired his further probing and exploring. To any lengths. But then, "tumultuous vultures of stern passion." She had to fight with herself.

But Ligeia wanted to go on and on with the craving, with the love, with the sensation, with the probing, with the knowing, on and on to the end.

There is no end. There is only the rupture of death. That's where men, and women, are "had." Man is always sold, in his search for final KNOWLEDGE.

"That she loved me I should not have doubted; and I might have been easily aware that, in a bosom such as hers, love would have reigned no ordinary passion. But in death only was I fully impressed with the strength of her affection. For long hours, detaining my hand, would she pour out before me the overflowing of a heart whose more than passionate devotion amounted to idolatry." (Oh, the indecency of all this endless intimate talk!) "How had I deserved to be so blessed by such confessions?" (Another man would have felt himself cursed.) "How had I deserved to be so cursed with the removal of my beloved in the hour of her making them? But upon this subject I cannot bear to dilate. Let me say only that in Ligeia's more than womanly abandonment to a love, alas! all unmerited, all unworthily bestowed, I at length recognized the principle of her longing, with so wildly earnest a desire, for the life which was now fleeing so rapidly away. It is this wild longing—it is this eager vehemence of desire for life—*but* for life, that I have no power to portray, no utterance capable of expressing."

Well, that is ghastly enough, in all conscience.

"And from them that have not shall be taken away even that which they have."

"To him that hath life shall be given life, and from him that hath not life shall be taken away even that life which he hath." Or her either.

These terribly conscious birds, like Poe and his Ligeia, deny the very life that is in them; they want to turn it all into talk, into *knowing*. And so life, which will not be known, leaves them.

But poor Ligeia, how could she help it? It was her doom. All the centuries of the SPIRIT, all the years of American rebellion against the Holy Ghost, had done it to her.

She dies, when she would rather do anything than die. And when she dies the clue, which he only lived to grasp, dies with her.

Foiled!

Foiled!

No wonder she shrieks with her last breath.

On the last day Ligeia dictates to her husband a poem. As poems go, it is rather false, meretricious. But put yourself in Ligeia's place, and it is real enough, and ghastly beyond bearing.

> Out—out are all the lights—out all!
>   And over each quivering form
> The curtain, a funeral pall,
>   Comes down with the rush of a storm,
> While the angels, all pallid and wan,
>   Uprising, unveiling, affirm
> That the play is the tragedy, 'Man,'
>   And its hero, the Conqueror Worm.

Which is the American equivalent for a William Blake poem. For Blake, too, was one of these ghastly, obscene "Knowers."

"'O God!' half shrieked Ligeia, leaping to her feet and extending her arms aloft with a spasmodic movement, as I made an end of these lines—'O God! O Divine Father! shall these things be undeviatingly so? Shall this conqueror be not once conquered? Are we not part and parcel in Thee? Who—who knoweth the mysteries of the will with its vigour? Man doth not yield him to the angels, *nor unto death utterly*, save only through the weakness of his feeble will.'"

So Ligeia dies. And yields to death at least partly. *Anche troppo*.

As for her cry to God—has not God said that those who sin against the Holy Ghost shall not be forgiven?

And the Holy Ghost is within us. It is the thing that prompts us to be real, not to push our own cravings too far, not to submit to stunts and high-falutin, above all, not to be too egoistic and wilful in our conscious self, but to change as the spirit inside us bids us change, and leave off when it bids us leave off, and laugh when we must laugh, particularly at ourselves, for in deadly earnestness there is always something a bit ridiculous. The Holy Ghost bids us never be too deadly in our earnestness, always to laugh in time, at ourselves and everything. Particularly at our sublimities. Everything has its hour of ridicule—everything.

Now Poe and Ligeia, alas, couldn't laugh. They were frenziedly earnest. And frenziedly they pushed on this vibration of consciousness and unison in consciousness. They sinned against the Holy Ghost that bids us all laugh and forget, bids us know our own limits. And they weren't forgiven.

Ligeia needn't blame God. She had only her own will, her gigantic volition" to thank, lusting after more consciousness, more beastly KNOWING.

Ligeia dies. The husband goes to England, vulgarly buys or rents a gloomy, grand old abbey, puts it into some sort of repair, and furnishes it with exotic, mysterious, theatrical splendour. Never anything open and real. This theatrical "volition" of his. The bad taste of sensationalism.

Then he marries the fair-haired, blue-eyed Lady Rowena Trevanion, of Tremaine. That is, she would be a sort of Saxon-Cornish blue-blood damsel. Poor Poe!

"In halls such as these—in a bridal chamber such as this—I passed, with the Lady of Tremaine, the unhallowed hours of the first month of our marriage—passed them with but little disquietude. That my wife dreaded the fierce moodiness of my temper—that she shunned me and loved me but little—I could not help perceiving, but it gave me rather pleasure than otherwise. I loathed her with a hatred belonging more to demon than to man. My memory flew back (oh, with what intensity of regret!) to Ligeia, the beloved, the august, the beautiful, the entombed. I revelled in recollections of her purity . . ." etc.

Now the vampire lust is consciously such.

In the second month of the marriage the Lady Rowena fell ill. It is the shadow of Ligeia hangs over her. It is the ghostly Ligeia who pours poison into

Rowena's cup. It is the spirit of Ligeia, leagued with the spirit of the husband, that now lusts in the slow destruction of Rowena. The two vampires, dead wife and living husband.

For Ligeia has not yielded unto death utterly. Her fixed, frustrated will comes back in vindictiveness. She could not have her way in life. So she, too, will find victims in life. And the husband, all the time, only uses Rowena as a living body on which to wreak his vengeance for his being thwarted with Ligeia. Thwarted from the final KNOWING her.

And at last from the corpse of Rowena, Ligeia rises. Out of her death, through the door of a corpse they have destroyed between them, reappears Ligeia, still trying to have her will, to have more love and knowledge, the final gratification which is never final, with her husband.

For it is true, as William James and Conan Doyle and the rest allow, that a spirit can persist in the after-death. Persist by its own volition. But usually, the evil persistence of a thwarted will, returning for vengeance on life. Lemures, vampires.

It is a ghastly story of the assertion of the human will, the will-to-love and the will-to-consciousness, asserted against death itself. The pride of human conceit in KNOWLEDGE.

There are terrible spirits, ghosts, in the air of America.

Eleanora, the next story, is a fantasy revealing the sensational delights of the man in his early marriage with the young and tender bride. They dwelt, he, his cousin and her mother, in the sequestered Valley of Many-coloured Grass, the valley of prismatic sensation, where everything seems spectrum-coloured. They looked down at *their own images* in the River of Silence, and drew the god Eros from that wave: out of their own self-consciousness, that is. This is a description of the life of introspection and of the love which is begotten by the self in the self, the self-made love. The trees are like serpents worshipping the sun. That is, they represent the phallic passion in its poisonous or mental activity. Everything runs to consciousness: serpents worshipping the sun. The embrace of love, which should bring darkness and oblivion, would with these lovers be a daytime thing bringing more heightened consciousness, visions, spectrum—visions, prismatic. The evil thing that daytime love-making is, and all sex-palaver.

In *Berenice* the man must go down to the sepulchre of his beloved and pull out her thirty-two small white teeth, which be carries in a box with him. It is repulsive and gloating. The teeth are the instruments of biting, of resistance, of antagonism. They often become symbols of opposition, little instruments or entities of crushing and destroying. Hence the dragon's teeth in the myth.

Hence the man in *Berenice* must take possession of the irreducible part of his mistress. "*Toutes ses dents étaient des idées,*" he says. Then they are little fixed ideas of mordant hate, of which he possesses himself.

The other great story linking up with this group is *The Fall of the House of Usher*. Here the love is between brother and sister. When the self is broken, and the mystery of the recognition of *otherness* fails, then the longing for identification with the beloved becomes a lust. And it is this longing for identification, utter merging, which is at the base of the incest problem. In psychoanalysis almost every trouble in the psyche is traced to an incest-desire. But it won't do. Incest-desire is only one of the modes by which men strive to get their gratification of the intensest vibration of the spiritual nerves, without any resistance. In the family, the natural vibration is most nearly in unison. With a stranger, there is greater resistance. Incest is the getting of gratification and the avoiding of resistance.

The root of all evil is that we all want this spiritual gratification, this flow, this apparent heightening of life, this knowledge, this valley of many-coloured grass, even grass and light prismatically decomposed, giving ecstasy. We want all this *without* resistance. We want it continually. And this is the root of all evil in us.

We ought to pray to be resisted, and resisted to the bitter end. We ought to decide to have done at last with craving.

The motto to *The Fall of the House of Usher* is a couple of lines from Béranger.

Son coeur est un luth suspendu;
Sitôt qu'on le touche il résonne.

We have all the trappings of Poe's rather overdone, vulgar fantasy. "I reined my horse to the precipitous brink of a black and lurid tarn that lay in unruffled lustre by the dwelling, and gazed down—but with a shudder even more thrilling than before—upon the remodelled and inverted images of the grey sedge, and the ghastly tree-stems, and the vacant and eye-like windows." The House of Usher, both dwelling and family, was very old. Minute fungi overspread the exterior of the house, hanging in festoons from the eaves. Gothic archways, a valet of stealthy step, sombre tapestries, ebon black floors, a profusion of tattered and antique furniture, feeble gleams of encrimsoned light through latticed panes, and over all "an air of stern, deep, and irredeemable gloom"—this makes up the interior.

The inmates of the house, Roderick and Madeline Usher, are the last remnants of their incomparably ancient and decayed race. Roderick has the same large, luminous eye, the same slightly arched nose of delicate Hebrew model, as characterized Ligeia. He is ill with the nervous malady of his family. It is he whose nerves are so strung that they vibrate to the unknown quiverings of the ether. He, too, has lost his self, his living soul, and becomes a sensitized instrument of the external influences; his nerves are verily like an aeolian harp which must vibrate. He lives in "some struggle with the grim phantasm, Fear," for he is only the physical, post-mortem reality of a living being.

It is a question how much, once the true centrality of the self is broken, the instrumental consciousness of man can register. When man becomes selfless, wafting instrumental like a harp in an open window, how much can his elemental consciousness express? The blood as it runs has its own sympathies and responses to the material world, quite apart from seeing. And the nerves we know vibrate all the while to unseen presences, unseen forces. So Roderick Usher quivers on the edge of material existence.

It is this mechanical consciousness which gives "the fervid facility of his impromptus." It is the same thing that gives Poe his extraordinary facility in versification. The absence of real central or impulsive being in himself leaves him inordinately mechanically sensitive to sounds and effects, associations of sounds, associations of rhyme, for example—mechanical, facile, having no root in any passion. It is all a secondary, meretricious process. So we get Roderick Usher's poem, *The Haunted Palace*, with its swift yet mechanical subtleties of rhyme and rhythm, its vulgarity of epithet. It is all a sort of dream-process, where the association between parts is mechanical, accidental as far as passional meaning goes.

Usher thought that all vegetable things had sentience. Surely all material things have a form of sentience, even the inorganic: surely they all exist in some subtle and complicated tension of vibration which makes them sensitive to external influence and causes them to have an influence on other external objects, irrespective of contact. It is of this vibration or inorganic consciousness that Poe is master: the sleep-consciousness. Thus Roderick Usher was convinced that his whole surroundings, the stones of the house, the fungi, the water in the tarn, the very reflected image of the whole, was woven into a physical oneness with the family, condensed, as it were, into one atmosphere—the special atmosphere in which alone the Ushers could live. And it was this atmosphere which had moulded the destinies of his family.

But while ever the soul remains alive, it is the moulder and not the moulded. It is the souls of living men that subtly impregnate stones, houses, mountains, continents, and give these their subtlest form. People only become subject to stones after having lost their integral souls.

In the human realm, Roderick had one connection: his sister Madeline. She, too, was dying of a mysterious disorder, nervous, cataleptic. The brother and sister loved each other passionately and exclusively. They were twins, almost identical in looks. It was the same absorbing love between them, this process of unison in nerve-vibration, resulting in more and more extreme exaltation and a sort of consciousness, and a gradual breakdown into death. The exquisitely sensitive Roger, vibrating without resistance with his sister Madeline, more and more exquisitely, and gradually devouring her, sucking her life like a vampire in his anguish of extreme love. And she asking to be sucked.

Madeline died and was carried down by her brother into the deep vaults of the house. But she was not dead. Her brother roamed about in incipient madness—a madness of unspeakable terror and guilt. After eight days they were suddenly startled by a clash of metal, then a distinct, hollow metallic, and clangorous, yet apparently muffled, reverberation. Then Roderick Usher, gibbering, began to express himself: "*We have put her living in the tomb!* Said I not that my senses were acute! I *now* tell you that I heard her first feeble movements in the hollow coffin. I heard them—many, many days ago—yet I dared not—*I dared not speak.*"

It is the same old theme of "each man kills the thing he loves." He knew his love had killed her. He knew she died at last, like Ligeia, unwilling and unappeased. So, she rose again upon him. "But then without those doors there *did* stand the lofty and enshrouded figure of the lady Madeline of Usher. There was blood upon her white robes, and the evidence of some bitter struggle upon every portion of her emaciated frame. For a moment she remained trembling and reeling to and fro upon the threshold, then, with a low moaning cry, fell heavily inward upon the person of her brother, and in her violent and now final death-agonies bore him to the floor a corpse, and a victim to the terrors he had anticipated."

It is lurid and melodramatic, but it is true. It is a ghastly psychological truth of what happens in the last stages of this beloved love, which cannot be separate, cannot be isolate, can not listen in isolation to the isolate Holy Ghost. For it is the Holy Ghost we must live by. The next era is the era of the Holy Ghost. And the Holy Ghost speaks individually inside each individual: always, forever a ghost. There is no manifestation to the general world. Each isolate individual listening in isolation to the Holy Ghost within him.

The Ushers, brother and sister, betrayed the Holy Ghost in themselves. They would love, love, love, without resistance. They would love, they would merge, they would be as one thing. So they dragged each other down into death. For the Holy Ghost says you must *not* be as one thing with another being. Each must abide by itself, and correspond only within certain limits.

The best tales all have the same burden. Hate is as inordinate as love, and as slowly consuming, as secret, as underground, as subtle. All this underground vault business in Poe only symbolizes that which takes place *beneath* the consciousness. On top, all is fair-spoken. Beneath, there is awful murderous extremity of burying alive. Fortunato, in *The Cask of Amontillado*, is buried alive out of perfect hatred, as the lady Madeline of Usher is buried alive out of love. The lust of hate is the inordinate desire to consume and unspeakably possess the soul of the hated one, just as the lust of love is the desire to possess, or to be possessed by, the beloved, utterly. But in either case the result is the dissolution of both souls, each losing itself in transgressing its own bounds.

The lust of Montresor is to devour utterly the soul of Fortunato. It would be no use killing him outright. If a man is killed outright his soul remains integral, free to return into the bosom of some beloved, where it can enact itself. In walling-up his enemy in the vault, Montresor seeks to bring about the indescribable capitulation of the man's soul, so that he, the victor, can possess himself of the very being of the vanquished. Perhaps this can actually be done. Perhaps, in the attempt, the victor breaks the bonds of his own identity, and collapses into nothingness, or into the infinite. Becomes a monster.

What holds good for inordinate hate holds good for inordinate love. The motto, *Nemo me impune lacessit*, might just as well be *Nemo me impune amat*.

In *William Wilson* we are given a rather unsubtle account of the attempt of a man to kill his own soul. William Wilson the mechanical, lustful ego succeeds in killing William Wilson the living self. The lustful ego lives on, gradually reducing itself towards the dust of the infinite.

In the *Murders in the Rue Morgue* and *The Gold Bug* we have those mechanical tales where the interest lies in the following out of a subtle chain of cause and effect. The interest is scientific rather than artistic, a study in psychologic reactions.

The fascination of murder itself is curious. Murder is not just killing. Murder is a lust to get at the very quick of life itself, and kill it—hence the stealth and the frequent morbid dismemberment of the corpse, the attempt to get at the very quick of the murdered being, to find the quick and to possess it. It is curious that the two men fascinated by the art of murder, though in different ways, should have been De Quincey and Poe, men so different in ways of life, yet perhaps not so widely different in nature. In each of them is traceable that strange lust for extreme love and extreme hate, possession by mystic violence of the other soul, or violent deathly surrender of the soul in the self: an absence of manly virtue, which stands alone and accepts limits. Inquisition and torture are akin to murder: the same lust. It is a combat between inquisitor and victim as to whether the inquisitor shall get at the quick of life itself, and pierce it. Pierce the very quick of the soul. The evil will of man tries to do this. The brave soul of man refuses to have the life-quick pierced in him. It is strange: but just as the thwarted will can persist evilly, after death, so can the brave spirit preserve, even through torture and death, the quick of life and truth. Nowadays society is evil. It finds subtle ways of torture, to destroy the life-quick, to get at the life-quick in a man. Every possible form. And still a man can hold out, if he can laugh and listen to the Holy Ghost.—But society is evil, evil, and love is evil. And evil breeds evil, more and more.

So the mystery goes on. La Bruyère says that all our human unhappiness *viennent de ne pouvoir être seuls.* As long as man lives he will be subject to the yearning of love or the burning of hate, which is only inverted love.

But he is subject to something more than this. If we do not live to eat, we do not live to love either.

We live to stand alone, and listen to the Holy Ghost. The Holy Ghost, who is inside us, and who is many gods. Many gods come and go, some say one thing and some say another, and we have to obey the God of the innermost hour. It is the multiplicity of gods within us make up the Holy Ghost.

But Poe knew only love, love, love, intense vibrations and heightened consciousness. Drugs, women, self-destruction, but anyhow the prismatic ecstasy of heightened consciousness and sense of love, of flow. The human soul in him was beside itself. But it was not lost. He told us plainly how it was, so that we should know.

He was an adventurer into vaults and cellars and horrible underground passages of the human soul. He sounded the horror and the warning of his own doom.

Doomed he was. He died wanting more love, and love killed him. A ghastly disease, love. Poe telling us of his disease: trying even to make his disease fair and attractive. Even succeeding.

Which is the inevitable falseness, duplicity of art, American art in particular.

—D.H. Lawrence, "Edgar Allan Poe,"
Studies in Classic American Literature, 1923

❖

WORKS

❖

POETRY

Although Poe is perhaps better known today for his tales, he was one of America's most important and influential poets in his own time. "The Raven" is still one of the central poems in American literature, and it was immensely popular when first published in 1845. Most readers were moved by the power and originality of Poe's poems. Poe's use of rhyme and meter makes him one of the great lyric poets of the nineteenth century.

The extracts in this section are arranged chronologically and focus on Poe's poetry. The selections begin with an essay by William Gilmore Simms, a southern writer who praises Poe's poetry, defending its greatness against the criticisms of some northern writers. Simms remarks that truly great poetry is not likely to be popular. In the next piece, Swinburne says that Poe was the only original American poet before Whitman, and then Whitman himself attests to Poe's brilliance. Whitman also criticizes Poe's seeming artificiality and lack of "heart." Such mixed praise is echoed in the two subsequent extracts, by Edmund Gosse and John Burroughs, respectively. They extol Poe's originality but lament his lack of humanity. Not lacking in confidence, Poe's view that "The Raven" was the greatest poem ever written is remembered by Joel Benton in a humorous anecdote; Benton adds that many people agree with Poe's less than modest assertion. Finally, Edmund Clarence Stedman comments on Poe's theory of poetry. Poe was opposed to Keats's equation ("Beauty is truth"), arguing instead that poetry has only to do with poetry and nothing to do with truth. Stedman concludes that Poe's greatest intellectual and imaginative achievements are found in his tales rather than in his poetry.

WILLIAM GILMORE SIMMS
"POE'S POETRY" (1845)

Simms was a southern writer who Poe once called the "best novelist" the country had yet produced, yet he is known today for his strident, proslavery views. Here Simms comments on Poe's notorious appearance at the Boston Lyceum, in which he read a metaphysical poem that was poorly received by the New England literati in attendance. Simms, citing a newspaper account of the event, argues that Poe's poetry was too good for that audience. He echoes the sentiment that "true" poetry is not likely to be popular, suggesting an elitism that is often associated with Poe. Students writing about "high art" versus popular culture might cite Simms's discussion of Poe.

―――――

Mr. Edgar A. Poe is one of the most remarkable, in many respects, among our men of letters. With singular endowments of imagination, he is at the same time largely possessed of many of the qualities that go to make an admirable critic;—he is methodical, lucid, forcible,—well-read, thoughtful, and capable, at all times, of rising from the mere consideration of the individual subject, to the principles, in literature and art, by which it should be governed. Add to these qualities, as a critic, that he is not a person to be overborne and silenced by a reputation;—that mere names do not control his judgement;—that he is bold, independent, and stubbornly analytical, in the formation of his opinions. He has his defects also;—he is sometimes the victim of capricious moods;—his temper is variable—his nervous organization being such, evidently, as to subject his judgements, sometimes, to influences that may be traced to the weather and the winds. He takes his colour from the clouds; and his sympathies are not unfrequently chilled and rendered ungenial, by the pressure of the atmosphere—the cold and vapors of a climate affecting his moral nature, through his physical, in greater degree than is usual among literary men,—who, by the way, are generally far more susceptible to these influences, than is the case with the multitude. Such are the causes which occasionally operate to impair the value and the consistency of his judgements as a Critic. As a Poet, Mr Poe's imagination becomes remarkably conspicuous, and to surrender himself freely to his own moods, would be to make all his writings in verse, efforts of pure imagination only. He seems to dislike the merely practical, and to shrink from the concrete. His fancy takes the ascendant in his Poetry, and wings his thoughts to such superior elevations, as to render it too intensely spiritual for the ordinary reader. With a genius thus endowed and constituted, it was a blunder with Mr Poe to accept the appointment, which called him to deliver himself in poetry before the Boston Lyceum. Highly imaginative men can scarcely succeed in such exhibitions. The sort of poetry called for on such occasions, is the very reverse of the spiritual, the fanciful or the metaphysical. To win the ears of a mixed audience, nothing more is required than moral or patriotic common places in rhyming heroics. The verses of Pope are just the things for such occasions. You must not pitch your flight higher than the penny-whistle elevation of

> Know then this truth, enough for man to know
> Virtue alone is happiness below.

Either this or declamatory verse,—something patriotic, or something satirical, or something comical. At all events, you must not be mystical.

You must not ask the audience to study. Your song must be such as they can read running, and comprehend while munching pèa-nuts. Mr Poe is not the writer for this sort of thing. He is too original, too fanciful, too speculative, too anything in verse, for the comprehension of any but 'audience fit though few'. In obeying this call to Boston, Mr Poe committed another mistake. He had been mercilessly exercising himself as a critic at the expense of some of their favorite writers. The swans of New England, under his delineation, had been described as mere geese, and these, too, of none of the whitest. He had been exposing the shortcomings and the plagiarisms of Mr Longfellow, who is supposed, along the banks of the Penobscot, to be about the comeliest bird that ever dipped its bill in Pieria. Poe had dealt with the favorites of Boston unsparingly, and they hankered after their revenges. In an evil hour, then, did he consent to commit himself in verse to their tender mercies. It is positively amusing to see how eagerly all the little witlings of the press, in the old purlieus of the Puritan, flourish the critical tomahawk about the head of the critic. In their eagerness for retribution, one of the papers before us actually congratulates itself and readers on the (asserted) failure of the poet. The good editor himself was not present, but he hammers away not the less lustily at the victim, because his objections are to be made at second hand. Mr Poe committed another error in consenting to address an audience in verse, who, for three mortal hours, had been compelled to sit and hear Mr Caleb Cushing in Prose. The attempt to speak after this, in poetry, and fanciful poetry, too, was sheer madness. The most patient audience in the world, must have been utterly exhausted by the previous inflictions. But it is denied that Mr Poe failed at all. He had been summoned to recite poetry. It is asserted that he did so. The *Boston Courier,* one of the most thoughtful journals of that city, gives us a very favourable opinion of the performance which has been so harshly treated. 'The Poem', says that journal, 'called "The Messenger Star", was an eloquent and classic production, based on the right principles, containing the essence of *true* poetry, mingled with a gorgeous imagination, exquisite painting, every charm of metre, and a graceful delivery. It strongly reminded us of Mr Home's *Orion,* and resembled it in the majesty of its design, the nobleness of its incidents, and its freedom from the trammels of productions usual on these occasions. The delicious word-painting of some of its scenes brought vividly to our recollection, Keats' *Eve of St Agnes,* and parts of *Paradise Lost.*

'That it was malapropos to the occasion, we take the liberty to deny. What is the use of repeating the "mumbling farce" of having invited a poet to deliver a poem? We (too often) find a person get up and repeat a hundred or two indifferent couplets of words, with jingling rhymes and stale witticisms, with scarcely a line of *poetry* in the whole, and which will admit of no superlative to describe it. If we are to have a poem, why not have the "true thing", that will be recognized as such,—for poems being written for people that can appreciate them, it would be as well to cater for their tastes as for individuals who cannot distinguish between the true and the false.'

The good sense of this extract should do much towards enforcing the opinion which it conveys; and it confirms our own, previously entertained and expressed, in regard to the affair in question. Mr Poe's error was not, perhaps, in making verses, nor making them after a fashion of his own; but in delivering them before an audience of mixed elements, and just after a discourse of three mortal hours by a prosing orator. That any of his hearers should have survived the two-fold infliction, is one of those instances of good fortune which should bring every person present to his knees in profound acknowledgement to a protecting providence.

—William Gilmore Simms, "Poe's Poetry,"
Charleston Southern Patriot, November 10, 1845

ALGERNON CHARLES SWINBURNE (1872)

Swinburne writes that, prior to Walt Whitman, Poe's poetry was the only original verse written in the United States. All else was either mere imitation or simply of poor quality.

Never did a country need more than America such an influence as [Whitman's]. We may understand and even approve his reproachful and scornful fear of the overweening "British element" when we see what it has hitherto signified in the literature of his country. Once as yet, and once only, has there sounded out of it all one pure note of original song—worth singing, and echoed from the singing of no other man; a note of song neither wide nor deep, but utterly true, rich, clear, and native to the singer; the short exquisite music, subtle and simple and sombre and sweet, of Edgar Poe. All the rest that is not of mocking-birds is of corncrakes, varied but at best for an instant by some scant-winded twitter of linnet or of wren.

—Algernon Charles Swinburne,
Under the Microscope, 1872

WALT WHITMAN
"EDGAR POE'S SIGNIFICANCE"
(1882)

Whitman, one of the great poets of nineteenth-century America, here praises Poe's brilliance while also criticizing his lack of warmth. Echoing a theme of Poe's critics, Whitman suggests that Poe has great technical abilities, but that his poetry lacks "heart" and thus seems artificial. Whitman notes that Poe's "incorrigible propensity toward nocturnal themes" might say something about the age in which the poems were written.

Almost without the first sign of moral principle, or of the concrete or its heroisms, or the simpler affections of the heart, Poe's verses illustrate an intense faculty for technical and abstract beauty, with the rhyming art to excess, an incorrigible propensity toward nocturnal themes, a demoniac undertone behind every page—and, by final judgment, probably belong among the electric lights of imaginative literature, brilliant and dazzling, but with no heat. There is an indescribable magnetism about the poet's life and reminiscences, as well as the poems. To one who could work out their subtle retracing and retrospect, the latter would make a close tally no doubt between the author's birth and antecedents, his childhood and youth, his physique, his so-call'd education, his studies and associates, the literary and social Baltimore, Richmond, Philadelphia and New York, of those times—not only the places and circumstances in themselves, but often, very often, in a strange spurning of, and reaction from them all. . . .

By its popular poets the calibres of an age, the weak spots of its embankments, its sub-currents, (often more significant than the biggest surface ones,) are unerringly indicated. The lush and the weird that have taken such extraordinary possession of Nineteenth century verse-lovers—what mean they? The inevitable tendency of poetic culture to morbidity, abnormal beauty—the sickliness of all technical thought or refinement in itself—the abnegation of the perennial and democratic concretes at first hand, the body, the earth and sea, sex and the like—and the substitution of something for them at second or third hand—what bearings have they on current pathological study?

—Walt Whitman, "Edgar Poe's Significance,"
Critic, June 3, 1882, p. 147

EDMUND GOSSE "HAS AMERICA PRODUCED A POET?" (1893)

Gosse was a reputed English poet and art critic. Here he notes that, while American critics still do not have as much appreciation for Poe as they might, Poe's poetry remains powerful and original, inspiring other English-language poets even forty years later. Gosse suggests that, even if such a legacy does not make Poe one of the "Great Poets," it at least earns him the right to be honored in his own country.

It is understood that Edgar Allan Poe is still unforgiven in New England. "Those singularly valueless verses of Poe," was the now celebrated *dictum* of a Boston prophet. It is true that, if "that most beguiling of all little divinities, Miss Walters of the *Transcript*," is to be implicitly believed, Edgar Poe was very rude and naughty at the Boston Lyceum in the spring of 1845. But surely bygones should be bygones, and Massachusetts might now pardon the *Al Aaraaf* incident. It is not difficult to understand that there were many sides on which Poe was likely to be long distasteful to Boston, Cambridge, and Concord. The intellectual weight of the man, though unduly minimised in New England, was inconsiderable by the side of that of Emerson. But in poetry, as one has to be always insisting, the battle is not to the strong; and apart from all faults, weaknesses, and shortcomings of Poe, we feel more and more clearly, or we ought to feel, the perennial charm of his verses. The posy of his still fresh and fragrant poems is larger than that of any other deceased American writer, although Emerson may have one or two single blossoms to show which are more brilliant than any of his. If the range of the Baltimore poet had been wider, if Poe had not harped so persistently on his one theme of remorseful passion for the irrecoverable dead, if he had employed his extraordinary, his unparalleled gifts of melodious invention, with equal skill, in illustrating a variety of human themes, he must have been with the greatest poets. For in Poe, in pieces like "The Haunted Palace," "The Conqueror Worm," "The City in the Sea," and "For Annie," we find two qualities which are as rare as they are invaluable, a new and haunting music, which constrains the hearer to follow and imitate and a command of evolution in lyrical work so absolute that the poet is able to do what hardly any other lyrist has dared to attempt, namely, as in "To One in Paradise," to take a normal stanzaic form, and play with it as a great pianist plays with an air.

So far as the first of these attributes is concerned, Poe has proved himself to be the Piper of Hamelin to all later English poets. From Tennyson to

Austin Dobson there is hardly one whose verse-music does not show traces of Poe's influence. To impress the stamp of one's personality on a succeeding generation of artists, to be an almost (although not wholly) flawless technical artist one's self, to charm within a narrow circle to a degree that shows no sign, after forty years, of lessening, is this to prove a claim to rank with the Great Poets? No, perhaps not quite; but at all events it is surely to have deserved great honour from the country of one's birthright.

—Edmund Gosse, "Has America Produced a Poet?" (1889),
Questions at Issue, 1893, pp. 88–90

John Burroughs
"Mr. Gosse's Puzzle over Poe" (1893)

Burroughs, an essayist and naturalist, was a great admirer of Emerson, Thoreau, and Whitman. Not surprisingly perhaps, he criticizes Poe for lacking their warmth and optimistic views of humankind. Burroughs cites Poe's lack of "humanity" as his greatest flaw. Like other critics, Burroughs acknowledges Poe's technical skills but argues that Poe's poetry lacks the connection to human reality that is necessary for lasting artistic greatness.

Poe, like Swinburne, was a verbal poet merely; empty of thought, empty of sympathy, empty of love for any real thing: a graceful and nimble skater up and down over the deeps and shallows of life,—deep or shallow, it was all the same to him. Not one real thing did he make more dear to us by his matchless rhyme; not one throb of the universal heart, not one flash of the universal mind, did he seize and put in endearing form for his fellow men. Our band of New England poets have helped enrich and ennoble human life; the world is fairer, life is sweeter, because they lived and sang; character, heroism, truth, courage, devotion, count for more since Emerson and Longfellow and Whittier and Lowell were inspired by these themes. I am not complaining that Poe was not didactic: didacticism is death to poetry. I am complaining that he was not human and manly, and that he did not touch life in any helpful and liberating way. His poems do not lay hold of real things. I do not find the world a more enjoyable or beautiful place because he lived in it. I find myself turning to his poems, not for mental or spiritual food, as I do to Wordsworth or Emerson or Whitman, or for chivalrous human sentiments as in Tennyson, but to catch a glimpse of the weird, the fantastic, and, as it were, of the night-side or dream-side of things.

> You are not wrong who deem
> That my days have been a dream.

But the man whose days are a dream, no matter with what skill he portrays his dream, will never take deep hold upon men's hearts. Think of the difference, for instance, between Burns and Poe. We are drawn to Burns the man; he touches our most tender and human side; his art does not occupy our attention. With Poe it is quite the reverse: we care nothing for the man, nothing for the matter of his poems; his art alone seems important, and elicits our admiration. . . .

I would not undervalue Poe. He was a unique genius. But I would account for his failure to deeply impress his own countrymen, outside the professional literary guild. His fund of love and sympathy was small. He was not broadly related to his fellows, as were Longfellow and Whittier and Whitman. His literary equipment was remarkable; his human equipment was not remarkable: hence his failure to reach the general fame of the New England poets.

—John Burroughs, "Mr. Gosse's Puzzle over Poe,"
Dial, October. 16, 1893, pp. 214–15

Joel Benton
"Poe's Opinion of 'The Raven'" (1897)

Benton, an American literary critic, tells the story of Poe's less than humble assessment of his own poem "The Raven." After the amusing anecdote, Benton notes that many critics now agree with Poe.

The brief story I have to tell about ("The Raven") I got orally from an author who once had some vogue, but who is now nearly completely forgotten. His name was at one time in many of our best periodicals; and the old *Democratic Review* once had a considerable critique upon his poetic position and promise. He was likened by the writer of the review article to Shelley and Keats; and there were passages of his verse given which brought out, as I remember, a considerable of the suggested resemblance. Probably, though, his poem of "The Sword of Bunker Hill"—which was set to music—best typifies his prevailing poetic style, which was, in the main, noted for being eloquent and patriotic.

William Ross Wallace (for it is he to whom I refer) was not unlike Poe in both temperament and habits. He was not a little like him in physique—in brightness of the eye, and in a superb courtliness of manner. He had the same, or a similar, irresolute will; but he was a delightful companion to meet if you met him at the right time. He was, I believe, a Southerner by birth, as Poe was by acclimation.

Wallace told me (in the early war-time when I first met him) that he knew Poe tolerably well. They were, he said, on pleasant and familiar terms; and, it would seem (as Keats and Reynolds did), they read over to each other their not yet published poetical work. It was in obedience to this habit that Poe, on meeting Wallace one day, told him in some such words as these (I will be sponsor now only for their substance, and not for their form, or for the form of the colloquy between the known and the now-unknown poet):

"Wallace," said Poe, "I have just written the greatest poem that ever was written."

"Have you?" said Wallace. "That is a fine achievement."

"Would you like to hear it?" said Poe.

"Most certainly," said Wallace.

Thereupon Poe began to read the soon to be famous verses in his best way—which I believe was always an impressive and captivating way. When he had finished he turned to Wallace for his approval of them—when Wallace said:

"Poe—they are fine; uncommonly fine."

"Fine?" said Poe, contemptuously. "Is that all you can say for this poem? I tell you it's the greatest poem that was ever written."

And then they separated—not, however, before Wallace had tried to placate, with somewhat more pronounced praise, the pettish poet.

And to-day there are critics who say—not knowing Poe's own opinion of "The Raven"—that it is "the greatest poem ever written." Whether it is or not, it bids fair to be the one that will be the most and the longest talked about.

—Joel Benton, "Poe's Opinion of 'The Raven'" (1897),
In the Poe Circle, 1899, pp. 57–60

Edmund Clarence Stedman
"Edgar Allan Poe" (1885)

A poet and critic, Stedman produced one of the first comprehensive anthologies of American literature, and he also co-edited a collection of Poe's works. Stedman reiterates the theme of Poe's dual nature, the artist and the person, and notes that, with the passage of time, the image of the heroic individual overshadows the real person. Stedman comments on Poe's theory of poetry and on how Poe's poems exemplify that theory. He also notes that Poe displayed a musical sensibility in creating his poems, employing "beautiful words" to achieve his poetic effects. Students writing about Poe's poetry might look at Stedman's analysis here.

Notwithstanding his admiration for the poetry, Stedman believes Poe's "intellectual strength and rarest imagination" can be found manifest in his tales. Stedman contrasts Poe with Hawthorne, suggesting that the latter was the greater artist. According to Stedman, Hawthorne was able to draw the beauty from common things, whereas Poe relied too heavily on shock or surprise. Students interested in comparing Hawthorne and Poe might use Stedman's essay to help draw distinctions between the two storytellers.

Stedman argues that Poe is the consummate artist. Even in his failures—Stedman specifically mentions Poe's inability to write genuine humor—Poe sought to create beauty, which for him was the sole purpose of art. Poe denied Keats's axiom, "Beauty is truth, truth beauty," arguing instead that truth had nothing to do with art. Readers exploring topics related to aesthetic theory could look at Stedman's analysis of Poe.

⟞⟊⟍⟋⟊⟍ ⟞⟊⟍⟋⟊⟍ ⟞⟊⟍⟋⟊⟍

I

Upon the roll of American authors a few names are written apart from the many. With each of these is associated some accident of condition, some memory of original or eccentric genius, through which it arrests attention and claims our special wonder. The light of none among these few has been more fervid and recurrent than that of Edgar Allan Poe. But, as I in turn pronounce his name, and in my turn would estimate the man and his writings, I am at once confronted by the question, Is this poet, as now remembered, as now portrayed to us, the real Poe who lived and sang and suffered, and who died but little more than a quarter-century ago?

The great heart of the world throbs warmly over the struggles of our kind; the imagination of the world dwells upon and enlarges the glory and the shame of human action in the past. Year after year, the heart-beats are more warm, the conception grows more distinct with light and shade. The person that was is made the framework of an image to which the tender, the romantic, the thoughtful, the simple, and the wise add each his own folly or wisdom, his own joy and sorrow and uttermost yearning. Thus, not only true heroes and poets, but many who have been conspicuous through force of circumstances, become idealized as time goes by. The critic's first labor often is the task of distinguishing between men, as history and their works display them, and the ideals which one and another have conspired to urge upon his acceptance.

The difficulty is increased when, as in the case of Poe, a twofold ideal exists, of whose opposite sides many that have written upon him seem to observe but one. In the opinion of some people, even now, his life was not only pitiful, but odious, and his writings are false and insincere. They speak of his morbid genius, his unjust criticisms, his weakness and ingratitude, and scarcely can endure the mention of his name. Others recount his history as that of a sensitive, gifted being, most sorely beset and environed, who was tried beyond his strength and prematurely yielded, but still uttered not a few undying strains. As a new generation has arisen, and those of his own who knew him are passing away, the latter class of his reviewers seems to outnumber the former. A chorus of indiscriminate praise has grown so loud as really to be an ill omen for his fame; yet, on the whole, the wisest modern estimate of his character and writings has not lessened the interest long ago felt in them at home and abroad.

It seems to me that two things at least are certain. First, and although his life has been the subject of the research which is awarded only to strange and suggestive careers, he was, after all, a man of like passions with ourselves,—one who, if weaker in his weaknesses than many, and stronger in his strength, may not have been so bad, nor yet so good, as one and another have painted him. Thousands have gone as far toward both extremes, and the world never has heard of them. Only the gift of genius has made the temperament of Poe a common theme. And thus, I also think, we are sure, in once more calling up his shade, that we invoke the manes of a poet. Of his right to this much-abused title there can be little dispute, nor of the claim that, whatever he lacked in compass, he was unique among his fellows,—so different from any other writer that America has produced as really to stand alone. He must have had genius to furnish even the basis for an ideal which excites this persistent interest. Yes, we are on firm ground with relation to his genuineness as a poet. But his narrowness of range, and the slender body of his poetic remains, of themselves should make writers hesitate to pronounce him our greatest one. His verse is as conspicuous for what it shows he could not do as for that which he did. He is another of those poets, outside the New England school, of whom each has made his mark in a separate way,—among them all, none more decisively than Poe. So far as the judgment of a few rare spirits in foreign lands may be counted the verdict of "posterity," an estimate of him is not to be lightly and flippantly made. Nor is it long since a group of his contemporaries and successors, in his own country, spoke of him as a poet whose works are a lasting monument, and of his "imperishable" fame.

After every allowance, it seems difficult for one not utterly jaded to read his poetry and tales without yielding to their original and haunting spell. Even as we drive out of mind the popular conceptions of his nature, and look only at the portraits of him in the flesh, we needs must pause and contemplate, thoughtfully and with renewed feeling, one of the marked ideal faces that seem—like those of Byron, De Musset, Heine—to fulfil all the traditions of genius, of picturesqueness, of literary and romantic effect. . . .

IV

Few and brief are (the) *reliquiæ* which determine his fame as a poet. What do they tell us of his lyrical genius and method? Clearly enough, that he possessed an exquisite faculty, which he exercised within definite bounds. It may be that within those bounds he would have done more if events had not hindered him, as he declared, "from making any serious effort" in the field of his choice. In boyhood he had decided views as to the province of song, and he never afterward changed them. The preface to his West Point edition, rambling and conceited as it is,—affording such a contrast to the proud humility of Keats's preface to *Endymion*,—gives us the gist of his creed, and shows that the instinct of the young poet was scarcely less delicate than that of his nobler kinsman. Poe thought the object of poetry was pleasure, not truth; the pleasure must not be definite, but subtile, and therefore poetry is opposed to romance; music is an *essential*, "since the comprehension of sweet sound is our most indefinite conception." Metaphysics in verse he hated, pronouncing the Lake theory a new form of didacticism that had injured even the tuneful Coleridge. For a neophyte this was not bad, and after certain reservations few will disagree with him. Eighteen years later, in his charming lecture, "The Poetic Principle," he offered simply an extension of these ideas, with reasons why a long poem "cannot exist." One is tempted to rejoin that the standard of length in a poem, as in a piece of music, is relative, depending upon the power of the maker and the recipient to prolong their exalted moods. We might, also, quote Landor's "Pentameron," concerning the greatness of a poet, or even Beecher's saying that "pint measures are soon filled." The lecture justly denounces the "heresy of the didactic," and then declares poetry to be the child of Taste,—devoted solely to the Rhythmical Creation of Beauty, as it is in music that the soul most nearly attains the supernal end for which it struggles. In fine, Poe, with "the mad pride of intellectuality," refused to look beyond the scope of his own gift, and would restrict the poet to one method and even to a single theme. In his *ex post facto* analysis of "The Raven" he conceives the highest tone of beauty to be sadness, caused by the pathos of existence and our inability to grasp the unknown. Of all beauty that of a beautiful woman is the supremest, her death is the saddest loss—and therefore "the most poetical topic in the world." He would treat this musically by application of the refrain, increasing the sorrowful loveliness of his poem by contrast of something homely, fantastic, or quaint.

Poe's own range was quite within his theory. His juvenile versions of what afterward became poems were so very "indefinite" as to express almost nothing; they resembled those marvellous stanzas of Dr. Chivers, that sound magnificently,—I have heard Bayard Taylor and Swinburne rehearse them with shouts of delight—and that have no meaning at all. Poe could not remain a Chivers, but sound always was his forte. We rarely find his highest imagination in his verse, or the creation of poetic phrases such as came to the lips of Keats without a summons. He lacked the dramatic power of combination, and produced no symphony in rhythm,—was strictly a melodist, who achieved wonders in a single strain. Neither Mrs. Browning nor any other poet had "applied" the refrain in Poe's fashion, nor so effectively. In "The Bells" its use is limited almost to one word, the only English word, perhaps, that could be repeated incessantly as the burden of such a poem. In "The Raven," "Lenore," and elsewhere, he employed the repetend also, and with still more novel results:—

An anthem for the queenliest dead that ever died so young,
A dirge for her, the doubly dead, in that she died so young.
        Our talk had been serious and sober,
    But our thoughts they were palsied and sere,
    Our memories were treacherous and sere.

One thing profitably may be noted by latter-day poets. Poe used none but elementary English measures, relying upon his music and atmosphere for their effect. This is true of those which seem most intricate, as in "The Bells" and "Ulalume." "Lenore" and "For Annie" are the simplest of ballad forms. I have a fancy that our Southern poet's ear caught the music of "Annabel Lee" and "Eulalie," if not their special quality, from the plaintive, melodious negro songs utilized by those early writers of "minstrelsy" who have been denominated the only composers of a genuine American school.

This suggestion may be scouted, but an expert might suspect the one to be a patrician refinement upon the melody, feeling, and humble charm of the other.

Poe was not a single-poem poet, but the poet of a single mood. His materials were seemingly a small stock in trade, chiefly of Angels and Demons, with an attendance of Dreams, Echoes, Ghouls, Gnomes and Mimes, ready at hand. He selected or coined, for use and re-use, a number of what have been called "beautiful words,"—"albatross," "halcyon," "scintillant," "Ligeia," "Weir," "Yaanek," "Auber," "D'Elormie," and the like. Everything was subordinate to sound. But his poetry, as it places us under the spell of the senses, enables us to enter, through their reaction upon the spirit, his indefinable mood; nor should we forget that Coleridge owes his specific rank as a poet, not to his philosophic verse, but to melodious fragments, and greatly to the rhythm of *The Ancient Mariner* and of *Christabel.* Poe's melodies lure us to the point where we seem to hear angelic lutes and citherns, or elfin instruments that make music in "the land east of the sun and west of the moon." The enchantment may not be that of Israfel, nor of the harper who exorcised the evil genius of Saul, but it is at least that of some plumed being of the middle air, of a charmer charming so sweetly that his numbers are the burden of mystic dreams.

V

If Poe's standing depended chiefly upon these few poems, notable as they are, his name would be recalled less frequently. His intellectual strength and rarest imagination are to be found in his *Tales.* To them, and to literary criticism, his main labors were devoted.

The limits of this chapter constrain me to say less than I have in mind concerning his prose writings. As with his poems, so with the "Tales,"—their dates are of little importance. His irregular life forced him to alternate good work with bad, and some of his best stories were written early. He was an apostle of the art that refuses to take its color from a given time or country, and of the revolt against commonplace, and his inventions partook of the romantic and the wonderful. He added to a Greek perception of form the Oriental passion for decoration. All the materials of the wizard's craft were at his command. He was not a pupil of Beckford, Godwin, Maturin, Hoffman, or Fouque; and yet if these writers were to be grouped we should think also of Poe, and give him no second place among them. "The young fellow is highly imaginative, and a little given to the terrific," said Kennedy, in his honest way. Poe could not have written a novel, as we term it, as well as the feeblest of Harper's or Roberts's yearlings. He vibrated between two points, the realistic and the mystic, and made no attempt to combine people or situations in ordinary life, though he knew how to lead up to a dramatic tableau or crisis. His studies of character were not made from observation, but from acquaintance with himself; and this subjectivity, or egoism, crippled his invention and made his "Tales" little better than prose poems. He could imagine a series of adventures—the experience of a single narrator—like *Arthur Gordon Pym,* and might have been, not Le Sage nor De Foe, but an eminent raconteur in his own field. His strength is unquestionable in those clever pieces of ratiocination, "The Murders in the Rue Morgue," "The Mystery of Marie Roget," "The Purloined Letter"; in some of a more fantastic type, "The Gold Bug" and "Hans Pfaall"; and especially in those with elements of terror and morbid psychology added, such as "The Descent into the Maelstrom," "The Black Cat," "The Tell-Tale Heart," and the mesmeric sketches. When composing these he delighted in the exercise of his dexterous intellect, like a workman testing his skill. No poet is of a low grade who possesses, besides an ear for rhythm, the resources of a brain so fine and active. Technical gifts being equal, the more intellectual of two poets is the greater. "Best bard, because the wisest."

His artistic contempt for metaphysics is seen even in those tales which appear most transcendental. They are charged with a feeling that in the realms of psychology we are dealing with something ethereal, which is none the less substance if we might but capture it. They are his resolute attempts to find a clew to the invisible world. Were he living now, how much he would make of our discoveries in light and sound, of the correlation of forces! He strove by a kind of divination to put his hand upon the links of mind and matter, and reach the hiding-places of the soul. It galled him that anything should lie outside the domain of human intelligence. His imperious intellect rebelled against the bounds that shut us in, and found passionate expression in works of which "Ligeia," "The Fall of the House of Usher," and "William Wilson" are the best types. The tales in which lyrics are introduced are full of complex beauty, the choicest products of his genius. They are the offspring of yearnings that lifted him so far above himself as to make us forget his failings and think of him only as a creative artist, a man of noble gifts.

In these short, purely ideal efforts—finished as an artist finishes a portrait, or a poet his poem—Poe had few equals in recent times. That he lacked sustained power of invention is proved, not by his failure to complete an extended work, but by his under-estimation of its value. Such a man measures everything by his personal ability, and finds plausible grounds for the resulting standard. Hawthorne had the growing power and the staying

power that gave us *The Scarlet Letter* and *The House of the Seven Gables.* Poe
and Hawthorne were the last of the romancers. Each was a master in his way,
and that of Poe was the more obvious and material. He was expert in much
that concerns the structure of works, and the modelling touches of the
poet left beauty-marks upon his prose. Yet in spiritual meaning his tales
were less poetic than those of Hawthorne. He relied upon his externals,
making the utmost of their gorgeousness of color, their splendor and gloom
of light and shade. Hawthorne found the secret meaning of common things,
and knew how to capture, from the plainest aspects of life, an essence of
evasive beauty which the senses of Poe often were unable to perceive. It was
Hawthorne who heard the melodies too fine for mortal ear. Hawthorne was
wholly masculine, with the great tenderness and gentleness which belong to
virile souls. Poe had, with the delicacy, the sophistry and weakness of a nature
more or less effeminate. He opposed to Hawthorne the fire, the richness,
the instability of the tropics, as against the abiding strength and passion
of the North. His own conceptions astonished him, and he often presents
himself "with hair on end, at his own wonders." Of these two artists and
seers, the New Englander had the profounder insight; the Southerner's
magic was that of the necromancer who resorts to spells and devices, and,
when some apparition by chance responds to his incantations, is bewildered
by the phantom himself has raised.

Poe failed to see that the Puritanism by which Hawthorne's strength
was tempered was also the source from which it sprang; and in his general
criticism did not pay full tribute to a genius he must have felt. In some of his
sketches, such as "The Man of the Crowd," he used Hawthorne's method, and
with inferior results. His reviews of other authors and his occasional literary
notes have been so carefully preserved as to show his nature by a mental
and moral photograph. His *Marginalia,* scrappy and written for effect, are
the notes of a thinking man of letters. The criticisms raised a hubbub in their
day, and made Poe the bogy of his generation—the unruly censor whom
weaklings not only had cause to fear, but often regarded with a sense of cruel
injustice. I acknowledge their frequent dishonesty, vulgarity, prejudice, but
do not, therefore, hold them to be worthless. Even a scourge, a pestilence,
has its uses; before it the puny and frail go down, the fittest survive. And so it
was in Poe's foray. Better that a time of unproductiveness should follow such
a thinning out than that false and feeble things should continue. I suspect
that *The Literati* made room for a new movement, sure though long delayed,
in American authorship. Mr. Higginson, however, is entirely right when he
intimates that Margaret Fuller, by her independent reviews in *The Tribune,*

sustained her full and early part in the chase against "such small deer." The shafts of Dian were more surely sped, and much less vindictively, than the spear of her brother-huntsman. Poe's sketches are a prose Dunciad, waspish and unfair, yet not without touches of magnanimity. He had small respect for the feeling that it is well for a critic to discover beauties, since any one can point out faults. When, as in the cases of Tennyson, Mrs. Browning, Taylor, and others, he pronounced favorably upon the talents of a claimant, and was uninfluenced by personal motives, his judgments not seldom have been justified by the after-career. Besides, what a cartoon he drew of the writers of his time,—the corrective of Griswold's optimistic delineations! In the description of a man's personal appearance he had the art of placing the subject before us with a single touch. His tender mercies were cruel; he never forgot to prod the one sore spot of the author he most approved,—was especially intolerant of his own faults in others, and naturally detected these at once. When meting out punishment to a pretentious writer, he revelled in his task, and often made short work, as if the pleasure was too great to be endurable. The keenness of his satire, just or unjust, is mitigated by its obvious ferocity: one instinctively takes part with the victim. Nothing in journalistic criticism, even at that time, was more scathing and ludicrous than his conceit of a popular bookwright in the act of confabulation with the Universe. But he marred the work by coarseness, telling one man that he was by no means a fool, although he did write "De Vere," and heading a paper on the gentlest and most forbearing of poets—"Mr. Longfellow and Other Plagiarists." In short, he constantly dulled the edge and temper of his rapier, and resorted to the broad-axe, using the latter even in his deprecation of its use by Kit North. Perhaps it was needed in those salad days by offenders who could be put down in no other wise; but I hold it a sign of progress that criticism by force of arms would now be less effective.

VI

Some analysis of Poe's general equipment will not be out of place. Only in the most perfect tales can his English style be called excellent, however significant his thought. His mannerisms—constant employment of the *dash* for suggestiveness, and a habit of italicizing to make a point or strengthen an illusion—are wearisome, and betray a lack of confidence in his skill to use plain methods. While asserting the power of words to convey absolutely any idea of the human mind, he relied on sound, quaintness, surprise, and other artificial aids. His prose is inferior to Hawthorne's; but sometimes he excels Hawthorne in qualities of form and proportion which are specially at the service of authors who are also poets. The abrupt beginnings of his stories often are artistic:—

> We had now reached the summit of the loftiest crag. For some minutes the old man seemed too much exhausted to speak. ("Descent into the Maelstrom.")
>
> The thousand injuries of Fortunato I had borne as best I could; but when he ventured upon insult, I vowed revenge. ("The Cask of Amontillado.")

His endings were equally good, when he had a clear knowledge of his own purpose, and some of his conceptions terminate at a dramatic crisis. The tone, also, of his masterpieces is well sustained throughout. In "The Fall of the House of Usher," the approach to the fated spot, the air, the landscape, the tarn, the mansion itself, are a perfect study, equal to the ride of Childe Roland,—and here Poe excels Browning: we not only come with him to the dark tower, but we enter and partake its mystery, and alone know the secret of its accursed fate. The poet's analytic faculty has been compared to that of Balzac, but a parallel goes no farther than the material side. In condensation he surpassed either Balzac or Hawthorne.

His imagination was not of the highest order, for he never dared to trust to it implicitly; certainly not in his poetry, since he could do nothing with a measure like blank verse, which is barren in the hands of a mere songster, but the glory of English metrical forms when employed by one commanding the strength of diction, the beauty and grandeur of thought, and all the resources of a strongly imaginative poet. Neither in verse nor in prose did he cut loose from his minor devices, and for results of sublimity and awe he always depends upon that which is grotesque or out of nature. Beauty of the fantastic or grotesque is not the highest beauty. Art, like nature, must be fantastic, not in her frequent, but in her exceptional moods. The rarest ideal dwells in a realm beyond that which fascinates us by its strangeness or terror, and the votaries of the latter have masters above them as high as Raphael is above Dore.

In genuine humor Poe seemed utterly wanting. He also had little of the mother-wit that comes in flashes and at once; but his powers of irony and satire were so great as to make his frequent lapses into invective the more humiliating. The command of humor has distinguished men whose genius was both high and broad. If inessential to exalted poetic work, its absence is hurtful to the critical and polemic essay. Poe knew this as well as any one, but a measureless self-esteem would not acknowledge the flaw in his armor. Hence efforts which involved the delusion that humor may come by works and not by inborn gift. Humor is congenital and rare, the fruit of natural mellowness, of sensitiveness to the light and humane phases of life. It is, moreover, set in action by an unselfish heart. Such is the mirth of Thackeray, of Cervantes and Moliere, and of the one master of English song. Poe's consciousness of his defect, and his refusal to believe it incurable, are manifest in trashy sketches for which he had a market, and which are humorous only to one who sees the ludicrous side of their failure. He analyzed mirth as the product of incongruity, and went to work upon a theory to produce it. The result is seen not only in the extravaganzas to which I refer,—and it is a pity that these should have been hunted up so laboriously,—but in the use of what he thought was humor to barb his criticisms, and as a contrast to the exciting passages of his analytical tales. One of his sketches, "The Due de l'Omelette," after the lighter French manner, has grace and jaunty persiflage, but most of his whimsical "pot-boilers" are deplorably absurd. There is something akin to humor in the sub-handling of his favorite themes,—such as the awe and mystery of death, the terrors of pestilence, insanity, or remorse. The grotesque and nether side of these matters presents itself to him, and then his irony, with its repulsive fancies, is as near humor as he ever approaches. That is to say, it is grave-yard humor, the kind which sends a chill down our backs, and implies a contempt for our bodies and souls, for the perils, helplessness, and meanness of the stricken human race.

Poe is sometimes called a man of extraordinary learning. Upon a first acquaintance, one might receive the impression that his scholarship was not only varied, but thorough. A study of his works has satisfied me that he possessed literary resources and knew how to make the most of them. In this he resembled Bulwer, and, with far less abundant materials than the latter required, employed them as speciously. He easily threw a glamour of erudition about his work, by the use of phrases from old authors he had read, or among whose treatises he had foraged with special design. It was his knack to cull sentences which, taken by themselves, produce a weird or impressive effect, and to reframe them skilfully. This plan was clever, and resulted in something that could best be muttered "darkly, at dead of night"; but it partook of trickery, even in its art. He had little exact scholarship, nor needed it, dealing, as he did, not with the processes of learning, but with results that could subserve the play of his imagination. Shakespeare's anachronisms and illusions were made as he required them, and with a fine disdain. Poe resorted to them of malice aforethought, and under pretence of correctness. Still, the work of a romancer and poet is not that of a bookworm. What he needs is a good reference-knowledge, and this Poe had. His irregular school-boy training was not likely to give him the scholastic habit, nor would his impatient manhood otherwise have confirmed it. I am sure that we may consider that portion of his youth to have been of most worth which was devoted, as in the case of many a born writer, to the unconscious education obtained from the reading, for the mere love of it, of *all* books to which he had access. This training served him well. It enabled him to give his romance an alchemic air, by citation from writers like Chapman, Thomas More, Bishop King, etc., and from Latin and French authors in profusion. His French tendencies were natural, and he learned enough of the language to read much of its current literature and get hold of modes unknown to many of his fellow-writers. I have said that his stock in trade was narrow, but for the adroit display of it examine any of his tales and sketches,—for example, "Berenice," or "The Assignation."

In knowledge of what may be called the properties of his romance, he was more honestly grounded. He had the good fortune to utilize the Southern life and scenery which he knew in youth. It chanced, also, that during some years of his boyhood—that formative period whose impressions are indelible—he lived in a characteristic part of England. He had seen with his own eyes castles, abbeys, the hangings and tapestries and other by-gone trappings of ancient rooms, and remembered effects of decoration and color which always came to his aid. These he used as if he were born to them; never, certainly, with the surprise at their richness which vulgarizes Disraeli's *Lothair*. In some way, known to genius, he also caught the romance of France, of Italy, of the Orient, and one tale or another is transfused with their atmosphere; while the central figure, however disguised, is always the image of the romancer himself. His equipment, on the whole, was not a pedant's, much less that of a searcher after truth; it was that of a poet and a literary workman. Yet he had the hunger which animates the imaginative student, and, had he been led to devote himself to science, would have contributed to the sum of knowledge. In writing *Eureka* he was unquestionably sincere, and forgot himself more nearly than in any other act of his professional life. But here his inexact learning betrayed him. What was begun in conviction—a swift generalization from scientific theories of the universe—grew to be so far beyond the data at his command, or so inconsistent with them, that he finally saw he had written little else than a prose poem, and desired that it should be so regarded. Of all sciences, astronomy appeals most to the imagination. What is rational in *Eureka* mostly is a re-statement of accepted theories: otherwise the treatise is vague and nebulous,—a light dimmed by its own vapor. The work is curiously saturated with our modern Pantheism; and although in many portions it shows the author's weariness, yet it was a notable production for a layman venturing within the precincts of the savant. The poetic instinct hits upon truths which the science of the future confirms; but as often, perhaps, it glorifies some error sprung from a too ardent generalization. Poe's inexactness was shown in frequent slips,—sometimes made unconsciously, sometimes in reliance upon the dulness of his rivals to save him from detection. He was on the alert for other people's errors; for his own facts, were he now alive, he could not call so lightly upon his imagination. Even our younger authors, here and abroad, now are so well equipped that their learning seems to handicap their winged steeds. Poe had, above all, the gift of poetic induction. He would have divined the nature of an unknown world from a specimen of its flora, a fragment of its art. He felt himself something more than a bookman. He was a creator of the beautiful, and hence the conscious struggle of his spirit for the sustenance it craved. Even when he was most in error, he labored as an artist, and it is idle criticism that judges him upon any other ground.

Accept him, then, whether as poet or romancer, as a pioneer of the art feeling in American literature. So far as he was devoted to art for art's sake, it was for her sake as the exponent of beauty. No man ever lived in whom the passion for loveliness more plainly governed the emotions and convictions. His service of the beautiful was idolatry, and he would have kneeled with Heine at the feet of Our Lady of Milo, and believed that she yearned to help him. This consecration to absolute beauty made him abhor the mixture of sentimental-ism, metaphysics, and morals, in its presentation. It was a foregone conclusion that neither Longfellow, Emerson, Lowell, nor Hawthorne should wholly satisfy him. The question of "moral" tendency concerned him not in the least. He did not feel with Keats that "Beauty is truth, truth beauty," and that a divine perfection may be reached by either road. This deficiency narrowed his range both as a poet and as a critic. His sense of justice was a sense of the fitness of things, and—strange to say—when he put it aside he forgot that he was doing an unseemly thing. Otherwise, he represents, or was one of the first to lead, a rebellion against formalism, commonplace, the spirit of the bourgeois. In this movement Whitman is his countertype at the pole opposite from that of art; and hence they justly are picked out from the rest of us and associated in foreign minds. Taste was Poe's supreme faculty. Beauty, to him, was a definite and logical reality, and he would have scouted Veron's claim that it has no fixed objective laws, and exists only in the nature of the observer. Although the brakes of art were on his imagination, his taste was not wholly pure; he vacillated between the classic forms and those allied with color, splendor, Oriental decoration; between his love for the antique and his impressions of the mystical and grotesque. But he was almost without confraternity. An artist in an unartistic period, he had to grope his way, to contend with stupidity and coarseness. Again, his imagination, gloating upon the possibilities of taste, violated its simplicity. Poe longed for the lamp of Aladdin, for the riches of the Gnomes. Had unbounded wealth been his, he would have outvied Beckford, Landor, Dumas, in barbaric extravagance of architecture. His efforts to apply the laws of the beautiful to imaginary decoration, architecture, landscape, are very fascinating as seen in "The Philosophy of Furniture," "Landscape Gardening," and "Landor's Cottage." "The Domain of Arnheim" is a marvellous dream of an earthly paradise, and the close is a piece of word-painting as effective as the language contains. Regarding this sensitive artist, this original poet, it seems indeed a tragedy that a man so ideal in either realm, so unfit for contact with ugliness, dulness, brutality, should have come to eat husks with the swine, to be misused by their human counterparts, and to die the death of a drunkard, in the refuge which society offers to the most forlorn and hopeless of its castaways.

—Edmund Clarence Stedman, "Edgar Allan Poe,"
Poets of America, 1885, pp. 225–28, 248–64

GENERAL PROSE

Poe was an enormously productive writer of prose. From 1833, when he published his first short story, "MS. Found in a Bottle," to his death in 1849, Poe wrote constantly, often publishing several pieces under different names in the same magazine issue. He wrote tales, sketches, commentary, literary criticism and theory, book reviews, and more. His prose works are generally divided into fiction and nonfiction, but within these larger categories Poe's writings could be labeled as any number of subgenres (including horror, humor, satire, science fiction, and detective fiction). Some of his nonfiction might be considered essays in science or philosophy.

The extracts in this and the following sections are divided into four broad areas: General Prose, Tales, *Eureka*, and Criticism. In the general overview, Henry Wadsworth Longfellow and John Mackinnon Robertson discuss Poe's fiction. Longfellow, in a letter to Poe, states that he thinks Poe could be one of the country's greatest "romancers," that is, writers of imaginative fiction. Robertson defends Poe against those who think his stories are puerile, material enjoyed by children but not by serious adults. Robertson argues that Poe's realistic presentation of fantastic events is a mark of his greatness.

In the Tales section, several writers weigh in on the value of Poe's short stories. Margaret Fuller hails Poe as one of the best writers of the time, while Martin Farquhar Tupper criticizes the tales for being unbelievable or immoral. Brander Matthews then suggests that no writer has matched Poe's ability to bring together both analysis and imagination. Robert Louis Stevenson, however, argues that much of Poe's fiction involves a great deal of trickery; although it exhibits technical mastery, Stevenson says, it does not amount to art. In his essay on "Poe and the Detective Story," Brander Matthews states that Poe invented the genre and details the ways in which this form differs from mere mystery. Francis Thompson also praises Poe's detective fiction, asserting that it outshines all of its popular imitations at the end of the nineteenth century. Finally, Lewis Gates argues that Poe's best poetry actually lies in his prose tales, although Gates goes on to condemn Poe's "inhumanity" and his artificiality, especially when it comes to developing meaningful characters.

Even though George Woodberry's extract is the only one devoted to the "prose poem," *Eureka* deserves its own section because it is a nearly uncategorizable literary work. In it, Poe discourses on the origins of the universe, the making of the world itself, and the role of a deity. *Eureka* is a work of philosophy and a work of physics, a poem and a scientific treatise rolled up in one. Woodberry argues that the effect is not salutary and that the work is a failure.

It is perhaps fitting to end the volume with a section discussing Poe's criticism. Poe was a careful, and often harsh, critic of others, and he wrote numerous book reviews and essays criticizing the writers of his day. Poe made a number of enemies based on his criticism. Hawthorne, despite having tasted a bit of the acid pen of Poe, asserts that he prefers Poe's tales to his criticism. Eugene Benson has less equanimity, blasting Poe for selectively dismantling the great works of others in a mean-spirited or unfair manner. Henry James, in his book on Hawthorne, also finds Poe's criticism to be vindictive, but he acknowledges as well that Poe was one of America's first insightful critics. In the last text, Barrett Wendell defends Poe's criticism, saying that Poe was severe because of his passion for the art itself. He holds, as many do, that Poe brought the same energy and intensity to his critical works as he did to his fiction and poetry.

HENRY WADSWORTH LONGFELLOW (1841)

Longfellow, the "American Tennyson," was a popular and influential poet
who Poe famously accused of plagiarism. Specifically, Poe charged him
with stealing verses from Tennyson himself. Nevertheless, in this letter,
Longfellow offers praise for Poe's talents as a writer of fiction.

―――――――

You are mistaken in supposing that you are not "favorably known to me."
On the contrary, all that I have read from your pen has inspired me with a
high idea of your power; and I think you are destined to stand among the first
romance-writers of the country, if such be your aim.

—Henry Wadsworth Longfellow,
Letter to Edgar Allan Poe (May 19, 1841)

JOHN MACKINNON ROBERTSON "POE" (1897)

Robertson, a British journalist and politician, here upbraids Poe's critics
for underestimating Poe's work. He specifically mentions Henry James,
who famously declared that taking Poe "with more than a certain degree
of seriousness is to lack seriousness oneself." Robertson points out that
this attitude is likely the result of the critic's own boyhood interest in
Poe. That is, if one liked Poe as a child, one is not supposed to like Poe
as an adult. Robertson suggests that this theory would depreciate such
classics as *Gulliver's Travels*, a book enjoyed by the young as well as held
in high esteem by adult readers. This notion raises several questions:
Can a work of literature be "great" if inexperienced readers (such as
children) enjoy it? What about writing intended for children, can it also
be esteemed and identified as literature? What kind of definition of literature is used when certain works get included or excluded? Students
exploring the idea of literature or interested in children's literature could
use Robertson's essay as a starting point.

Robertson cites Poe's "The Unparalleled Adventures of One Hans
Pfall," a hoax of a tale about a balloon trip to the moon, as an example
of Poe's detailed, powerful storytelling. Robertson calls Poe's special
faculty of imagination, "sanity raised to a higher power," and he argues
that Poe—for all the fantastic imagery in his tales—is in fact a realist. He
notes that Poe used science in exposing the marvelous and the marvelous
in exploring science. Students writing about realism or fantasy in Poe
might examine Robertson's argument here. Those drawn to Poe's science
fiction writings might also turn to Robertson's article.

―――――――

As a poet Poe has a commanding distinction; but if we find him remarkable in that regard, what shall we say of the range and calibre of the mind which produced the manifold achievement of his prose? The more one wanders through that, out of all comparison the more extensive part of his work, the more singular appear those estimates of the man which treat him merely as a poet of unhappy life and morbid imagination. Perhaps it is that in all seriousness the literary world inclines to Mr. Swinburne's conviction that poets as such are the guardian angels of mankind, and all other mind-workers their mere satellites; perhaps that, despite Goethe's services to biology, it has a hereditary difficulty in conceiving a poet as an effective intelligence in any other walk than that of his art, and accordingly excludes instinctively from view whatever tends to raise the point. Or is it that the sense of the abnormality of feeling in Poe's verse, and in his best-known stories, gives rise to a vague notion that his performances in the line of normal thought can be of no serious account? It is difficult to decide; but certain it is that most of his critics have either by restrictedness of view or positive misjudgment done him serious wrong.

It is Mr. Henry James who . . . makes the remark: "With all due respect to the very original genius of the author of the *Tales of Mystery,* it seems to me that to take him with more than a certain degree of seriousness is to lack seriousness oneself. An enthusiasm for Poe is the mark of a decidedly primitive stage of reflection." One cannot guess with any confidence as to the precise "degree of seriousness" which Mr. James would concede; or how much seriousness he brings to bear on any of his own attachments; or what the stage of reflection was at which he cultivated an enthusiasm for, say, Theophile Gautier. One therefore hesitates to put oneself in competition with Mr. James in the matter of seriousness of character. But one may venture to suggest that the above passage throws some light on the rather puzzling habit of depreciation of Poe among American men of letters. Themselves given mainly to the study of modern fiction, they seem to measure Poe only as a fictionist; and, even then, instead of fairly weighing his work on its merits, they test it by the calibre of the people who prefer the *Tales of Mystery* to novels of character. Remembering that as boys they enjoyed Poe when they did not enjoy the novel of character, they decide that the writer who thus appeals to boyish minds can be of no great intellectual account. This is a very fallacious line of reasoning. It would make out Defoe to be an artist of the smallest account, though Mr. James has a way of connecting intellectual triviality with "very original genius," which somewhat confuses the process of inference. It would relegate Swift to a rather low standing, because boys notoriously enjoy *Gulliver's Travels.*

That result would surely not do. It surely does not follow that Mr. Stevenson is intellectually inferior to Mr. Howells because the former wrote *Treasure Island,* beloved of boys, while Mr. Howells' books appeal only to people who know something of life. The fair, not to say the scientific method, surely, is to take an author's total performance, and estimate from that his total powers. This, Mr. James has not done, I think, as regards Poe, or he would not have written as he has done about "seriousness;" and, if one may say such a thing about impertinence, the kind of culture specially affected by Mr. James is too much in the ascendant among the very intelligent reading public of the States. These white-handed students of the modern novel are not exactly the people to estimate an endowment such as Poe's.[1]

If one critical impression can be said to be predominant for an attentive reader of Poe's prose, it is perhaps a wondering sense of the perfection which may belong to what Lamb called "the sanity of true genius," even where the genius borders on the formless clime we name insanity. This is no idle paradox. What I say is that while Poe's work again and again gives evidence of a mind tending to alienation, it yet includes a hundred triumphs of impeccable reason; and that for the most part his intellectual faculty is sanity itself. It opens up a curious view of things to compare the opaque, lethargic, chaotic state of mind which in respectable society so securely passes for sanity, with the pure electric light, the cloudless clearness, of Poe's intelligence in its normal state; and to reflect that he has been called mad, and is sometimes described as a charlatan. How would his detractors, for instance, have compared with Poe in thinking power if they had had to deal with such a problem as that of the *prima facie* credibility of the "Moon Hoax," which Poe is falsely accused of imitating? The Moon Hoax was a celebrated narrative, the work of Mr. Richard Adams Locke, which appeared in the *New York Sun* some three weeks *after* Poe's "Hans Pfaall" had been published in the *Southern Literary Messenger,* and which made a great sensation at the time. The "Moon Story" gravely professed to describe the inhabitants, animals, vegetation, and scenery of the moon, as having been lately made out by Sir John Herschel with a new telescope; while Poe gave a minute narrative, touched at points with banter, of a balloon journey to the same orb; but there was little detailed resemblance in the narratives, and Poe accepted Mr. Locke's declaration that he had not seen the "Adventure" when he concocted his hoax. The point of interest for us here is that the hoax was very widely successful; and that Poe found it worth while afterwards to show in detail how obvious was the imposition, and how easily it should have been seen through by intelligent readers. "Not one person in ten," he records, "discredited it, and the doubters were chiefly those who doubted without being able to say why—the ignorant, those uninformed in astronomy—people who *would not* believe because the thing was so novel, so entirely "out of the usual way. A grave professor of mathematics in a Virginian college told me seriously that he had *no doubt* of the truth of the whole affair!" Accordingly, Poe appended to his "Hans Pfaall" story, on republishing it, an analysis of the other story, than which there could not be a more luminous exercise of psychological logic. His scientific and other knowledge, and his power of scrutiny, enabled him to detect a dozen blunders and clumsinesses; but perhaps the most characteristic touch is his remark on the entire absence from the narrative of any expression of surprise at a phenomenon which, on the assumptions made, must have been part of the discoverer's vision—namely, the curious appearance presented by the moon's alleged inhabitants, in that their heads would be towards the terrestrial gazer, and that they would appear to hang to the moon by their feet. The demand for an expression of astonishment at this was that of an intelligence which had carried the action of imagination to a high pitch of methodic perfection. The processes of sub-conscious inference which initiate conviction, the polarity of average thinking, the elements of evidence, all had been pondered and perceived by Poe with an acumen that is as singular as most forms of genius. And the result of the demonstration was no mere protraction of subtle introspection, but the masterly solution of an abstruse concrete problem. His facility in the explication of cypher-writing was astounding: witness his triumph over all challengers when he dealt with the subject in a Philadelphia journal and in *Graham's Magazine;* his unravelling of a cryptograph in which were employed seven alphabets, without intervals between the words or even between the lines; and his crowning conquest of a cypher so elaborate that no outsider succeeded in solving it *with the key* when Poe offered a reward as an inducement. Take, again, the essay on "Maelzel's Chess Player," in which he bends his mind on the question whether that was or was not an automaton; examines with an eye like a microscope the features of the object; passes in review previous attempts at explanation; and evolves with rigorous logic an irresistible demonstration that the machine was worked by a man, and of the manner of the working. The power to work such a demonstration is as rare, as remarkable, as almost any species of faculty that can be named. It is sanity raised to a higher power. Such performances, to say nothing of his prediction of the plot of *Barnaby Rudge* from the opening chapters, should give pause to those who incline to the view, endorsed by some respectable critics, that there was nothing extraordinary in Poe's feats of analytic fiction, seeing that he himself tied the knots he untied. But that criticism is invalid on the face of it. Why is Poe so unrivalled in his peculiar line if it is so easy to tie and untie complex knots of incident, and to forge chains of causation in narrative? Does any one ever dream of denying skill in plot-construction to Scribe and Sardou because they deliberately lead up to their *denouments?* Is it the tyro who propounds deep problems in chess, or the schoolboy who imagines new theorems in geometry? The matter is hardly worth discussing. That the author of "The Murders in the Rue Morgue," "The Adventure of Hans Pfaall," and "The Mystery of Marie Roget" could be a mere intellectual charlatan, differing only from his fellows in power of make-believe, is what De Quincey would call a "fierce impossibility."

As a narrator and as a thinker Poe has half a dozen excellences any one of which would entitle him to fame. The general mind of Europe has been fascinated by his tales; but how far has it realised the quality of the work in them? It has for the most part read Poe as it has read Alexandre Dumas. Poe, indeed, wrote to interest the reading public, and he was far too capable an artist not to manage what he wanted; but it was not in his nature to produce work merely adequate to the popular demand. Hundreds of popular stories are produced and are forgotten, for the plain reason that while the writer has somehow succeeded in interesting a number of his contemporaries, his work lacks the intellectual salt necessary for its preservation to future times. Posterity reads it and finds nothing to respect; neither mastery of style nor subtlety nor closeness of thought. But Poe's best stories have a quality of pure mind, an intensity of intelligised imagination, that seems likely to impress men centuries hence as much as it did his more competent readers in his own day. Even at the present moment, when his *genre* is almost entirely uncultivated, such a hard-headed critic as Professor Minto sums up that "there are few English writers of this century whose fame is likely to be more enduring. The feelings to which he appeals are simple but universal, and he appeals to them with a force that has never been surpassed." To that generously just verdict I am disposed, however, to offer a partial demurrer, in the shape of a suggestion that it is not so much in the universality of the "feelings" to which he appeals as in the manifest and consummate faculty with which he is seen to frame his appeal, that Poe's security of renown really lies. Doubtless many readers will, as hitherto, see the narrative and that only; just as Poe himself points out that "not one person in ten—nay, not one person in five hundred—has, during the perusal of *Robinson Crusoe,* the most remote conception that any particle of genius, or even of common talent, has been employed in its creation. Men do not look upon it in the light of a literary performance." But one fancies that the age of critical reading is evolving, in which, notwithstanding a random saying of Poe's own to the contrary, men will combine delight in the artist's skill with due susceptibility to the result.

Even among those who perceive the immense importance of naturalism in fiction, there are, it is to be feared, some who are so narrow as to see no value in any work of which the naturalism is not that species of absolute realism that, selection apart, is substantially contended for by M. Zola, and is variously exemplified in his and other modern novels of different countries and correspondingly different flavours. Now, the effective vindication of Poe, to my mind, is that, weird and *bizarre* and abnormal as are the themes he affected, he is essentially a realist in his method. Granted that he turns away from experience, ordinary or otherwise, for his subjects, what could be more perfect than the circumspection with which he uses every device of arrangement and tone, of omission and suggestion, to give his fiction the air of actuality? Take his "Hans Pfaall." Hardly any critic, save Dr. Landa in his preface to his Spanish translation of some of the Tales, has done justice to the exactitude and verisimilitude with which Poe has there touched in his astronomical, physical, and physiological details; and employed them to the point of carrying illusion to its possible limit even while he has artistically guarded himself from the downright pretence by the fantastic fashion of his introduction. There is realism and realism. It was Poe's idiosyncrasy as a fictionist to examine, not the interplay of the primary human and social emotions either in the open or in half lights, not to be either a Thackeray or a Hawthorne, but to trace the sequences and action of thinking faculty in its relation to the leading instincts and feelings of the individual; and this he does partly by studying himself and partly by comparing himself with others—precisely the method of ordinary humanist fiction. He is always an observer in this direction. His objection to the "Moon Hoax" was that it not merely showed ignorant blundering in its details but was wanting in proper calculation of the attitude of good observers; so in his paper on "Maelzel's Chess Player" he unhesitatingly rejects one of Brewster's explanations as assuming too commonplace a stratagem; so, in easily unravelling a friend's cypher, he laughs at the "shallow artifice" he sees in it; and so in his Parisian stories he derides, in the police officer, the cunning which he finds so inferior to true sagacity.

Even the story of "The Black Cat" is realistic—realistic in the very wildness of its action. Any one in reading Poe can see how he consciously constructed tales by letting his creative faculty follow the line of one of those morbid fancies that probably in some degree occur at times to all of us, and of which, alas! he must have had a tremendous share; giving the recapitulation a gruesome lifelikeness by vigilant embodiment of the details he had noted in following the track of the sinister caprice. And so "The Tell-Tale Heart," and "William Wilson," and "The Cask of Amontillado" are realistic—realistic in the sense that they have had a psychologic basis in the perversities of a disturbed imagination: hence the uncanny fascination of these and other stories of his in a similar taste.[2] Whether that particular species of fiction will retain a hold on men is a matter on which it would be rash to prophesy; and indeed it may be that not only this but another class of Poe's productions—that which includes "The Fall of the House of Usher," "Ligeia," "The Masque of the Red Death," "The Assignation," and "Berenice"—may, as mankind progresses in rational culture, lose that peculiar impressiveness they have for so many readers to-day. These strange creations, whelmed in shade, seem to belong to some wild region, out of the main road of human evolution. To my own taste, I confess, they are less decisively and permanently impressive than such feats of daylight imagination, so to speak, as *Arthur Gordon Pym*, "Hans Pfaall," "The Pit and the Pendulum," or even "The Murders in the Rue Morgue," and "The Purloined Letter"; but there is no overlooking the element of power, the intension of idea, which makes itself felt in the twilight studies as in the others. Like every man who has to live by steady pen-work, Poe produced some inferior stuff and some downright trash; but wherever his faculty comes at all fully into play it puts a unique stamp of intellect on its product, a stamp not consisting in mere force or beauty of style, though these are involved, but in a steady, unfaltering pressure of the writer's thought on the attention of his reader. And when we recognise this pregnancy and intensity, and take note that such a critic as Mr. Lowell was so impressed by the "serene and sombre beauty" of "The Fall of the House of Usher" as to pronounce it sufficient by itself to prove Poe a man of genius and the master of a classic style, we shall see cause to doubt whether any considerable portion of Poe's imaginative work belongs to the perishable order of literature.

As for the group of tales of the saner type, with their blazing vividness and tense compactness of substance—beyond insisting on the importance of the capacity implied in these results, and the essential realism of the stories within the limits of their species, there can be little need to claim for them either attention or praise. Their fascination as narratives is felt by all: the only drawback is the tendency to argue that, because the non-realistic novel is potentially inferior to the realistic, this class of story is inferior to the realistic novel or story of ordinary life. To reason so is to confuse types. Lytton is a worse novelist than Thackeray because, professing both explicitly and implicitly to portray character and society, he is less true in every respect; and the idealistic element in George Eliot is of less value than her work of observation because it claims acceptance on the same footing while its title is, in the terms of the case, awanting. Here we are dealing with comparable things, with performances to be judged in relation to each other. But in Poe we deal with quite a different species of art. That familiar objection to his tales on the score of their lack of human or moral colour, expressed by Mr. Lowell, in his *Fable for Critics,* in the phrase "somehow the heart seems squeezed out by the mind," is the extension of the confusion into downright injustice. It lies on the face of his work that Poe never aims at reproducing every-day life and society, with its multitude of minute character-phenomena forming wholes for artistic contemplation, but—to put it formally—at working out certain applications and phases of the faculties of reflection and volition, as conditioning and conditioned by abnormal tendencies and incidents. He does not seek or profess to draw "character" in the sense in which Dickens or Balzac does; he has almost nothing to do with local colour or sub-divisions of type; his fisherman in "The Descent into the Maelstrom" is an unspecialised intelligent person; Arthur Gordon Pym similarly is simply an observing, reasoning, and energising individual who goes through and notes certain experiences: in short, these personages are abstractions of one aspect of Poe.[3] On the other hand Usher and the speakers in "The Black Cat" and "The Imp of the Perverse" merely represent a reversal of the formula; peculiar idiosyncrasy in their case being made the basis of incident, whereas in the other pure incident or mystery was made the motive. No matter which element predominates, normal character study is excluded; Poe's bias, as we said, being toward analysis or synthesis of processes of applied reason and psychal idiosyncrasy, not to reproduction of the light and shade of life pitched on the everyday plane. It was not that he was without eye for that. On the contrary, his criticisms show he had a sound taste in the novel proper; and we find him rather critically alert than otherwise in his social relation to the personalities about him. It was that his artistic bent lay in another direction.

As a tale-teller, then, he is to be summed up as having worked in his special line with the same extraordinary creative energy and intellectual mastery as distinguish his verse; giving us narratives "of imagination all compact," yet instinct with life in every detail and particle, no matter how strange, how aloof from common things, may be the theme. As Dr. Landa remarks, he has been the first story-writer to exploit the field of science in the department of the marvellous; and he has further been the first to exploit the marvellous in morbid psychology with scientific art. These are achievements as commanding, as significant of genius, as the most distinguished success in any of the commoner walks of fiction; and a contrary view is reasonably to be described as a fanatical development of an artistic doctrine perfectly sound and of vital importance in its right application, but liable, like other cults, to incur reaction when carried to extremes. After "The Idiot Boy" and *The Prelude* came *The Lady of Shalott* and the *Idylls of the King;* after Trollope came King Romance again; and even if Poe were eclipsed for a time, posterity would still be to reckon with.

Notes

1. Mr. Howells, it may be remembered, has followed Mr. James in speaking slightingly of Poe; and, indeed, the general current of American criticism is still in that direction. In face of these judgments, which dispose not only of performance but of calibre, one is driven to wonder how the writers estimate their own total powers, as against Poe's.

2. See the *Saturday Review* of Nov. 28, 1885, for a well-expressed criticism to the same effect, published a few weeks after the foregoing, but doubtless by a writer who had never seen that. Cp. Hennequin, *Ecrivaim Francises,* pp. 120–130.

3. The unfinished "Journal of Julius Rodman" (published in Mr. Ingram's *edition de luxe* of the tales and poems) presents us with a somewhat more individualised type, but there too the interest centres in the incidents.

—John Mackinnon Robertson, "Poe," (1885)
New Essays Towards a Critical Method, 1897, pp. 92–104

TALES

MARGARET FULLER "POE'S TALES" (1845)

In this book review, Fuller, an American writer, critic, and early feminist thinker, praises Poe's gifts for writing short stories at a time when so many poor examples of the form are proliferating.

⟫⟫⟫   ⟫⟫⟫   ⟫⟫⟫

Mr. Poe's tales need no aid of newspaper comment to give them popularity; they have secured it. We are glad to see them given to the public in this neat form, so that thousands more may be entertained by them without injury to their eyesight.

No form of literary activity has so terribly degenerated among us as the tale. Now that everybody who wants a new hat or bonnet takes this way to earn one from the magazines or annuals, we are inundated with the very flimsiest fabrics ever spun by mortal brain. Almost every person of feeling or fancy could supply a few agreeable and natural narratives, but when instead of using their materials spontaneously they set to work with geography in hand to find unexplored nooks of wild scenery in which to locate their Indians or interesting farmers' daughters, or with some abridgment of history to hunt monarchs or heroes yet unused to become the subjects of their crude coloring, the sale-work produced is a sad affair indeed and "gluts the market" to the sorrow both of buyers and lookers-on.

In such a state of things the writings of Mr. Poe are a refreshment, for they are the fruit of genuine observations and experience, combined with an invention which is not "making up," as children call their way of contriving stories, but a penetration into the causes of things which leads to original but credible results. His narrative proceeds with vigor, his colors are applied with discrimination, and where the effects are fantastic they are not unmeaningly so.

The "Murders in the Rue Morgue" especially made a great impression upon those who did not know its author and were not familiar with his mode of treatment. Several of his stories make us wish he would enter the higher walk of the metaphysical novel and, taking a mind of the self-possessed and deeply marked sort that suits him, give us a deeper and longer acquaintance with its life and the springs of its life than is possible in the compass of these tales.

As Mr. Poe is a professed critic and of all the band the most unsparing to others, we are surprised to find some inaccuracies in the use of words, such as these: "he had with him many books, but rarely *employed* them."—"His results have, in truth, the *whole air* of intuition."

The degree of skill shown in the management of revolting or terrible circumstances makes the pieces that have such subjects more interesting than the others. Even the failures are those of an intellect of strong fiber and well-chosen aim.

—Margaret Fuller,
"Poe's Tales," New York *Daily Tribune,*
July 11, 1845

Martin Farquhar Tupper
"American Romance" (1846)

Tupper was a British poet best known for his *Proverbial Philosophy*. He criticizes many of Poe's tales for being either immoral or unbelievable (or both), but he admires the technical achievements of "The Gold Bug," "The Murders in the Rue Morgue," and "A Descent into the Maelstrom."

"Fresh fields and pastures new" are obviously the likeliest places wherein to look for inventive genius and original power; accordingly, we are not surprised to hear that the author of this remarkable volume is an American. His work has come to our shores recommended by success upon its own; and that such success is no more than it deserves we will undertake to demonstrate to our readers, before we put the finishing point to our note of admiration.

First, however, and by way of getting a troublesome duty out of the way at once, we must qualify our coming praises, by a light and wholesome touch of censure. This, in a general way, and without descending into a specification of instances, must be held to apply to such a tale as the "Black Cat," which is impossible and revolting; to such an argument as "Mesmeric Revelation," which far too daringly attempts a solution of that deepest of riddles, the nature of the Deity; to such a dialogue as "Lionising," simply foolish; and to such a juvenile production as the "Fall of the House of Usher." These, though not without their own flashes of genius, might have been omitted to great advantage: and the remainder of the volume, acute, interesting and graphic, would then have stood consistent with itself—*totus, teres, atque rotundus.*

Induction, and a microscopic power of analysis, seem to be the pervading characteristics of the mind of Edgar Poe. Put him on any trail, and he traces it as keenly as a Blackfoot or Ojibway; give him any clue, and he unravels the whole web of mystery: never was bloodhound more sagacious in scenting out a murderer; nor Oedipus himself more shrewd in solving an enigma. He would make a famous Transatlantic Vidocq, and is capable of more address and exploit than a Fouché; he has all his wits about him ready for use, and could calmly investigate the bursting of a bombshell; he is a hound never at fault, a moral tightrope dancer never thrown from his equilibrium; a close keen reasoner, whom no sophistry distracts—nothing foreign or extraneous diverts him from his inquiry.

But it is time to present the reader with specimens of some of our author's peculiarities. "The Gold-Bug," a strange tale of treasure-seeking, forcibly demonstrates how able an ally Dr. Young and M. Champollion would have found in Edgar Poe, whilst engaged in deciphering Egyptian hieroglyphics.

Take, again, the marvellous train of analytical reasoning whereby he arrives at truth in the "Rue Morgue Murders"; a tale wherein the horror of the incidents is overborne by the acuteness of the arguments; and is introduced by a specimen of mind-reading which Dr. Elliotson's Adolphe or Okey might vainly attempt to equal. "The Mystery of Marie Rogêt" is similar in keenness; and to us at least the only mystery in the matter now is,—why was, not the "dark sailor" apprehended? Additional interest is given to these twin tales of terror from their historic truth; and from the strange fact that the guesser's sagacity has anticipated in the last case the murderer's confession.

Let us now turn to other pages equally brightened by genius, while they are untarnished with the dread details of crime. "A Descent into the Maelström" has but one fault; it is too deliberate; there is too little in it of the rushing havoc, the awful eddying of that northern sea's black throat. Still there is magnificent writing in the tale; and a touch is given below of our author's peculiar presence of mind which would stand him in good stead on a barrel of invited gunpowder. . . .

The "Conversation Between Eiros and Charmion" is full of terror and instruction; true to philosophy and to holy writ, it details the probable mode of the final conflagration:

> If the *Vestiges of Creation* have obtained so much celebrity from attempting to shew and explain to mankind the *Beginning* of things, we may surely anticipate fame for the author who has thus, in a like philosophizing excursus, depicted to us their *Ending*.

Let us, in conclusion, draw the reader's attention to the only piece of Poe-try—(the pun is quite irresistible)—wherewith Mr. Poe has favoured us in this book. It occurs in the otherwise condemned tale of "Usher"; and not only half redeems that ill-considered production, but makes us wish for many more such staves. Its title is the "Haunted Palace," and it purports to be a madman's rhapsody on his own mind:

> After perusing these extracts, and our own honest verdict of the book, we are sure that our readers will not long be strangers to the Tales of Edgar Poe.

—Martin Farquhar Tupper, "American Romance,"
London *Literary Gazette*, January 31, 1846

Robert Louis Stevenson (1875)

Stevenson is best known for his novels *Treasure Island*, *Kidnapped*, and *The Strange Case of Dr. Jekyll and Mr. Hyde*. In this review, he criticizes Poe's lack of humanity as well as his highly artificial writing style, both common themes among those who dislike Poe. Stevenson acknowledges Poe's technical capabilities, but he argues that Poe uses tricks to make his impressions: "he cheats with gusto." Stevenson concludes that whatever else Poe's work may be, it is not art.

The tales themselves (in *The Works of Edgar Allan Poe*, ed. John H. Ingram, Vols. 1 and 2) are all before us in these two volumes; and though Mr. Ingram does not tell us whether they are there printed in chronological order, I fancy we shall not be mistaken in regarding some of the last stories in the second volume, as being also among the last he wrote. There is no trace, in these, of the brilliant and often solid workmanship of his better moments. The stories are ill-conceived and written carelessly. There is much laughter; but it is a very ghastly sort of laughter at best—the laughter of those, in his own words, "who laugh, but smile no more." He seems to have lost respect for himself, for his art, and for his audience. When he dealt before with horrible images, he dealt with them for some definite enough creative purpose, and with a certain measure and gravity suitable to the occasion; but he scatters them abroad in these last tales with an indescribable and sickening levity, with something of the ghoul or the furious lunatic that surpasses what one had imagined to oneself of Hell. There is a duty to the living more important than any charity to the dead; and it would be criminal in the reviewer to spare one harsh word in the expression of his own loathing and horror, lest, by its absence, another victim should be permitted to soil himself with the perusal of the infamous "King Pest." He who could write "King Pest" had ceased to be a human being. For his own sake, and out of an infinite compassion for so lost a spirit, one is glad to think of him as dead. But if it is pity that we feel towards Poe, it is certainly not pity that inspires us as we think of Baudelaire, who could sit down in cold blood, and dress out in suitable French this pointless farrago of horrors. There is a phase of contempt that, if indulged, transcends itself and becomes a phase of passionate self-satisfaction; so for the weal of our own spirits, it is better to think no more of Baudelaire or "King Pest."

It is not the fashion of Poe's earlier tales to be pointless, however it may be with these sorry ones of the end. Pointlessness is, indeed, the very last charge that could be brought reasonably against them. He has the true story-teller's instinct. He knows the little nothings that make stories, or mar them. He knows how to enhance the significance of any situation, and give colour and life with seemingly irrelevant particulars. Thus, the whole spirit of "The Cask of Amontillado" depends on Fortunato's carnival costume of cap and bells and motley. When Poe had once hit upon this device of dressing the victim grotesquely, he had found the key of the story; and so he sends him with uneven steps along the catacombs of the Montresors, and the last sound we hear out of the walled-up recess is the jingling of the bells upon his cap. Admirable, also, is the use he makes of the striking clock at Prince Prospero's feast, in "The Mask of the Red Death." Each time the clock struck (the reader will remember), it struck so loudly that the music and the dancing must cease perforce until it had made an end; as the hours ran on towards midnight, these pauses grew naturally longer; the maskers had the more time to think and look at one another, and their thoughts were none the more pleasant. Thus, as each hour struck, there went a jar about the assemblage; until, as the reader will remember, the end comes suddenly. Now, this is quite legitimate; no one need be ashamed of being frightened or excited by such means; the rules of the game have been respected; only, by the true instinct of the story-teller he has told his story to the best advantage, and got full value for his imaginations. This is not so always, however; for sometimes he will take a high note falsetto; sometimes, by a sort of conjuring trick, get more out of his story than he has been able to put into it; and, while the whole garrison is really parading past us on the esplanade, continue to terrify us from the battlements with sham cannon and many fierce-looking shakos upon broomsticks. For example, in "The Pit and the Pendulum," after having exhausted his bedevilled imagination in the conception of the pendulum and the red-hot collapsing walls, he finds he can figure forth nothing more horrible for the pit; and yet the pit was to be the crowning horror. This is how he affects his purpose (vol. i. p. 214):—

> Amid the thought of the fiery destruction that impended, the idea of the coolness of the well came over my soul like balm. I rushed to its deadly brink. I threw my straining vision below. The glare from the enkindled roof illumined its inmost recesses. Yet for a wild moment did my spirit refuse to comprehend the meaning of what I saw. At length it forced—it wrestled its way into my soul—it burned itself in upon my shuddering reason. O for a voice to speak! oh horror! oh, any horror but this!

And that is all. He knows no more about the pit than you or I do. It is a pure imposture, a piece of audacious, impudent thimble-rigging; and yet, even with such bugs as these he does manage to frighten us. You will find the same artifice repeated in "Hans Pfaal," about the mysteries of the moon; and again, though with a difference, in the abrupt conclusion of *Arthur Gordon Pym*. His imagination is a willing horse; but three times, as you see, he has killed it under him by over-riding, and come limping to the post on foot. With what a good grace does he not turn these failures to advantage, and make capital out of each imaginative bankruptcy! Even on a critical retrospect, it is hard to condemn him as he deserves; for he cheats with gusto.

After this knowledge of the stage, this cleverness at turning a story out, perhaps the most striking of Poe's peculiarities is an almost incredible insight into the debateable region between sanity and madness. The "Imp of the Perverse," for example, is an important contribution to morbid psychology; so, perhaps, is "The Man of the Crowd;" "Berenice," too, for as horrible as it is, touches a chord in one's own breast, though perhaps it is a chord that had better be left alone; and the same idea recurs in "The Tell-Tale Heart." Sometimes we can go with him the whole way with a good conscience; sometimes—instead of saying, yes, this is how I should be if I were just a little more mad than ever I was—we can say frankly, this is what I am. There is one passage of analysis in this more normal vein, in the story of "Ligeia," as to the expression of Ligeia's eyes. He tells us how he felt ever on the point of understanding their strange quality, and ever baffled at the last moment, just as "in our endeavours to recall to memory something long forgotten, we often find ourselves upon the very verge of remembrance, without being able in the end to remember;" and how, in streams of running water, in the ocean, in the falling of a meteor, in the glances of unusually aged people, in certain sounds from stringed instruments, in certain passages from books, in the commonest sights and sensations of the universe, he found ever and anon some vague inexplicable analogy to the expression and the power of these loved eyes. This, at least, or the like of it, we all know. But, in the general, his subtlety was more of a snare to him than anything else. "Nil sapientiae odiosius," he quotes himself from Seneca, "nil sapientiae odiosius acumine nimio." And though it is delightful enough in the C. Auguste Dupin trilogy—it was Baudelaire who called it a trilogy—yet one wearies in the long run of this strain of ingenuity; one begins to marvel at the absence of the good homespun motives and sentiments that do the business of the everyday world; although the demonstrator is clever, and the cases instructive and probably unique, one begins to weary of going round this madhouse, and long for the society of some plain harmless person, with business habits and a frock coat, and nerves not much more shattered than the majority of his plain and harmless contemporaries. Nor did this exaggerated insight make him wearisome only; it did worse than that—it sometimes led him astray. Thus, in "The Pit and the Pendulum," when the hero has been condemned, "the sound of the inquisitorial voices," he says, seemed merged in one dreamy indeterminate hum. "It conveyed to my soul the idea of *revolution,* perhaps from its association in fancy with the burr of a mill-wheel." Now, it wants but a moment's reflection to prove how much too clever Poe has been here, how far from true reason he has been carried by this *nimium acumen.* For—the man being giddy—the "idea of revolution" must have preceded the merging of the inquisitorial voices into an indeterminate hum, and most certainly could not have followed it as any fanciful deduction. Again, as before in the matter of effect, one cannot help fearing that some of the subtlety is fustian. To take an example of both sorts of imagination—the fustian and the sincere—from the same story *Arthur Gordon Pym:* the four survivors on board the brig *Grampus* have lashed themselves to the windlass, lest they should be swept away; one of them, having drawn his lashings too tight, is ready to yield up his spirit for a long while, is nearly cut in two, indeed, by the cord about his loins. "No sooner had we removed it, however," Poe goes on, "than he spoke and seemed to experience instant relief—being able to move with much greater ease than either Parker or myself" (two who had not tied themselves so closely). *"This was no doubt owing to the loss of blood."* Now, whether medically correct or not, this is, on the face of it, sincerely imagined. Whether correct or not in fact, it is correct in art. Poe evidently believed it true; evidently it appeared to him that thus, and not otherwise, the thing would fall out. Now, turn a page back, and we shall find (ii. 78), in the description of the visions that went before Pym while thus bound, something to be received very much more deliberately. "I now remember," he writes,

> that in all which passed before my mind's eye, *motion* was a predominant idea. Thus I never fancied any stationary object, such as a house, a mountain, or anything of that kind; but windmills, ships, large birds, balloons, people on horseback, carriages driving furiously, and similar moving objects presented themselves in endless succession.

This may be true; it may be the result of great erudition in the thoughts of people in such sore straits; but the imagination does not adopt these details, they do not commend themselves to our acceptance, it is nowise apparent why stationary objects should *not* present themselves to the fancy of a man tied to the windlass of a dismasted brig; and, this being so, the whole passage, as art, stands condemned. If it be mere causeless fancy (as it seems), it is fustian of the most unpardonable sort; if it be erudition,—well then, it may be erudition, but never art. Things are fit for art so far only as they are both true and apparent. To make what I mean clear: Mr. Ruskin, in some one or other of his delightful books, quotes and approves a poet (I think it was Homer) who said of a brave man that he was as brave as a fly; and proceeds, in his usual happy manner, to justify the epithet. The fly, he tells us, is in very deed the most madly courageous of all created beings. And therefore the simile is good—excellent good. And yet the reader's instinct would tell him, I am sure, that the simile is a vile simile. Let him prefer his instinct before Mr. Ruskin's natural history. For, though it be based on what is true, this comparison is not based upon a truth that is apparent; it does not commend itself to our acceptance; it is not art.

—Robert Louis Stevenson,
Academy, January 2, 1875, pp. 1–2

BRANDER MATTHEWS (1885)

Matthews, a literature professor, revisits Lowell's appreciation of Poe's genius, especially as it combines analytical detail with imagination. Matthews points out that the best of Poe's tales have never been matched by any writer.

Although it may be doubted whether the fiery and tumultuous rush of a volcano, which might be taken to typify Poe, is as powerful or impressive in the end as the calm and inevitable progression of a glacier, to which, for the purposes of this comparison only, we may liken Hawthorne, yet the weight and influence of Poe's work are indisputable. One might hazard the assertion that in all Latin countries he is the best known of American authors. Certainly no American writer has been so widely accepted in France. Nothing better of its kind has ever been done than the 'Pit and the Pendulum,' or than the 'Fall of the House of Usher' (which has been compared aptly with Browning's *Childe Roland to the Dark Tower Came* for its power of suggesting intellectual desolation). Nothing better of its kind has ever been done than the 'Gold Bug,' or than the 'Purloined Letter,' or than the 'Murders in the Rue Morgue.' The 'Murders in the Rue Morgue' is indeed a story of the most marvellous skill: it was the first of its kind, and to this day it remains a model, not only unsurpassed, but unapproachable. It was the first of detective stories; and it has had thousands of imitations and no rival. The originality, the ingenuity, the verisimilitude of this tale and of its fellows are beyond all praise. Poe had a faculty which one may call imaginative ratiocination to a degree beyond all other writers of fiction. He did not at all times keep up to the high level, in one style, of the 'Fall of the House of Usher,' and, in another, of the 'Murders in the Rue Morgue,' and it was not to be expected that he should. Only too often did he sink to the grade of the ordinary 'Tale from *Blackwood*,' which he himself satirised in his usual savage vein of humour.

And yet there is no denying that even in his flimsiest and most tawdry tales we see the truth of Mr. Lowell's assertion that Poe had "two of the prime qualities of genius,—a faculty of vigorous yet minute analysis, and a wonderful fecundity of imagination." Mr. Lowell said also that Poe combined "in a very remarkable manner two faculties which are seldom found united,—a power of influencing the mind of the reader by the impalpable shadows of mystery, and a minuteness of detail which does not leave a pin or a button unnoticed. Both are, in truth, the natural results of the predominating quality of his mind, to which we have before alluded,—analysis." In Poe's hands, however, the enumeration of pins and buttons, the exact imitation of the prosaic facts of humdrum life in this workaday world, is not an end, but a means only, whereby he constructs and intensifies the shadow of mystery which broods over the things thus realistically portrayed.

—Brander Matthews, *The Philosophy of the Short-Story*
(1885), 1901, pp. 44–48

Lewis E. Gates "Edgar Allan Poe" (1900)

Gates, a Harvard literature professor, asserts that Poe's best poetry is actually to be found in his prose. He says that Poe's short stories are really prose poems, works that artistically present situations, characters, and events in such a way as to produce a particular effect—humor or terror, for instance—in the reader. Students could use this essay to explore the differences between poetry and prose, especially looking at Poe's theory of each.

Gates suggests that Poe's tales have a superficial quality; Poe is less interested in a detailed picture of characters than in using a character to create a desired effect on the reader. In other words, characters are merely devices in Poe's fiction, not actual recognizable individuals.

Gates calls this Poe's "successful artificiality." Students writing character studies might examine Gates's assertions. Is it true that Poe has no fully developed characters? How does a character's given personality work to achieve the author's aims?

Gates also criticizes Poe's "inhumanity." He argues that Poe seems callous when presenting unpleasant details and often comes off as dry or insensitive. Gates further suggests that this dryness leads to a kind of insincerity, as Poe manipulates his readers to feel certain things, rather than eliciting more authentic emotions. These are fairly common criticisms of Poe. Students might look at certain Poe stories to challenge or confirm these views.

Gates concludes that Poe was a master of technique and of the intellect but lacked the real personality needed to produce great literature. Gates argues that Poe adroitly manipulates the reader's mind but does not move the reader on a more visceral level. As such, Poe becomes more of a clever chess player, arranging the pieces into a successful pattern to achieve victory, than a genuine writer who can create real emotional feelings. Students might use this essay to look at the difference between a true artist and a creator of effects, perhaps by comparing Poe's stories with Hawthorne's or Melville's.

***

Poe is a better poet in his prose than in his poetry. A reader of Poe's poetry, if he be quick to take umbrage at artificiality and prone to cavil, feels, after a dozen poems, like attempting an inventory of Poe's literary workshop—the material Poe uses is so uniform and the objects he fashions are so few and inevitable. The inventory might run somewhat as follows: One plaster bust of Pallas slightly soiled; one many-wintered Raven croaking *Nevermore;* a parcel of decorative names—Auber, Yaanek, Zante, Israfel; a few robes of sorrow, a somewhat frayed funeral pall, and a coil of Conqueror Worms; finally, one beautiful lay figure whom the angels name indifferently Lenore, Ulalume, and Annabel Lee. Masterly as is Poe's use of this poetical outfit, subtle as are his cadences and his sequences of tone-colour, it is only rarely that he makes us forget the cleverness of his manipulation and wins us into accepting his moods and imagery with that unconscious and almost hypnotic subjection to his will which the true poet secures from his readers.

In the best of his visionary *Tales,* on the other hand, Poe is much more apt to have his way with us. He works with a far greater variety of appliances, which it is by no means easy to number and call by name; the effects he aims at are manifold and not readily noted and classified; and the details that his imagination elaborates come upon us with a tropical richness and apparent confusion that mimic well the splendid lawlessness and undesignedness of nature. Moreover, even if the artifice in these tales were more palpable than it is, it would be less offensive than in poetry, inasmuch as the standard of sincerity is in such performances confessedly less exacting. The likeness in aim and in effect between the tales and the poems, however, cannot be missed—between such tales as "Ligeia" and "Eleonora" and such poems as "The Raven" and "Ulalume." Mr. Leslie Stephan has somewhere spoken of De Quincey's impassioned prose as aiming to secure in unmeasured speech very many of the same effects that Keats's *Odes* produce in authentic verse. This holds true also of the best of Poe's romances; they are really prose-poems. And, indeed, Poe has himself recognized in his essay on Hawthorne the close kinship between tale and poem, assigning to the poem subjects in the treatment of which the creation of beauty is the ruling motive, and leaving to the prose tale the creation of all other single effects, such as horror, humour, and terror. Both poem and tale must be brief, absolutely unified, and must create a single overwhelming mood.

The world that Poe's genuinely fantastic tales take us into has the burnish, the glow, the visionary radiance of the world of Romantic poetry; it is as luxuriantly unreal, too, as phantasmagoric—though it lacks the palpitating, buoyant loveliness of the nature that such poets as Shelley reveal, and is somewhat enamelled or metallic in its finish. Its glow and burnish come largely from the concreteness of Poe's imagination, from his inveterate fondness for sensations, for colour, for light, for luxuriant vividness of detail. Poe had the tingling senses of the genuine poet, senses that vibrated like delicate silver wire to every impact. He was an amateur of sensations and loved to lose himself in the O *Altitudo* of a perfume or a musical note. He pored over his sensations and refined upon them, and felt to the core of his heart the peculiar thrill that darted from each. He had seventy times seven colours in his emotional rainbow, and was swift to fancy the evanescent hue of feeling that might spring from every sight or sound—from the brazen note, for example, of the clock in "The Masque of the Red Death," from "the slender stems" of the ebony and silver trees in "Eleonora," or from the "large and luminous orbs" of Ligeia's eyes. Out of the vast mass of these vivid sensations— "passion-winged ministers of thought"—Poe shaped and fashioned the world in which his romances confine us, a world that is, therefore, scintillating and burnished and vibrant, quite unlike the world in Hawthorne's tales, which is woven out of dusk and moonlight.

Yet, curiously enough, this intense brilliancy of surface does not tend to exorcise mystery, strangeness, terror from Poe's world, or to transfer his stories into the region of everyday fact. Poe is a conjurer who does not need to have the lights turned down. The effects that he is most prone to aim at are, of course, the shivers of awe, crispings of the nerves, shuddering thrills that come from a sudden, overwhelming sense of something uncanny, abnormal, ghastly, lurking in the heart of life. And these nervous perturbations are even more powerfully excited by those of his stories that, like "Eleonora" and "Ligeia," have a lustrous finish, than by sketches that, like "Shadow" and "Silence," deal with twilight lands and half-visualized regions. In "The Masque of the Red Death," in "The Fall of the House of Usher," and in "A Descent into the Maelstrom," the details of incident and background flash themselves on our imaginations with almost painful distinctness.

The terror in Poe's tales is not the terror of the child that cannot see in the dark, but the terror of diseased nerves and morbid imaginations, that see with dreadful visionary vividness and feel a mortal pang. Poe is a past master of the moods of diseased mental life, and in the interests of some one or other of these semi-hysterical moods many of his most uncannily prevailing romances are written. They are prose-poems that realize for us such half-frenetic glimpses of the world as madmen have; and *suggest* in us for the moment the breathless, haggard mood of the victim of hallucinations.

It must not, however, be forgotten that Poe wrote tales of ratiocination as well as romances of death. In his ability to turn out with equal skill stories bordering on madness and stories where intellectual analysis, shrewd induction, reasoning upon evidence, all the processes of typically sane mental life, are carried to the utmost pitch of precision and effectiveness, lies one of the apparent anomalies of Poe's genius and art. In "The Murders in the Rue Morgue," "The Mystery of Marie Roget," and "The Purloined Letter," Poe seems sanity incarnate, pure mental energy untouched by moods or passions, weaving and unweaving syllogisms and tracking out acutely the subtlest play of thought. What in these stories has become of Poe the fancy-monger, the mimic maniac, the specialist in moodiness and abnormality?

After all, the difficulty here suggested is only superficial and yields speedily to a little careful analysis. We have not really to deal with a puzzling case of double personality, with an author who at his pleasure plays at being Dr. Jekyll or Mr. Hyde. In all Poe's stories the same personality is at work, the same methods are followed, and the material used, though at first sight it may seem in the two classes of tales widely diverse, will also turn out to be quite the same, at any rate in its artificiality, in its remoteness from real complex human nature, and in its origin in the mind of the author. Certain instructions that in an essay on Hawthorne Poe has given to would-be writers of tales are delightfully serviceable to the anxious unraveller of the apparent contradictions in Poe's personality. . . .

The shallowness of Poe's treatment of life and character is almost too obvious to need illustration. Not only does he disdain, as Hawthorne disdains, to treat any individual character with minute realistic detail, but he does not even portray typical characters in their large outlines, with a view to opening before us the permanent springs of human action or putting convincingly before us the radical elements of human nature. The actors in his stories are all one-idea'd creatures, monomaniac victims of passion, or grief, or of some perverse instinct, or of an insane desire to guess riddles. They are magniloquent *poseurs,* who dine off their hearts in public, or else morbidly ingenious intellects for the solving of complicated problems. The worthy Nietzsche declares somewhere that the actors in Wagner's music-dramas are always just a dozen steps from the mad-house. We may say the same of Poe's characters, with the exception of those that are merely Babbage calculating machines. Complex human characters, characters that are approximately true to the whole range of human motive and interest, Poe never gives us. He conceives of characters merely as means for securing his artificial effects on the nerves of his readers.

The world, too, into which Poe takes us, burnished as it is, vividly visualized as it is, is a counterfeit world, magnificently false like his characters. Sometimes it is a phantasmagoric world, full of romantic detail and sensuous splendour. Its bright meadows are luxuriant with asphodels, hyacinths, and acanthuses, are watered with limpid rivers of silence that lose themselves shimmeringly in blue Da Vinci distances, are lighted by tripletinted suns, and are finally shut in by the "golden walls of the universe." When not an exotic region of this sort, Poe's world is apt to be a dextrously contrived toy universe, full of trap-doors, unexpected passages, and clever mechanical devices of all sorts, fit to help the conjurer in securing his effects. Elaborately artificial in some fashion or other, Poe's world is sure to be, designed with nice malice to control the reader's imagination and put it at Poe's mercy. In short, in all that he does, in the material that he uses, in the characters that he conjures up to carry on the action of his stories, in his methods of weaving together incident and description and situation and action, Poe is radically artificial, a calculator of effects, a reckless scorner of fact and of literal truth.

And, indeed, it is just this successful artificiality that for many very modern temperaments constitutes Poe's special charm; he is thoroughly irresponsible; he whistles the commonplace down the wind and forgets everything but his dream, its harmony, its strenuous flight, its splendour and power. The devotees of art for art's sake have now for many years kept up a tradition of unstinted admiration for Poe. This has been specially true in France, where, indeed, men of all schools have joined in doing him honour. Barbey d'Aurevilly wrote an eulogistic essay on him as early as 1853, an essay to which he has since from time to time made various additions, the last in 1883. Baudelaire translated Poe's tales in several instalments between 1855 and 1865. Emile Hennequin published, a few years ago, an elaborate study and life of Poe; and Stephane Mallarme has of late conferred a new and perhaps somewhat dubious immortality upon the "Raven," through a translation into very symbolistic prose. In truth, Poe was a decadent before the days of decadence, and he has the distinction of having been one of the earliest defiant practisers of art for art's sake. In his essay on the "Poetic Principle," he expressly declared that a poem should be written solely "for the poem's sake,"—a phrase which almost anticipates the famous formula of modern Eestheticism. The drift of this essay, Poe's opinion elsewhere recorded, and his practice as a story-teller, all agree in implying or urging that art is its own justification, that the sole aim of art is the creation of beauty, and that art and actual life need have nothing to do with one another. To be sure, Poe's comments on everyday life have not acquired quite the exquisite contempt and the epigrammatic finish characteristic of modern decadence; yet the root of the matter was in Poe—witness a letter in which he boasts of his insensibility to the charms of "temporal life," and of being "profoundly excited" solely "by music and by some poems."

Poe and his heroes curiously anticipate, in many respects, the morbid dreamers whom French novelists of the decadent school have of recent years repeatedly studied, and of whom Huysmans's Des Esseintes may be taken as a type. The hero in "The Fall of the House of Usher," with his "cadaverousness of complexion," his "eye large, liquid, and luminous beyond comparison," his "habitual trepidancy," his "hollow-sounding enunciation," "his morbid acuteness of the senses," and his suffering when exposed to the odours of certain flowers and to all sounds save those of a few stringed instruments, might be a preliminary study for Huysmans's memorable Des Esseintes. Usher has not the French hero's sophistication and self-consciousness; he suffers dumbly, and has not Des Esseintes's consolation in knowing himself a "special soul," supersensitive and delicate beyond the trite experience of nerves and senses prescribed by practical life. He does not carry on his morbid experimentations debonairly as does Des Esseintes, and he takes his diseases too seriously. But he nevertheless anticipates Des Esseintes astonishingly in looks, in nerves, in physique, and even in tricks of manner. Poe's heroes, too, are forerunners of modern decadents in their refinings upon sensation, in their fusion of the senses, and in their submergence in moods. As Herr Nordau says of the Symbolists, they have eyes in their ears; they see sounds; they smell colours. One of them hears rays of light that fall upon his retina. They are all extraordinarily alive to the "unconsidered trifles" of sensation. The man in the "Pit and the Pendulum" smells the odour of the sharp steel blade that swings past him. They detect with morbid delicacy of perception shades of feeling that give likeness to the most apparently diverse sensations. The lover in "Ligeia" feels in his "intense scrutiny of Ligeia's eyes" the same sentiment that at other times overmasters him "in the survey of a rapidly growing vine, in the contemplation of a moth, a butterfly, . . . in the falling of a meteor, . . . in the glances of unusually aged people," and when listening to "certain sounds from stringed instruments." Moods become absorbing and monopolizing in the lives of these vibrating temperaments. "Men have called me mad," the lover in "Eleonora" ingratiatingly assures us; "but the question is not yet settled whether madness is or is not the loftiest intelligence; whether much that is glorious, whether all that is profound, does not spring from disease of thought—from moods of mind exalted at the expense of the general intellect." Finally, Poe's heroes anticipate the heroes of modern decadence in feeling the delicate artistic challenge of sin and of evil: they hardly reach the audacities of French Diabolism and Sadism; but at least they have the whim of doing or fancying moral evil that aesthetic good may come.

All these characteristics of Poe's work may be summed up by saying that his heroes are apt to be neuropaths or degenerates. And doubtless Poe himself was a degenerate, if one cares to use the somewhat outworn idiom of the evangelist of the Philistines. He had the ego-mania of the degenerate, a fact which shows itself strikingly in his art through his preoccupation with death. In his poetry and prose alike the fear of death as numbing the precious core of personality is an obsession with him, and such subjects as premature burial, metempsychosis, revivification after death, the sensations that may go with the change from mortality to immortality (see the "Colloquy of Monos and Una"), had an irresistible fascination for him. Moreover, throughout Poe's art there are signs of ego-mania in the almost entire lack of the social sympathies. Where in Poe's stories do we find portrayed the sweet and tender relationships and affections that make human life endurable? Where are friendship and frank comradeship and the love of brothers and sisters and of parents and children?

Where are the somewhat trite but after all so necessary virtues of loyalty, patriotism, courage, pity, charity, self-sacrifice? Such old-fashioned qualities and capacities, the stuff out of which what is worth while in human nature has heretofore been wrought, are curiously unrecognized and unportrayed in Poe's fiction. They seem to have had no artistic meaning for him—these so obvious and commonplace elements in man and life. Perhaps they simply seemed to him not the stuff that dreams are made of.

When all is said, there is something a bit inhuman in Poe, which, while at times it may give a special tinge to our pleasure in his art, occasionally vitiates or destroys that pleasure. His taste is not immaculate; he will go any length in search of a shudder. Sometimes he is fairly repulsive because of his callous recital of loathsome physical details, for example in his description of the decimated Brigadier-General, in "The Man That Was Used Up." In "King Pest," "The Premature Burial," and "M. Valdemar," there is this same almost vulgar insensibility in the presence of the unclean and disgusting. At times, this callousness leads to artistic mischance, and causes a shudder of laughter where Poe wants a shiver of awe. Surely this is apt to be the case in "Berenice," the story where the hero is fascinated by the beautiful teeth of the heroine, turns amateur dentist after her death, and in a frenzy of professional enthusiasm breaks open her coffin, and extracts her incisors, bicuspids, and molars, thirty-two altogether—the set was complete.

When this inhumanity of Poe's does not lead to actual repulsiveness or to unintentional grotesqueness, it is nevertheless responsible for a certain aridity and intellectual cruelty that in the last analysis will be found pervading pretty much all he has written. This is what Barbey d'Aurevilly has in mind when he speaks of Poe's *secheresse*, the terrible dryness of his art. And looking at the matter wholly apart from the question of ethics, this dryness is a most serious defect in Poe's work as an artist. His stories and characters have none of the buoyancy, the tender, elastic variableness, and the grace of living things; they are hard in finish, harsh in surface, mechanically inevitable in their working out. They seem calculated, the result of ingenious calculation, not because any particular detail impresses the reader as conspicuously false—Poe keeps his distance from life too skilfully and consistently for this—but because of their all-pervading lack of deeply human imagination and interest, because of that shallowness in Poe's hold upon life that has already been noted. The stories and the characters seem the work of pure intellect, of intellect divorced from heart; and for that very reason they do not wholly satisfy, when judged by the most exacting artistic standards. They seem the product of some ingenious mechanism for the manufacture of fiction, of some surpassing rival of Maelzel's chess-playing automaton. This faultily faultless accuracy and precision of movement may very likely be a penalty Poe has to submit to because of his devotion to art for art's sake. He is too much engrossed in treatment and manipulation; his dexterity of execution perhaps presupposes, at any rate goes along with, an almost exclusive interest in technical problems and in "effects," to the neglect of what is vital and human in the material he uses.

Closely akin to this dryness of treatment is a certain insincerity of tone or flourish of manner, that often interferes with our enjoyment of Poe. We become suddenly aware of the gleaming eye and complacent smile of the concealed manipulator in the writing-automaton. The author is too plainly lying in wait for us; or he is too ostentatiously exhibiting his cleverness and resource, his command of the tricks of the game. One of the worst things that can be said of Poe from this point of view is that he contains the promise and potency of Mr. Robert Hichens, and of other cheap English decadents. Poe himself is never quite a mere acrobat; but he suggests the possible coming of the acrobat, the clever tumbler with the ingenious grimace and the palm itching for coppers.

The same perfect mastery of technique that is characteristic of Poe's treatment of material is noticeable in his literary style. When one stops to consider it, Poe's style, particularly in his romances, is highly artificial, an exquisitely fabricated medium. Poe is fond of inversions and involutions in his sentence-structure, and of calculated rhythms that either throw into relief certain picturesque words, or symbolize in some reverberant fashion the mood of the moment. He seems to have felt very keenly the beauty of De Quincey's intricate and sophisticated cadences, and more than once he actually echoes some of the most noteworthy of them in his own distribution of accents. Special instances of this might be pointed out in "Eleonora" and in "The Premature Burial." Poe's fondness for artificial musical effects is also seen in his emphatic reiteration of specially picturesque phrases, a trick of manner that every one associates with his poetry, and that is more than once found in his prose writings. "And, all at once, the moon arose through the thin ghastly mist, and was crimson in color. And mine eyes fell upon a huge gray rock which stood by the shore of the river, and was lighted by the light of the moon. And the rock was gray, and ghastly, and tall—and the rock was gray." Echolalia, Herr Nordau would probably call this trick in Poe's verse and prose, and he would regard it as an incontestable proof of Poe's degeneracy. Nevertheless, the beauty of the effects to which this mannerism leads in Poe's more artificial narratives is very marked.

In Poe's critical essays his style takes on an altogether different tone and movement, and becomes analytical, rapid, incisive, almost acrid in its severity and intellectuality. The ornateness and the beauty of cadence and colour that are characteristic of his decorative prose disappear entirely. Significantly enough, Macaulay was his favourite literary critic. "The style and general conduct of Macaulay's critical papers," Poe assures his readers, "could scarcely be improved." A strange article of faith to find in the literary creed of a dreamer, an amateur of moods, an artistic epicure. Yet that Poe was sincere in this opinion is proved by the characteristics of his own literary essays. He emulates Macaulay in his briskness, in the downrightness of his assertions, in his challengingly demonstrative tone, and in his unsensitiveness to the artistic shade. Of course, he is far inferior to Macaulay in knowledge and in thoroughness of literary training, while he surpasses him in acuteness of analysis and in insight into technical problems.

Poe's admiration for Macaulay and his emulation of him in his critical writings are merely further illustrations of the peculiar intellectual aridity that has already been noted as characteristic of him. Demonic intellectual ingenuity is almost the last word for Poe's genius as far as regards his real personality, the quintessential vital energy of the man. His intellect was real; everything else about him was exquisite feigning. His passion, his human sympathy, his love of nature, all the emotions that go into his fiction, have a counterfeit unreality about them. Not that they are actually hypocritical, but that they seem unsubstantial, mimetic, not the expression of a genuine nature. There was something of the cherub in Poe, and he had to extract his feelings from his head. Much of the time a reader of Poe is cajoled into a delighted forgetfulness of all this unreality, Poe is so adroit a manipulator, such a master of technique. He adapts with unerring tact his manner to his matter and puts upon us the perfect spell of art. Moreover, even when a reader forces himself to take notice of Poe's artificiality, he may, if he be in the right temper, gain only an added delight, the sort of delight that comes from watching the exquisitely sure play of a painter's firm hand, adapting its action consciously to all the difficulties of its subject. Poe's precocious artistic sophistication is one of his rarest charms for the appreciative amateur. But if a reader be exorbitant and relentless and ask from Poe something more than intellectual resource and technical dexterity, he is pretty sure to be disappointed; Poe has little else to offer him. Doubtless it is Philistinish to ask for this something more; but people have always asked for it in the past, and seem likely to go on asking for it, even despite the fact that Herr Max Nordau has almost succeeded in reducing the request to an absurdity.

—Lewis E. Gates, "Edgar Allan Poe,"
Studies and Appreciations, 1900, pp. 110–28

Francis Thompson
"A Dreamer of Things Impossible" (1901)

Thompson, an English poet, begins by pointing out that Poe actually originated two of the most popular genres in British fiction: the detective story (most commonly associated with Arthur Conan Doyle) and science fiction or fantasy (represented by H.G. Wells). Thompson notes that Poe's genius was closely linked to his perceived madness, and Thompson compares Poe's tales to an opium dream, in which beauty is forever linked to terror.

It is a singular and not very creditable fact that (as we have recently experienced) the tales of Edgar Allan Poe should be difficult to procure in their entirety—apart from complete editions of his works. It is the more regrettable and singular because these creations of genius touch on two sides of the most popular modern schools of British fiction. Perhaps, indeed, this is the explanation of it: that the derivative has ousted the original. On the one side they have relation to the "detective" fiction of Dr. Conan Doyle, on the other they are in contact with the fantastic fiction of Mr. Wells. And between these two extremes is enthroned the very Poe—single, singular, with no predecessor and no authentic successor—unless it be the Stevenson of *Dr. Jekyll and Mr. Hyde*. That central and—artistically—supreme class of his tales is difficult to describe, for, indeed, to describe it is to describe Poe himself. It has been the tendency of the modern romantic school, and of modern poets in general, to make themselves the heroes of their own work. Chateaubriand, Byron, Shelley, are instances that come at once to one's mind, and Byron had strong influence on the early Poe. But not Byron, not even the author of *Epipsychidion* and *Alastor*, hardly the author of *Atala*, had such a peculiar gift for arabesquing their own lives, for transcendentalising themselves, their happenings, and environment. In nearly all these tales of idealistic terror or beauty, of which the "House of Usher" is an example, the hero is Poe himself; while they constantly revolve round situations suggested by his own history. To consider Poe is to consider these tales, to consider the tales is to consider Poe.

It is significant that his family was alleged to be descended from the Irish family of Le Poer—one of the English Pale, it is true, but thoroughly Irished by long residence and intermixture. The spirit of his work is Celtic, if the form of his poetry be not, indeed, of direct Celtic origin. It is at least possible that he should have seen some of Mangan's poems, and that unfortunate Irish poet anticipates Poe's peculiar form so strikingly that it is difficult to believe the resemblance can be accident alone. Yet, hardly less singular than such a coincidence would be, is the coincidence between the lives of the two men—identical in drudgery, misery, poverty, bondage to stimulants, and not far from identical in their deaths. It is the visionary and ethereal spirit of Celtic romance which informs the central group of tales no less than the poems. The Celtic temperament would go far to explain Poe's weakness and strength; his brilliant caprice, his pride and passion, his literary quarrels, his lack of robust moral stamina, his ready enslavement to alcohol. The Celtic visionariness, with its lack of hold on earth, is further accentuated in him by the love of strange ways in reading which he shared with Shelley. The trait is constantly appearing—implicit or explicit—in his heroes. The hero of the scarcely-sane "Ligeia" relates:

> With how vast a triumph, with how vivid a delight, with how much of all that is ethereal in hope did I feel—as she bent over me in studies but little sought, but less known—that delicious vista by slow degrees expanding before me, down whose long, gorgeous, and all untrodden path I might at length pass onward to the goal of a wisdom too divinely precious not to be forbidden?

His quotations testify to the same thing. Glanville, Raymond Lully, Platonists like Henry King; by his citation of them he indicates the shadowy and mysterious authors whom he found congenial to his mind. But not to penetrate them, so far as we can see, with the zeal of the thinker. He loved, as he says himself, "those who feel rather than those who think." They give him dreams, suggest the stuff of tales or poetry; they are indeed, to him, in no disparaging sense, "such stuff as dreams are made on." When a mind thus exalted, and of such natural development in one supermundane direction applies itself to fiction, the result must needs be strange, almost monstrous. The pearl is an abnormality, the result of external irritation which provokes the precious excretion. These tales are no less precious and abnormal. One feels the reading of them as it were an unlawful pleasure, wrung from pain, disease, calamity, and the fruitage of delirium. The cost is too great, and the pleasure itself scarcely human. We said of "Ligeia" that it was hardly sane; we might have said thus of all the group to which we refer. Poe was conscious of this, and absolutely suggested—before Lombroso—a relation between madness and genius. For the hero of "Eleonora" surely speaks in the name of Poe:

> Men [he says] have called me mad, but the question is not yet settled whether madness is or is not the loftiest intelligence, whether much that is glorious, whether all that is profound, does not spring from disease of thought, from *moods* of mind exalted at the expense of the general intellect. They who dream by day are cognisant of many things which escape those who dream only by night. In their grey visions they obtain glimpses of eternity, and thrill, in waking, to find that they have been upon the verge of the great secret. In snatches they learn something of the wisdom which is of good and more of the mere knowledge which is of evil. They penetrate, however rudderless or compassless, into the vast ocean of the "light ineffable."

This perilous doctrine is at least not far from descriptive of Poe's own genius. There was something uncanny about the man which forbade intimacy, almost approach. Of the hero (there is virtually but one) who paces through these tales in Poe's image you feel that no woman could live with him without going mad—or dying. And death, accordingly, is Poe's gift to all his women. The tales are vital with a wrongful vitality. They are told by heroes whose sensitive nerves have the preternatural acuteness of initial insanity; colour, sound, scent—every detail of description in their rendering becomes morbidly distinct to us, like the ticking of a clock in the dark. In the "House of Usher" this feature becomes conscious of itself; the hero hears the beating of a woman's heart while she stands without the closed door. Beauty and terror are alike portentous, "larger than human," like figures in a mist. The landscapes are preterhuman, painted as with fire, and blinded with a light such as only streams from the fountains of the dreaming brain. The heroes live by choice in chambers out of nightmare, where curtains like molten silver fall in cataracts on carpets of burning gold, lighted by coloured flames which writhe from antique lamps, and perfumed from carven censers; on golden tapestries phantasmal figures waver in the rushing of a continuous wind. Amid such surroundings women of unearthly beauty, or the shadow of Poe's own child-wife, pass and die, and dying, give rise to tragedies of impermissible terror; the Red Death incarnates itself among the fated revellers; or a man flies through life pursued by the visible presence of himself. Beauty which cannot separate itself from terror, terror haunted by beauty, are the powers which rule this world of an opium-dream.

It is the deliberate turning away of a man from the normal; it is the obsession by the desire for better bread than is made from wheat. When Poe theorises on landscape-gardening, he avows his preference for the artificial style, but must have a "spiritualised " artificiality, an artifice which suggests the more than mortal. Yet this world at which the human heart aches becomes real while we read—there is the genius. The art is admirable in its sureness and delicacy. The imagination has seized these things of beauty and terror with more than the closeness of a poet—with the closeness of a dream; and there is no closeness, either to terror or beauty, so appalling as that of a dream. The scope is strange and narrow, but the mastership is absolute.

Yet the same man who can thus handle ideal horror and loveliness with the touch and arts of a poet is also, on another side, and within the limits of romance, one of the most convincing of realists. The man who wrote "The Fall of the House of Usher" and "The Masque of the Red Death" wrote also *The Narrative of Arthur Gordon Pym* and "The Descent into the Maelstrom." For the dreamer was also a keen analyst and an amateur of science; and had his active days in youth. Mr. Wells himself has not combined romance and realism more startlingly than that feat is achieved in *Arthur Gordon Pym*. The seizure of the ship, and, above all, the whole episode of the storm and subsequent starvation, are done with amazing wealth and verisimilitude of imaginative detail. In reading the description of the escape from the Maelstrom, in the other tale we have mentioned, it is hard to realise that Poe, in all probability, never was in the neighbourhood of the Scandinavian seas. The little vivid touches seem the result of experience. . . .

Finally, this wonderfully original artist has struck out and set the method for yet another class of tale—the "detective story" now represented by Dr. Conan Doyle. For, with Mr. Blatchford, we refuse to concede that the deductive method is undeveloped in Poe's tales of this class.

Certain applications of the deductive method Dr. Doyle has developed from his medical experience which are not to be found in Edgar Poe. But the deductive method itself is used by Poe with consummate skill. Dr. Doyle may also pride himself that in many cases he has trusted his mystery entirely to the ingenuity of the problem: whereas Poe holds back the essential clues the better to effect his surprise. But the merit of the tales lies deeper than their display of analysis. It is the finished art of construction and narrative, bringing out the ghastly element or the thrill of excitement with exact *crescendo* of effect; the beauty of the exposition; and, over all, the style of a master, which can endow with immortality a thing in its essence so ephemeral as this species has shown itself in other hands. Let it be, if you will, that the great Dupin was the bungling pretender which the great Holmes, we know, once declared him to be. Yet Poe makes us believe in his greatness—and that is *the* thing which matters in art. Perhaps the truth is that Dr. Doyle, too, is an artist, and knows the artistic value of "bounce" in the right place. From the artistic standpoint, however, these latter tales—"The Murders in the Rue Morgue" and their kind—though they were the first to make Poe's fame as a tale-writer, will be the last to keep it. It is on the two former classes that his fame must chiefly rest—and rest securely.

—Francis Thompson, "A Dreamer of Things Impossible"
(1901), *Literary Criticisms,* ed. Terence L. Connolly,
1948, pp. 317–22

BRANDER MATTHEWS
"POE AND THE DETECTIVE STORY" (1907)

Poe is now credited with inventing the detective fiction genre, in such tales as "The Murders in the Rue Morgue" and "The Purloined Letter." Going beyond just asserting this, Matthews here shows how Poe created this new literary form. Matthews starts by using Poe's own words to distinguish the detective story from "mere mystery." In the latter, the reader is kept in the dark about what is really going on until the moment that the mystery is solved; once the veil is lifted, the story is over. In detective fiction, by contrast, the reader becomes interested in the steps taken to solve the mystery; the mystery is less important than the analysis employed to solve it. In Poe, as in the works of Arthur Conan Doyle and other imitators, the main character is the amateur detective who uses careful observation and logical deduction to solve the case. An Auguste Dupin or a Sherlock Holmes is merely a smarter, more meticulous observer than the reader, and the reader (like the sidekick in the tales) is interested in learning how the detective figured "it" out.

Students interested in detective fiction should look at Matthews's article, since it clearly lays out the elements that make this genre distinctive from others. Students can also use this essay to look at how new literary genres are formed. Matthews talks about how critics are becoming like evolutionary biologists, searching for the origins of different species of literature. What does this say about the role of literary criticism? Is criticism a kind of science?

———◦◦◦—— ——◦◦◦—— ——◦◦◦——

In one of those essays which were often as speculative and suggestive as he claimed, the late John Addington Symonds called attention to three successive phases of criticism, pointing out that the critics had first set up as judges, delivering opinions from the bench and never hesitating to put on the black cap; that then they had changed into showmen, dwelling chiefly on the beauties of the masterpieces they were exhibiting; and that finally, and only very recently, they had become natural historians, studying "each object in relation to its antecedents and its consequences" and making themselves acquainted "with the conditions under which the artist grew, the habits of his race, the opinions of his age, his physiological and psychological peculiarities." And Symonds might have added that it is only in this latest phase, when the critics have availed themselves of the methods of the comparative biologists, that they are concerned with the interesting problems connected with the origin of the several literary species.

All over the world today devoted students are working at the hidden history of the lyric, for example, and of certain subdivisions of this species, such as the elegy, as it flowered long ago in Greece and as it has flourished in most of the literatures of modern Europe. To the "natural historian" of literary art, these subdivisions of a species are becoming more and more interesting, as he perceives more clearly how prone the poets have always been to work in accord with the pattern popular in their own time and to express themselves freely in the form they found ready to their hands. The student of the English drama is delighted when he can seize firmly the rise and fall of the tragedy of blood for one example, of the comedy of humors for another, and of sentimental comedy for a third; just as the investigator into the history of fiction is pleased to be able to trace the transformations of the pastoral, of the picaresque romance, and of the later short story.

The beginnings of a species, or of a subspecies, are obscure more often than not; and they are rarely to be declared with certainty. "Nothing is more difficult than to discover who have been in literature the first inventors" of a new form, so M. Jules Lemaitre once asserted, adding that innovations have generally been attempted by writers of no great value, and not infrequently by those who failed in those first efforts, unable to profit by their own originality. And it is natural enough that a good many sighting shots should be wasted on a new target before even an accomplished marksman could plump his bullet in the bull's-eye. The historical novel as we know it now must be credited to Scott, who preluded by the rather feeble "Waverly," before attaining the more boldly planned "Rob Roy" and "Guy Mannering." The sea tale is to be ascribed to Cooper, whose wavering faith in its successful accomplishment is reflected in the shifting of the successive episodes of the "Pilot" from land to water and back again to land; and it was only when he came to write the "Red Rover" that Cooper displayed full confidence in the form he was the first to experiment with. But the history of the detective story begins with the publication of the "Murders in the Rue Morgue," a masterpiece of its kind, which even its author was unable to surpass; and Poe, unlike most other originators, rang the bell the very first time he took aim.

The detective story which Poe invented sharply differentiates itself from the earlier tales of mystery, and also from the later narratives in which actual detectives figure incidentally. Perhaps the first of these tales of mystery is Walpole's "Castle of Otranto," which appears to us now clumsy enough, with its puerile attempts to excite terror. The romances of Mrs. Radcliffe are scarcely more solidly built—indeed, the fatigue of the sophisticated reader of to-day when he undertakes the perusal of these old-fashioned and long-winded chronicles may be ascribed partly to the flimsiness of the foundation which is supposed to support the awe-inspiring superstructure. Godwin's "Caleb Williams" is far more firmly put together; and its artful planning called for imagination as well as mere invention. In the "Edgar Huntley" of Charles Brockden Brown the veil of doubt skilfully shrouds the unsuspected and unsuspecting murderer who did the evil deed in his sleep—anticipating the somnambulist hero of Wilkie Collins' "Moonstone."

The disadvantages of this mystery-mongering have been pointed out by Poe with his wonted acuteness in his criticism of "Barnaby Rudge." After retelling the plot of Dickens' contorted narrative, and after putting the successive episodes into their true sequence, Poe asserted that "the thesis of the novel may thus be regarded as based upon curiosity," and he declared that "every point is so arranged as to perplex the reader and whet his desire for elucidation." He insisted "that the secret be well kept is obviously necessary," because if it leaks out "against the author's will, his purposes are immediately at odds and ends." Then he remarked that although "there can be no question that . . . many points . . . which would have been comparatively insipid even if given in full detail in a natural sequence, are endued with the interest of mystery; but neither can it be denied that a vast many more points are at the same time deprived of all effect, and become null, through the impossibility of comprehending them without the key." In other words, the novelist has chosen to sacrifice to the fleeting interest which is evoked only by wonder the more abiding interest which is aroused by the clear perception of the interplay of character and motive. Poe suggested that even "Barnaby Rudge"—in spite of its author's efforts to keep secret the real springs of action which controlled the characters—if taken up a second time by a reader put into possession of all that had been concealed, would be found to possess quadruple brilliance, "a brilliance unprofitably sacrificed at the shrine of the keenest interest of mere mystery."

Dickens was not the last novelist of note to be tempted and to fall into this snare. In the "Disciple," and again in "André Cornélis," M. Paul Bourget was lured from the path of psychologic analysis into the maze of mystery-mongering; but he had the tact to employ his secrets to excite interest only in the beginning of what were, after all, studies from life, each of them setting forth the struggle of a man with the memory of his crime. In "The Wreckers" Stevenson and his young collaborator attempted that "form of police novel or mystery story which consisted in beginning your yarn anywhere but at the beginning, and finishing it anywhere but at the end." They were attracted by its "peculiar interest when done, and the peculiar difficulties that attend its execution." They were "repelled by that appearance of insincerity and shallowness of tone which seems its inevitable drawback," because "the mind of the reader always bent to pick up clews receives no impression of reality or life, rather of an airless, elaborate mechanism; and the book remains enthralling, but insignificant, like a game of chess, not a work of human art." They hoped to find a new way of handling the old tale of mystery, so that they might get the profit without paying the price. But already in his criticism of "Barnaby Rudge" had Poe showed why disappointment was unavoidable, because the more artfully the dark intimations of horror are held out, the more certain it is that the anticipation must surpass the reality. No matter how terrific the circumstances may be which shall appear to have occasioned the mystery, "still they will not be able to satisfy the mind of the reader. He will surely be disappointed."

Even Balzac, with all his mastery of the novelist's art, lost more than he gained when he strove to arouse the interest of his readers by an appeal to their curiosity. His mystery-mongering is sometimes perilously close to blatant sensationalism and overt charlatanry; and he seems to be seeking the bald effect for its own sake. In the "Chouans," and again in the "Ténébreuse Affaire," he has complicated plots and counterplots entangled almost to confusion, but the reader "receives no impression of reality or life" even if these novels cannot be dismissed as empty examples of "airless, elaborate mechanism."

The members of the secret police appearing in these stories have all a vague likeness to Vidocq, whose alleged memoirs were published in 1828, a few years before the author of the "Human Comedy" began to deal with the scheming of the underworld. Balzac's spies and his detectives are not convincing, despite his utmost effort; and we do not believe in their preternatural acuteness. Even in the conduct of their intrigues we are lost in a murky mistiness. Balzac is at his best when he is arousing the emotions of recognition; and he is at his worst when he sinks to evoking the emotions of surprise.

In the true detective story as Poe conceived it in the "Murders in the Rue Morgue," it is not in the mystery itself that the author seeks to interest the reader, but rather in the successive steps whereby his analytic observer is enabled to solve a problem that might well be dismissed as beyond human elucidation. Attention is centred on the unravelling of the tangled skein rather than on the knot itself. The emotion aroused is not mere surprise, it is recognition of the unsuspected capabilities of the human brain; it is not a wondering curiosity as to an airless mechanism, but a heightening admiration for the analytic acumen capable of working out an acceptable answer to the puzzle propounded. In other words, Poe, while he availed himself of the obvious advantages of keeping a secret from his readers and of leaving them guessing as long as he pleased, shifted the point of attack and succeeded in giving a human interest to his tale of wonder.

And by this shift Poe transported the detective story from the group of tales of adventure into the group of portrayals of character. By bestowing upon it a human interest, he raised it in the literary scale. There is no need now to exaggerate the merits of this feat or to suggest that Poe himself was not capable of loftier efforts. Of course the "Fall of the House of Usher," which is of imagination all compact, is more valid evidence of his genius than the "Murders in the Rue Morgue," which is the product rather of his invention, supremely ingenious as it is. Even though the detective story as Poe produced it is elevated far above the barren tale of mystery which preceded it and which has been revived in our own day, it is not one of the loftiest of literary forms, and its possibilities are severely limited. It suffers to-day from the fact that in the half century and more since Poe set the pattern it has been vulgarized, debased, degraded by a swarm of imitators who lacked his certainty of touch, his instinctive tact, his intellectual individuality. In their hands it has been bereft of its distinction and despoiled of its atmosphere.

Even at its best, in the simple perfection of form that Poe bestowed on it, there is no denying that it demanded from its creator no depth of sentiment, no warmth of emotion, and no large understanding of human desire. There are those who would dismiss it carelessly, as making an appeal not far removed from that of the riddle and of the conundrum. There are those again who would liken it rather to the adroit trick of a clever conjurer. No doubt, it gratifies in us chiefly that delight in difficulty conquered, which is a part of the primitive play impulse potent in us all, but tending to die out as we grow older, as we lessen in energy, and as we feel more deeply the tragi-comedy of existence. But inexpensive as it may seem to those of us who look to literature for enlightenment, for solace in the hour of need, for stimulus to stiffen the will in the never-ending struggle of life, the detective tale, as Poe contrived it, has merits of its own as distinct and as undeniable as those of the historical novel, for example, or of the sea tale. It may please the young rather than the old, but the pleasure it can give is ever innocent; and the young are always in the majority.

In so far as Poe had any predecessor in the composing of a narrative, the interest of which should reside in the application of human intelligence to the solution of a mystery, this was not Balzac, although the American romancer was sufficiently familiar with the "Human Comedy" to venture an unidentified quotation from it. Nor was this predecessor Cooper, whom Balzac admired and even imitated, although Leatherstocking in tracking his redskin enemies revealed the tense observation and the faculty of deduction with which Poe was to endow his Dupin. The only predecessor with a good claim to be considered a progenitor is Voltaire, in whose "Zadig" we can find the method which Poe was to apply more elaborately. The Goncourts perceived this descent of Poe from Voltaire when they recorded in their "Journal" that the strange tales of the American poet seemed to them to belong to "a new literature, the literature of the twentieth century, scientifically miraculous story-telling by A + B, a literature at once monomaniac and mathematical, Zadig as district attorney, Cyrano de Bergerac as a pupil of Arago."

Voltaire tells us that Zadig by study gained "a sagacity which discovered to him a thousand differences where other men saw only uniformity"; and he describes a misadventure which befell Zadig when he was living in the kingdom of Babylon. One day the chief eunuch asked if he had seen the Queen's dog. "It is a female, isn't it?" returned Zadig; "a spaniel, and very small; she littered not long ago; she is lame of the left fore foot; and she has very long ears." "So you have seen her?" cried the eunuch. "No," Zadig answered; "I have never seen her; and I never even knew that the Queen had a dog."

About the same time the handsomest horse in the king's stables escaped; and the chief huntsman, meeting Zadig, inquired if he had not seen the animal. And Zadig responded: "It is the horse that gallops the best; he is five feet high; his shoe is very small; his tail is three and a half feet long; the knobs of his bit are of twenty-three carat gold; and he is shod with eleven-penny silver." And the chief huntsman asked, "Which way did he go?" To which Zadig replied: "I have not seen him; and I have never heard anything about him."

The chief eunuch and the chief huntsman naturally believed that Zadig had stolen the queen's dog and the king's horse; so they had him arrested and condemned, first to the knout, and afterward to exile for life in Siberia. And then both the missing animals were recovered; so Zadig was allowed to plead his case. He swore that he had never seen either the dog of the queen nor the horse of the king. This is what had happened: He had been walking toward a little wood and he had seen on the sand the track of an animal, and he judged that it had been a dog. Little furrows scratched in the low hillocks of sand between the footprints showed him that it was a female whose teats were pendent, and who therefore must have littered recently. As the sand was less deeply marked by one foot than by the three others, he had perceived the queen's dog to be lame.

As for the larger quadruped, Zadig, while walking in a narrow path in the wood, had seen the prints of a horse's shoes, all at an equal distance; and he had said to himself that here was a steed with a perfect stride. The path was narrow, being only seven feet wide, and here and there the dust had been flicked from the trees on either hand, and so Zadig had made sure that the horse had a tail three and a half feet long. The branches crossed over the path at the height of five feet, and as leaves had been broken off, the observer had decided that the horse was just five feet high. As to the bit, this must be of gold, since the horse had rubbed it against a stone, which Zadig had recognized as a touchstone and on which he had assayed the trace of precious metal. And from the marks left by the horse's shoes on another kind of stone Zadig had felt certain that they were made of eleven-penny silver.

Huxley has pointed out that the method of Zadig is the method which has made possible the incessant scientific discovery of the last century. It is the method of Wellington at Assaye, assuming that there must be a ford at a certain place on the river, because there was a village on each side. It is the method of Grant at Vicksburg, examining the knapsacks of the Confederate soldiers slain in a sortie to see if these contained rations, which would show that the garrison was seeking to break out because the place was untenable. It is also the method of Poe in the "Gold Bug" and in the "Murders in the Rue Morgue."

In his application of this method, not casually, playfully, and with satiric intent, as Voltaire had applied it, but seriously and taking it as the mainspring of his story, Poe added an ingenious improvement of his own devising. Upon the preternaturally acute observer who was to control the machinery of the tale, the American poet bestowed a companion of only an average alertness and keenness; and to this commonplace companion the romancer confided the telling of the story. By this seemingly simple device Poe doubled the effectiveness of his work, because this unobservant and unimaginative narrator of the unravelling of a tangled skein by an observant and imaginative analyst naturally recorded his own admiration and astonishment as the wonder was wrought before his eyes, so that the admiration and astonishment were transmitted directly and suggestively to the readers of the narrative.

In the "Gold Bug" the wonder worker is Legrand, and in both the "Murders in the Rue Morgue" and the "Purloined Letter" he is M. Dupin; and in all three tales the telling of the story is entrusted to an anonymous narrator, serving not only as a sort of Greek chorus to hint to the spectators the emotions they ought to feel, but also as the describer of the personality and peculiarities of Legrand and Dupin, who are thus individualized, humanized, and related to the real world. If they had not been accepted by the narrator as actual beings of flesh and blood, they might otherwise retain the thinness and the dryness of disembodied intelligences working in a vacuum.

This device of the transmitting narrator is indisputably valuable; and, properly enough, it reappears in the one series of detective tales which may be thought by some to rival Poe's. The alluring record of the investigations of Mr. Sherlock Holmes is the work of a certain Dr. Watson, a human being but little more clearly characterized than the anonymous narrators who have preserved for us the memory of Legrand and Dupin. But Poe here again exhibited a more artistic reserve than any of his imitators, in so far as he refrained from the undue laudation of the strange intellectual feats which are the central interest of these three tales. In the "Gold Bug" he even heightens his suspense by allowing the narrator to suggest that Legrand might be of unsound mind; and in the "Murders in the Rue Morgue" the narrator, although lost in astonishment at the acuteness of Dupin, never permits his admiration to become fulsome; he holds himself in, as though fearing that overpraise might provoke a denial. Moreover, Poe refrained from all exhibitions of Dupin's skill merely for its own sake—exhibitions only dazzling the spectators and not furthering his immediate purpose.

Nothing could be franker than Sir Conan Doyle's acknowledgment of his indebtedness. "Edgar Allan Poe, who, in his carelessly prodigal fashion, threw out the seeds from which so many of our present forms of literature have sprung, was the father of the detective tale, and covered its limits so completely that I fail to see how his followers can find any fresh ground which they can confidently call their own. For the secret of the thinness and also of the intensity of the detective story is that the writer is left with only one quality, that of intellectual acuteness, with which to endow his hero. Everything else is outside the picture and weakens the effect. The problem and its solution must form the theme, and the character drawing is limited and subordinate. On this narrow path the writer must walk, and he sees the footmarks of Poe always in front of him. He is happy if he ever finds the means of breaking away and striking out on some little side-track of his own."

The deviser of the adventures of Sherlock Holmes hit on a happy phrase when he declared that "the problem and its solution must form the theme." This principle was violated by Dumas, who gave us the solution before the problem, when he showed how d'Artagnan used the method of Zadig to deduce all the details of the duel on horseback, in the "Vicomte de Bragelonne," after the author had himself described to us the incidents of that fight. But when he was thus discounting his effect Dumas probably had in mind, not Poe, but Cooper, whose observant redskins he mightily admired and whom he frankly imitated in the "Mohicans of Paris."

Although Poe tells these three stories in the first person, as if he was himself only the recorder of the marvellous deeds of another, both Legrand and Dupin are projections of his own personality; they are characters created by him to be endowed with certain of his own qualifications and peculiarities. They were called into being to be possessed of the inventive and analytical powers of Poe himself. "To be an artist, first and always, requires a turn for induction and analysis"—so Mr. Stedman has aptly put it; and this turn for induction and analysis Poe had far more obviously than most artists. When he was a student he excelled in mathematics; in all his other tales he displays the same power of logical construction; and he delighted in the exercise of his own acumen, vaunting his ability to translate any cipher that might be sent to him and succeeding in making good his boast. In the criticism of "Barnaby Rudge," and again in the explanation of the Maelzel chess-player, Poe used for himself the same faculty of divination, the same power of seizing the one clue needful, however tangled amid other threads, which he had bestowed upon Legrand and Dupin.

If we may exclude the "Marie Rogêt" narrative in which Poe was working over an actual case of murder, we find him only three times undertaking the "tale of ratiocination," to use his own term; and in all three stories he was singularly happy in the problem he invented for solution. For each of the three he found a fit theme, wholly different from that employed in either of the others. He adroitly adjusted the proper accessories, and he created an appropriate atmosphere. With no sense of strain, and no awkwardness of manner, he dealt with episodes strange indeed, but so simply treated as to seem natural, at least for the moment. There is no violence of intrigue or conjecture; indeed Poe strives to suggest a background of the commonplace against which his marvels may seem the more marvellous. In none of his stories is Poe's consummate mastery of the narrative art, his ultimate craftsmanship, his certain control of all the devices of the most accomplished story-teller, more evident than in these three.

And yet they are but detective stories, after all; and Poe himself, never prone to underestimate what he had written, spoke of them lightly and even hinted that they had been overpraised. Probably they were easy writing—for him—and therefore they were not so close to his heart as certain other of his tales over which he had toiled long and more laboriously. Probably also he felt the detective story to be an inferior form. However superior his stories in this kind might be, he knew them to be unworthy of comparison with his more imaginative tales, which he had filled with a thrilling weirdness and which attained a soaring elevation far above any height to be achieved by ingenious narratives setting forth the solving of a puzzle.

It is in a letter to Philip Pendleton Cooke, written in 1848, that Poe disparaged his detective stories and declared that they "owe most of their popularity to being something in a new key. I do not mean to say that they are not ingenious—but people think them more ingenious than they are—on account of their method and air of method. In the 'Murders in the Rue Morgue,' for instance, where is the ingenuity of unravelling a web which you yourself (the author) have woven for the express purpose of unravelling? The reader is made to confound the ingenuity of the supposititious Dupin with that of the writer of the story." Here, surely, Poe is overmodest; at least he overstates the case against himself. The ingenuity of the author obviously lies in his invention of a web which seemingly cannot be unravelled and which nevertheless one of the characters of the tale, Legrand or Dupin, succeeds in unravelling at last. This ingenuity may be, in one way, less than that required to solve an actual problem in real life; but it is also, in another way, more, for it had to invent its own puzzle and to put this together so that the secret seemed to be absolutely hidden, although all the facts needed to solve it were plainly presented to the reader.

In the same letter to Cooke, Poe remarked on the "wide diversity and variety" of his tales when contrasted one with another; and he asserted that he did not consider any one better than another. "There is a vast variety of kinds, and in degree of value these kinds vary—but each tale is equally good *of its kind.*" He added that "the loftiest kind is that of the highest imagination." For this reason only he considered that "Ligeia" might be called the best of his stories. Now, after a lapse of threescore years, the "Fall of the House of Usher," with its "serene and sombre beauty," would seem to deserve the first place of all. And among the detective stories, standing on a lower plane as they do, because they were wrought by invention rather than by the interpreting imagination, the foremost position may be given to the "Murders in the Rue Morgue." In this tale Poe's invention is most ingenious and his subject is selected with the fullest understanding of the utmost possibilities of the detective story. At the core of it is a strange, mysterious, monstrous crime; and M. Anatole France was never wiser than when he declared the unfailing interest of mankind in a gigantic misdeed "because we find in all crimes that fund of hunger and desire on which we all live, the good as well as the bad." Before a crime such as this we seem to find ourselves peering into the contorted visage of primitive man, obeying no law but his own caprice.

The superiority of the poet who wrote the first detective story over all those who have striven to tread in the trail he blazed is obvious enough. It resides not only in his finer workmanship, his more delicate art, his finer certainty of execution, his more absolute knowledge of what it was best to do and of the way best to do this; it is to be seen not only in his command of verisimilitude, in his plausibility, in his faculty of enwrapping the figures of his narrative in the atmosphere most fit for them; it is not in any of these things or in all of them that Poe's supremacy is founded. The reason of that supremacy must be sought in the fact that, after all, Poe was of a truth a poet, and that he had the informing imagination of a poet, even though it was only the more prosaic side of the faculty divine which he chose to employ in these tales of ratiocination.

It is by their possession of poetry, however slight their portion might be, that Fitzjames O'Brien and M. Jean Richepin and Mr. Rudyard Kipling were kept from rank failure when they followed in Poe's footsteps and sought to imitate, or at least to emulate his more largely imaginative tales in the "Diamond Lens" of the Irish-American, in the "Morts Bizarres" of the Frenchman, and in half a dozen tales of the Anglo-Indian. But what tincture of poesy, what sweep of vision, what magic of style, is there in the attempts of the most of the others who have taken pattern by his detective stories?

None, and less than none. Ingenuity of a kind there is in Gaboriau's longer fictions, and in those of Fortuné de Boisgobey, and in those of Wilkie Collins; but this ingenuity is never so simply employed, and it is often artificial and violent and mechanical. It exists for its own sake, with little relation to the admitted characteristics of our common humanity. It stands alone, and it is never accompanied by the apparent ease which adds charm to Poe's handling of his puzzles.

Consider how often Gaboriau puts us off with a broken-backed narrative, taking up his curtain on a promising problem, presenting it to us in aspects of increasing difficulty, only at last to confess his impotence by starting afresh and slowly detailing the explanatory episodes which happened before the curtain rose. Consider how frequently Fortuné de Boisgobey failed to play fair. Consider how juiceless was the documentary method of Wilkie Collins, how mechanical and how arid, how futilely complicated, how prolonged, and how fatiguing. Consider all the minor members of the sorry brood hatched out of the same egg, how cheap and how childish the most of them are. Consider all these; and we are forced to the conclusion that if the writing of a good detective story is so rare and so difficult, if only one of Poe's imitators has been able really to rival his achievement, if this single success has been the result of an acceptance of Poe's formula and of a close adherence to Poe's practice, then, what Poe wrought is really unique; and we must give him the guerdon of praise due to an artist who has accomplished the first time of trying that which others have failed to achieve even after he had shown them how.

—Brander Matthews, "Poe and the Detective Story,"
Scribner's Magazine, September 1907

EUREKA

GEORGE E. WOODBERRY
"THE END OF THE PLAY" (1885)

Eureka is Poe's most ambitious work. It is almost uncategorizable, as it combines philosophy, astronomy, physics, and religion in what Poe called a "prose poem." Organized as a literary work, *Eureka* presents Poe's philosophy, in which he develops a cosmogony, literally explaining the origins of the universe. Poe upholds that the universe began when the "Deity" willed a primordial "particle" into being, which then set off a chain reaction in all directions to create the world. Poe's theory is similar to the atomism of such ancient philosophers as Epicurus and Lucretius, who believed that the world was made up of atoms in motion. *Eureka* is also "pantheistic" in its equation of God and Nature; in this, Poe follows the philosophers Spinoza and Leibniz.

Woodberry, a literature professor and biographer of Poe, dismisses the faulty science and muddled philosophy he finds in *Eureka*. As a work of science and philosophy, the "prose poem" does not really add to those fields of knowledge. Woodberry notes that Poe's speculations have been proved wrong and, in many cases, were already known to be false in Poe's time. While acknowledging Poe's literary genius, Woodberry states that Poe was out of his element when writing a treatise on science and philosophy.

Students discussing Poe's *Eureka* will want to look at Woodberry's claims in this extract. Those interested in the relationships between literature and science or between art and philosophy could also consult this piece. Students might want to compare Poe's *Eureka* to some of his other "science fiction." Would Woodberry's objections hold up against the fictional works as well?

In the history of Poe's mental development, *Eureka,* the principal work of his last years, necessarily occupies an important place. The earliest indication that such topics occupied his mind occurs in the review of Macaulay's Essays: "That we know no more today of the nature of Deity—of its purposes—and thus of man himself—than we did even a dozen years ago—is a proposition disgracefully absurd; and of this any astronomer could assure Mr. Macaulay. Indeed, to our own mind, the *only* irrefutable argument in support of the soul's immortality—or, rather, the only conclusive proof of man's alternate dissolution and rejuvenescence *ad infinitum*—is to be found in analogies deduced from the modern established theory of the nebular cosmogony." Shortly after this utterance the metaphysical tales begin, but the speculations of Poe were not fully developed until the publication of *Eureka*. In the following criticism, which necessarily partakes somewhat of the abstract nature of its subject, only what is peculiar to Poe will be dwelt on; and it may as well be premised that the end in view is not the determination of abstract truth, but simply the illustration alike of Poe's genius and character by the light of his speculations.

Poe's hypothesis is as follows: The mind knows intuitively—by inductive or deductive processes which escape consciousness, elude reason, or defy expression—that the creative act of Deity must have been the simplest possible; or, to expand and define this statement, it must have consisted in willing into being a primordial particle, the germ of all things, existing without relations to aught, or, in the technical phrase, unconditioned. This particle, by virtue of the divine volition, radiated into space uniformly in all directions a shower of atoms of diverse form, irregularly arranged among themselves, but all, generally speaking, equally distant from their source; this operation was repeated at intervals, but with decreased energy in each new instance, so that the atoms were impelled less far. On the exhaustion of the radiating force, the universe was thus made up of a series of concentric hollow spheres, like a nest of boxes, the crusts of the several spheres being constituted of the atoms of the several discharges. The radiating force at each of its manifestations is measured by the number of atoms then thrown off; or, since the number of atoms in any particular case must have been directly proportional with the surface of the particular sphere they occupied, and since the surfaces of a series of concentric spheres are directly proportional with the squares of their distances from the centre, the radiating force in the several discharges was directly proportional with the squares of the distances to which the several atomic showers were driven.

On the consummation of this secondary creative act, as the diffusion may be called, there occurred, says Poe, a recoil, a striving of the atoms each to each in order to regain their primitive condition; and this tendency, which is now being satisfied, is expressed in gravitation, the mutual attraction of atoms with a force inversely proportional with the squares of the distances. In other words, the law of gravitation is found to be the converse of the law of radiation, as would be the case if the former energy were the reaction of the latter as is claimed; furthermore, the distribution of the atoms in space is seen to be such as would result from the mode of diffusion described. The return of the atoms into their source, however, would take place too rapidly, adds Poe, and without accomplishing the Deity's design of developing out of the original homogeneous particle the utmost heterogeneity, were it not that God, in this case a true *Deus ex machina,* has interposed by introducing a repelling force which began to be generated at the very inception of the universal reaction, and ever becomes greater as the latter proceeds. Poe names this force electricity, while at the same time he suggests that light, heat, and magnetism are among its phases, and ascribes to it all vital and mental phenomena; but of the principle itself he makes a mystery, since he is intuitively convinced that it belongs to that spiritual essence which lies beyond the limits of human inquiry. In the grand reaction, then, the universe is through attraction becoming more condensed, and through repulsion more heterogeneous. Attraction and repulsion taken together constitute our notion of matter; the former is the physical element, the Body, the latter is the spiritual element, the Soul. Incidentally it should be remarked that since in a divine design, being perfect, no one part exists for the sake of others more than the others for its sake, it is indifferent whether repulsion be considered, as hitherto, an expedient to retard the attractive force, or, on the other hand, the attractive force as an expedient to develop repulsion; in other words, it is indifferent whether the physical be regarded as subordinate to the spiritual element, or *vice versa*. To return to the main thread, Poe affirms that repulsion will not increase indefinitely as the condensation of the mass proceeds, but when in the process of time it has fulfilled its purpose—the evolution of heterogeneity—it will cease, and the attractive force, being unresisted, will draw the atoms back into the primordial particle in which, as it has no parts, attraction will also cease; now, attraction and repulsion constituting our notion of matter, the cessation of these two forces is the same thing with the annihilation of matter, or in other words, the universe, at the end of the reaction which has been mentally followed out, will sink into the nihility out of which it arose. In conclusion Poe makes one last affirmation, to wit, that the diffusion and ingathering of the universe is the diffusion and ingathering of Deity itself, which has no existence apart from the constitution of things.

It is difficult to treat this hypothesis, taken as a metaphysical speculation, with respect. To examine it for the purpose of demolition would be a tedious, though an easy task; but fortunately there is no need to do more than point out a few of its confusions in order to illustrate the worthlessness of Poe's thought in this field, and to indicate the depth of the delusion under which he labored in believing himself a discoverer of new truth. For this purpose it will be best to take the most rudimentary metaphysical ideas involved. The primordial particle is declared to be unconditioned—"my particle proper is absolute Irrelation,"—or in other words it is the Absolute; but this is incompatible with its being willed into being by Deity, to which it would then necessarily stand related as an effect to its cause; on the contrary, it must itself, being the Absolute, be Deity with which Poe at last identifies it. In other words, when Poe has reached the conception of the primordial particle as first defined by him, he is just where he started, that is, at the conception of Deity, and at that point, as has been seen, he had to end. The difficulty which bars inquiry—the inconceivability of creation—remains as insuperable as ever, although Poe may have cheated himself into believing it overcome by the legerdemain of a phrase from physics; in the attempt to describe the generation of the phenomenal universe out of the unknowable, he has been foiled by the old obstacles—the impossibility of making an equation between nothing and something, of effecting a transformation of the absolute into the conditioned. If the primordial particle be material, it is only the scientific equivalent of the old turtle of the Hindoos, on which the elephant stands to support the globe; if it be immaterial, it is the void beneath.

Such a criticism as the above belongs to the primer of thought in this science; but objections as obvious, brief, and fatal may be urged against every main point of the argument. Without entering on such a discussion it is sufficient to observe, as characteristic illustrations of the density of Poe's ignorance in this department of knowledge, that he regards space not as created but as given, explains the condensation of the universe as being a physical reaction upon the immaterial will of God (for the original radiating force cannot be discriminated from and is expressly identified with the divine volition, just as the primordial particle cannot be discriminated from and is expressly identified with the divine essence), and lastly so confuses such simple notions as final and efficient causes that he contradistinguishes the force of repulsion from that of attraction as arising and disappearing in obedience to the former instead of the later sort. In a word, Poe's theory belongs to the infancy of speculation, to the period before physics was separated from ontology; in this sense, and in no other, Kennedy's remark that Poe wrote like "an old Greek philosopher," was just.

What Poe himself most prized in this hypothesis was its pantheistic portion. The sentence of Baron Bielfeld,—"nous ne connaissons rien de la nature ou de l'essence de Dieu;—pour savoir ce qu'il est, il faut etre Dieu meme,"—had made a deep impression on his mind early in life; it is one of the half-dozen French quotations that he introduces at every opportunity into his compositions; in *Eureka* he translates it, "We know absolutely *nothing* of the nature or essence of God; in order to comprehend what he is, we should have to be God ourselves,"—and he immediately adds, "I nevertheless venture to demand if this our present ignorance of the Deity is an ignorance to which the soul is *everlastingly* condemned." Now after reflection he boldly took the only road to such knowledge that was left open by the apothegm, and affirmed that he was God, being persuaded thereto by his memories of an ante-natal and his aspiration for an immortal existence, and in particular by his pride. "My whole nature utterly *revolts*," he exclaimed, "at the idea that there is any Being in the Universe superior to *myself!*" On reading so violent an expression of belief one involuntarily examines the matter more closely and pushes home the question whether Poe did actually so fool himself to the top of his bent; and after some little investigation one finds that, if he was his own dupe, the reason is not far to seek. It is necessary here to summarize the speculations which were put forth elsewhere by Poe, especially in the metaphysical tales, and either led up to or supplemented the views *of Eureka.*

According to these other statements, the Universe is made up of gross matter sensibly perceived and of fine matter so minutely divided that the atoms coalesce (this is, of course, a contradiction in terms) and form an unparticled substance which permeates and impels all things. This unparticled substance or imperceptible coalescent matter is the universal mind (into such unintelligible phraseology is the keen analyst forced); its being is Deity; its motion, regarded on the material or energetic side, is the divine volition, or, regarded on the mental or conscious side, is the creative thought. Deity and its activity, being such in its universal existence, is individualized, by means of gross matter made for that end, into particular creatures, among which are men; the human being, in other words, is a specialization of the universal, or is God incarnate, as is every other creature whatsoever. It is superfluous to follow Poe in his fantastic conception of the universe as the abode of countless rudimentary incarnations of the Deity, each a divine thought and therefore irrevocable; the peculiar form of his pantheism would not be more defined thereby. At the first glance one sees that his theory is built out of Cartesian notions, crudely apprehended, and rendered ridiculous by the effort to yoke them with thoroughly materialistic ideas. In fact, Poe's scraps of speculative philosophy came from such opposite quarters that when his mind began to work on such contradictory information he could not well help falling into inextricable confusion. On the one hand he had derived, early in life, from obscure disciples of the French *philosophes,* the first truth that a materialist ever learns,—the origin of all knowledge in experience, and the consequent limitation of the mind to phenomena; on the other hand he had at a later period gleaned some of the conceptions of transcendentalism from Coleridge, Schlegel, and other secondary sources; from the union of such principles the issue was naturally monstrous, two-natured, like the Centaur. Essentially Poe was a materialist; whether, by gradually refining and subdividing matter, he reaches the unparticled substance, or by reversing the evolution of nature he arrives at the fiery mist and the primordial particle, he seeks to find out God by searching matter; and even in adopting the radically spiritual idea of pantheism, he is continually endeavoring to give it a materialistic form. He persuaded himself, as it is easy for ignorance to do; subtle as his mind was, well furnished for metaphysical thought both by his powers of abstraction and of reasoning, he wrote the jargon that belongs to the babbling days of philosophy because he did not take the pains to know the results of past inquiry and to train himself in modern methods. By his quick perception and adroit use of analogies, and especially by his tireless imagination, he gave his confused dogmatism the semblance of a reasoned system; but in fact his metaphysics exhibit only the shallowness of his scholarship and the degrading self-delusion of an arrogant and fatuous mind.

It is probable that few readers of *Eureka* ever seriously tried to understand its metaphysics. Its power—other than the fascination which some readers feel in whatever makes of their countenances "a foolish face of wonder"—lies in its exposition of Laplace's nebular theory and its vivid and popular presentation of astronomical phenomena. In this physical portion of the essay it has been fancied that Poe anticipated some of the results of later science; but this view cannot be sustained with candor. His own position that matter came from nihility and consisted of centres of force had been put forth as a scientific theory by Boscovich in 1758-59, had been widely discussed, and had found its way into American text-books. The same theory in a modified form had just been revived and brought to the notice of scientists by Faraday in his lecture in 1844. It has not, however, occupied the attention of first-class scientific men since that time. There may be, in the claim that "the recent progress of scientific thought runs in Poe's lines," some reference to Sir William Thomson's vortex theory of the constitution of atoms, but its resemblance to Poe's theory of vortices is only superficial, for what he puts forth was merely a revival of one of the earliest attempts to explain the Newtonian law, long since abandoned by science. It is true that in several particulars, such as the doctrine of the evolution of the universe from the simple to the complex, Poe's line of thought has now been followed out in detail; these suggestions, however, were not at the time peculiar to Poe, were not originated or developed by him, but on the contrary were common scientific property, for he appropriated ideas, just as he paraphrased statements of fact, from the books he read. He was no more a forerunner of Spencer, Faraday, and Darwin than scores of others, and he did nothing to make their investigations easier.

Poe's purely scientific speculations are mainly contained in the unpublished *addenda* to a report of his lecture on "The Universe" sent to a correspondent, and consist either of mathematical explanations of Kepler's first and third laws; or of statements, "that the sun was condensed at once (not gradually according to the supposition of Laplace) into his smallest size," and afterwards "sent into space his substance in the form of a vapor" from which Neptune was made; or of similar theories. They exhibit once more Poe's tenacity of mind, the sleuth-hound persistence of his intellectual pursuit; but, like his metaphysics, they represent a waste of power. They are, moreover, characterized by extraordinary errors. Some of the data are quite imaginary, it being impossible to determine what are the facts; some of them are quite wrong. The density of Jupiter, for example, in a long and important calculation, is constantly reckoned as two and one half, whereas it is only something more than one fifth, and the densities of the planets are described as being inversely as their rotary periods, whereas in any table of the elements of the solar system some wide departures from this rule are observable. Again, it is stated that Kepler's first and third laws "cannot be explained upon the principle of Newton's theory;" but, in fact, they follow mathematical deduction from it. Poe's own explanation of them is merely a play upon figures. A striking instance of fundamental ignorance of astronomical science is his statement at various places that the planets rotate (on their own axes) in elliptical orbits, and the reference he frequently makes to the *breadth* of their orbits (the breadth of their paths through space) agreeably to this supposition. Such a theory is incompatible with the Newtonian law of gravitation, according to which any revolution in an elliptical orbit implies a source of attraction at the focus of the ellipse. Examples of bodies which have breadth of orbit in Poe's sense are found in the satellites of all the planets, each of which, however, has its primary as a source of attraction to keep it in its elliptical orbit; the primary by its revolution round the sun gives then the satellite a breadth of orbit. But to make the proper rotation of the planets themselves take place about a focus, which would be merely a point moving in an elliptical orbit about the sun, would be to give them an arbitrary motion with no force to produce it.

So far was Poe from being a seer of science, that he was fundamentally in error with regard to the generalizations which were of prime importance to his speculations. The one grand assumption of his whole speculation is the universality of the law of inverse squares as applied to attraction and repulsion, whereas it has been known since the beginning of study regarding them that that law does not explain all the forces involved, as, for example, molecular forces; and for this Boscovich himself had provided. Again, to illustrate his scientific foresight, he reproaches Herschel for his reluctance to doubt the stability of the universe, and himself boldly affirms, consistently with his theory, that it is in a state of ever swifter collapse; than this nothing could be more at variance with the great law of the conservation of energy. Undoubtedly Poe had talents for scientific investigation, had he been willing to devote himself to such work; but, so far as appears from this essay, he had not advanced farther in science that the elements of physics, mathematics, and astronomy, as he had learned them at school or from popular works, such as Dr. Nichol's *Architecture of the Heavens,* or from generalizations, such as the less technical chapters of Auguste Comte's *La Philosophie positif.* Out of such a limited stock of knowledge Poe could not by mere reflection generate any Newtonian truth; that he thought he had done so, measures his folly. In a word, for this criticism must be brought to a close, *Eureka* affords one of the most striking instances in literature of a naturally strong intellect tempted by overweening pride to an Icarian flight and betrayed, notwithstanding its merely specious knowledge, into an ignoble exposure of its own presumption and ignorance. The facts are not to be obscured by the smooth profession of Poe that he wished this work to be looked on only as a poem; for, though he perceived that his argument was too fragmentary and involved to receive credence, he was himself profoundly convinced that he had revealed the secret of eternity. Nor, were *Eureka* to be judged as a poem, that is to say, as a fictitious cosmogony, would the decision be more favorable; even then so far as it is obscure to the reader it must be pronounced defective, so far as it is understood, involving as it does in its primary conceptions incessant contradictions of the necessary laws of thought, it must be pronounced meaningless. Poe believed himself to be that extinct being, a universal genius of the highest order; and he wrote this essay to prove his powers in philosophy and in science. To the correspondent to whom he sent the *addenda* he declared, "As to the lecture, I am very quiet about it—but if you have ever dealt with such topics, you will recognize the novelty and *moment* of my views. What I have propounded will (in good time) revolutionize the world of Physical and Metaphysical science. I say this calmly, but I say it." Poe succeeded only in showing how egregiously genius may mistake its realm.

—George E. Woodberry, "The End of the Play,"
Edgar Allan Poe, 1885, pp. 286–301

CRITICISM

Nathaniel Hawthorne (1846)

Hawthorne, best known for his novel *The Scarlet Letter,* was also a prolific short story writer. Poe had given Hawthorne's collection *Twice-Told Tales* a mixed review, praising Hawthorne as one of America's best writers but

also criticizing his "monotony of tone." Hawthorne seems to acknowledge this, and he says that he prefers Poe's fiction to his criticism.

I presume the publishers will have sent you a copy of *Mosses from an Old Manse*—the latest (and probably the last) collection of my tales and sketches. I have read your occasional notices of my productions with great interest—not so much because your judgment was, upon the whole, favorable, as because it seemed to be given in earnest. I care for nothing but the truth; and shall always much more readily accept a harsh truth, in regard to my writings, than a sugared falsehood.

I confess, however, that I admire you rather as a writer of tales than as a critic upon them. I might often—and often do—dissent from your opinions in the latter capacity, but could never fail to recognize your force and originality in the former.

> —Nathaniel Hawthorne, Letter to Edgar Allan Poe
> (June 17, 1846), cited in George E. Woodberry, "Poe in
> New York," *Century Magazine,* October 1894, p. 860

EUGENE BENSON "POE AND HAWTHORNE" (1868)

Benson blasts Poe, claiming that his praise for Hawthorne was in reality a thinly veiled attack. Benson sees Poe as a mean-spirited critic who
delighted in picking apart the work of others, mocking their supposed
ignorance, and in several cases accusing them of plagiarism.

As a critic, Poe was illiberal and perverse, burning incense before second-rate writers, and stinging the author he professed to admire. His article on Hawthorne, like Antony's oration, with its blasting phrase, "Yet Brutus was an honorable man," leaves an impression contrary and fatal to the frequent professions of high appreciation which make the refrain of his article. As a critic, Poe spent himself upon questions of detail, and, in all cases, belittled his subject. He did not exercise the most engaging faculties of his mind. He is brilliant, caustic, stinging, personal without geniality, expressing an irritated mind. Reading his criticisms, we think his literary being might be said to resemble a bush that blossoms into a few perfect flowers, but always has its thorns in thickest profusion. Poe was what may be called a *technical critic.* He delighted to involve his reader in the mechanism of poetry, and convict his victim of ignorance, while he used his knowledge as a means to be exquisitely insolent. He was like an art critic stuffed with the jargon of studios, talking an unknown language; careless about the elements of the subject which, properly, are the chief and only concern of the public. That Poe was acute, that he was exact, that he was original, no one can question; but he was not stimulating, and comprehensive, and generous, like the more sympathetic critics, as, for example, Diderot or Carlyle. It was his misfortune to have been called to pronounce upon the ephemera of literature, conscious that he was *expected* to think them fixed stars. His critical notices of American men of letters show the incessant struggle of a supreme scorn muffled and quieted from time to time in the acknowledgment of mitigating circumstances to excuse the literary criminals that he had assembled. When he wishes to be indulgent and generous, it is the indulgence and generosity of a cat stroking a mouse—the claw is *felt* by the breathless victim. He probably *tore* his subject more than any critic that ever lived. In his criticisms, the sentences are sharp, stinging, pointed, and sparkling; they are like so many surgical knives—they lay open the living subject, quivering and fainting, to the bone. Poe had no indulgence for literary offenders. He had the instincts of a mole slaking its thirst over its prey. Poe scratched almost every one of his literary contemporaries, and, in nine cases out of ten, he was right in his destructive work. But he was virulent, mocking, incensing, seeming to be animated with a personal animosity for his subject; he was like a literary pirate, sparing neither friend nor foe, always accusing other people of stealing, while his own hands were not pure.

—Eugene Benson, "Poe and Hawthorne,"
Galaxy, December 1868, pp. 747–48

HENRY JAMES (1879)

James, a writer and critic best known for his novels (including *Portrait of a Lady* and *The Wings of the Dove*), considers Poe to have been one of America's first real literary critics, but he questions the value of Poe's criticism. Like Benson, James notes that Poe was often vulgar and vindictive, despite providing some useful insights into the writers of his day.

There was but little literary criticism in the United States at the time Hawthorne's earlier works were published; but among the reviewers Edgar Poe perhaps held the scales the highest. He, at any rate, rattled them loudest, and pretended, more than any one else, to conduct the weighing-process on scientific principles. Very remarkable was this process of Edgar Poe's, and very extraordinary were his principles; but he had the advantage of being a man of genius, and his intelligence was frequently great. His collection of critical sketches of the American writers flourishing in what M. Taine would call his *milieu* and *moment,* is very curious and interesting reading, and it has one quality which ought to keep it from ever being completely forgotten. It is probably the most complete and exquisite specimen of *provincialism* ever prepared for the edification of men. Poe's judgments are pretentious, spiteful, vulgar; but they contain a great deal of sense and discrimination as well, and here and there, sometimes at frequent intervals, we find a phrase of happy insight imbedded in a patch of the most fatuous pedantry.

—Henry James, *Hawthorne,* 1879, p. 62

BARRETT WENDELL (1900)

Wendell was the first professor to offer a systematic course in American literature at Harvard University. He views Poe's criticism as an extension of his art; Poe was severely critical of others at times, but only because his passion for the art made him want to see it done right.

His critical writings, collected in the sixth, seventh, and eighth volumes of Stedman and Woodberry's edition of his works, are the only ones in which he shows how he could deal with actual fact; and in dealing with actual fact he proved himself able. Though some of the facts he dealt with, however, were worthy of his pen,—he was among the first, for example, to recognise the merit of Tennyson and of Mrs. Browning,—most of them in the course of fifty years have proved of no human importance. For all this, they existed at the moment. Poe was a journalist, who had to write about what was in the air; and he wrote about it so well that in certain aspects this critical work seems his best. He dabbled a little in philosophy, of course, particularly on the aesthetic side; but he had neither the seriousness of nature—spiritual insight, one might call it,—which must underlie serious philosophising, nor yet the scholarly training which must precede lasting, solid thought. What he did possess to a rare degree was the temper of an enthusiastic artist, who genuinely enjoyed and welcomed whatever in his own art, of poetry, he found meritorious. No doubt he was more than willing to condemn faults; whoever remembers any of his critical activity, for example, will remember how vigorously he attacked Longfellow for plagiarism. We ought to recall with equal certainty how willingly Poe recognised in the same Longfellow those traits which he believed excellent. Poe's serious writing does not concern the eternities as did the elder range of American literature, nor yet does it touch on public matters. True or not, indeed, that grotesque story of his death typifies his relation to political affairs. His critical writing, all the same, deals with questions of fine art in a spirit which if sometimes narrow, often dogmatic, and never scholarly, is sincere, fearless, and generally eager in its impulsive recognition of merit.

—Barrett Wendell,
A *Literary History of America,* 1900, pp. 208–09

Chronology

1809   Born in Boston, January 19, as the second of three children of David Poe and his wife, Elizabeth Arnold, both actors. The father soon abandons the family.

1811   Death of Poe's mother in Richmond, Virginia. The children are taken into diverse households, Edgar into the home of John Allan, a Richmond merchant. Not legally adopted, he is nevertheless renamed Edgar Allan.

1815–20   Resident, with the Allans, first in Scotland, then in London.

1826   Enters the University of Virginia (founded by Thomas Jefferson the year before), where he studies languages. Gambling debts compel him to leave, after Allan refuses to pay them.

1827   Enlists in army in Boston, where his first book, *Tamerlane and Other Poems,* appears and is ignored.

1828–29   Honorably discharged as sergeant major and lives in Baltimore, where *Al Aaraaf, Tamerlane and Minor Poems* is published.

1830–31   Enters West Point in May 1830; does well in studies but is expelled in January 1831. Lives in Baltimore with his father's sister, Maria Clemm, and her daughter Virginia, then eight years old. Begins to write tales.

1832–35   Tutors cousin Virginia Clemm, while continuing to write stories. Death of John Allan, who neglects to recognize Poe in his will. Poe writes book reviews for *Southern Literary Messenger,* and becomes editorial assistant on magazine. Moves to Richmond with Virginia and Mrs. Clemm and becomes editor of the journal.

1836	May marriage to Virginia Clemm, who was fourteen; her mother stayed on as housekeeper. Busy with writing or revising reviews, poems, and stories for the *Messenger*.
1837–38	Resigns from *Messenger* and moves himself and household to New York City, where he is unable to secure editorial work. Publishes "Ligeia" and, in July 1838, *Pym*. Moves household to Philadelphia.
1839–40	Works for *Gentleman's Magazine*, where he prints "William Wilson" and "The Fall of the House of Usher." Publishes two-volume *Tales of the Grotesque and Arabesque* in Philadelphia, late in 1839. Fired by his employer and fails to found his own magazine.
1841–42	Is employed as an editor of *Graham's Magazine*, where he prints "The Murders in the Rue Morgue." In January 1842, Virginia Poe suffers a burst blood vessel while singing. She survives but is never the same.
1843–45	Rise in Poe's popularity with the prize-winning "The Gold Bug." Moves to New York City and helps edit the *Evening Mirror*, where "The Raven" is printed in January 1845 and causes a sensation. *Tales* published in July 1845, *The Raven and Other Poems* in November of the same year. Engages in literary quarrel, falsely accusing Longfellow of plagiarism. Virginia's condition worsens. Becomes owner and editor of the *Broadway Journal*.
1846	Abandons *Broadway Journal* because of depression and financial problems. Moves household to Fordham, New York.
1847	Death of Virginia on January 30. Poe becomes very sick but is nursed by Mrs. Clemm and recovers.
1848	Proposes marriage to poet Sarah Helen Whitman, who later breaks off the relationship. Publishes *Eureka* in June.
1849	A year of rapid decline, marked by heavy drinking and paranoid delusions. Travels to Richmond, where he is engaged to Elmira Royster Shelton. Sails to Baltimore and then vanishes. Discovered delirious outside a polling booth on October 3, thus suggesting the subsequent legend that he was dragged from poll to poll as an alcoholic "repeater." Dies on October 7, ostensibly of "congestion of the brain."

Index